What others are saying....

"Every meal is balanced, nutritious and absolutely delicious. Suzanne's dishes never leave you feeling deprived or unsatisfied. Her recipes will change the way you eat and feel, giving you more energy and vitality than you've had in years."—*Ellen Kreidman, Ph.D., Author of The New York Times best sellers,* Light His Fire *and* Light Her Fire.

"Suzanne's warmth and robust sense of humor are a great compliment to her forthright style. She transformed my kitchen into a cozy and nurturing environment. She possesses an extensive knowledge of macrobiotic and vegetarian nutrition and shares it all in this wonderful book."—*Pia Zadora, Actress/Singer, Beverly Hills, CA*

"Suzanne is uncommonly talented. She has a master's knowledge of nutrition and the effects of food on the body. I have lost weight while eating more luxurious than I thought possible and gained more energy to start exercising. Until you experience Suzanne's recipes, it is hard to believe that healthy food and nutrition can have such a major impact on the body, mind and soul."
—*Maryjo J McGrath, Esq., Santa Barbara, CA*

"Suzanne Landry has the wonderful gift of being able to share her passion for healthy food while making it very delicious. In addition, she writes and talks in an interesting and entertaining manner. To top it all off, she practices what she recommends and it shines in her face and in her life. I recommend her book to all who are serious and wish to be joyful about food and healthful eating."—*W. M. Lewis, M.D., Santa Barbara, CA*

"Suzanne Landry has been guiding our patients to a healthy lifestyle at Issels Medical Center since 2005. Her knowledge of proper food combining and how to fit it into daily life is invaluable to our patients. She is a wealth of information."
—*Dr. Christian Issels, N.D., Santa Barbara, CA*

"Suzanne Landry is a pioneer in the field of creating healthy, alternative, tasteful menus to satisfy the palate of clients who have diet and health issues in our programs at Issels Medical Center. Suzanne has maintained her commitment to pure and organic ingredients while providing great food and I encourage all to try any and all of her recipes."—*Vanessa Keyes, White Star Catering, Santa Barbara, CA*

"Opened up a whole new world of healthy cooking. It way exceeded my expectations. I haven't enjoyed being in the kitchen this much in years!"—*Jim S., Sarasota, FL*

"This book really helped me make some huge changes in my diet and the diet of my kids! Even after so many of my well-meaning friends had been unable to convince me to make more healthy choices. I always thought vegetarian dishes would taste bland—this is definitely not the case here!"—*Melinda H., Short Hills, NJ*

"I have learned more about food and its relationship to the human body and its functions than I have in any health class. Suzanne Landry's book, natural food cooking classes and blog are educational, fun and have opened up a world of knowledge necessary for a lifetime of proper eating."—*Sally S., Basking Ridge, NJ*

"Very informative, very clear, lots of helpful tips and easy ingredient preparations. Your classes are great demonstrations that are inspiring and fun. I've been looking forward to your cookbook!"—*Catherine H., Ventura, CA*

"The dishes were balanced, scrumptious, and realistically easy. Suzanne's instructions were clear and concise—even more enlightening were all of her extra bits of information from time-saving tips and chefs' shortcut secrets, to specific ideas for leftovers. I loved the entire book and can't wait to try more recipes and learn from her expertise."—*Walter K., Livingston, NJ*

"Everything was perfect for me. I got much more out of your book than I could have dreamed I would. The most fascinating thing was the nutritional and endless information I picked up regarding so many facets of eating, preparing, life, etc....Great!"
—*Sylvia L., San Luis Obispo, CA*

"Your book gave me a more balanced look and an experience of what healthy cooking means and how to apply it to my situation. All I need do now is to practice it daily. Loved your open way of sharing your own experience...we all benefited greatly—thank you!"—*Joan K., Camarillo, CA*

To Ellen
To Your vibrant
health!
Suzanne Landry
2015

The Passionate Vegetable

Health inspired recipes to revitalize your life
for vegetarians or meat lovers!

Suzanne Landry, CNC

Dedication

To my mom, Mary Rose, now 92 years old, for sharing your love through the food you prepared for your family. I take the same great pleasure in feeding and nourishing my family as you did. As a child our mealtimes were a time for family gathering and sharing of conversation and laughter. A "hot square meal" grounded this tradition. This ritual was so fundamentally important to me while growing up that even as a single mom I continued these dinner reunions. And oh, mom's wonderful pies! You inspired my curiosity with all the wonderful smells coming from your kitchen. You drew me into the magical world of cooking again and again. For your belief, love and faith in me, I dedicate these pages to you.

To my sons Aaron, David and Matthew, you are the reason I embarked on this exciting journey and exploration of the relationship between food and health. You were my original recipe tasters for all my new experiments. Now as adults, I am very proud to see that the journey and exploration continues as you make your own healthy choices.

Lastly to my husband, George, for your love, encouragement and infinite patience through this long project. For all your understanding and support on those many weekends I stayed home to work on my book and chose not to go sailing. For your willingness, even tonight, to eat leftovers so that I could make my deadline.

Suzanne Landry (Lemagie)

Contents

List of Recipes

AMBER WAVES OF GRAIN

BEAN CUISINE

VEGETABLES—NATURE'S BOUNTY

TO MEAT OR NOT TO MEAT

GOOD FOR YOU DESSERTS

A Note to My Readers

Over thirty years ago I started teaching vegetarian cooking classes. Even though my classes were sold out, I rarely had a vegetarian in my class. This is still true even today as I teach. What I have learned is that many people want to try more vegetarian dishes, even if they're not quite ready to let go of the convenience of animal protein. I call them "Vegetarians on the Verge" or "Flexitarians." I don't think Americans need to be encouraged to eat more animal protein. On the contrary, we need to be encouraged to eat more vegetables and high-fiber whole grains and beans. To that end, this book has been written for you.

I raised my children on this diet, one rich with whole grains, beans, soups, nuts, sea vegetables, and fresh vegetables. They grew up to be strong, healthy men that look first to their diet and lifestyle habits if they feel "off." Running to the pharmacy for an over-the-counter cure was never an option, nor was it ever needed.

Working in a clinic for alternative cancer treatment, I have seen many patients. When I've consulted with them about their diets, they often described meals predominantly based on animal food, packaged food, and frozen, canned and cooked vegetables. Many of the vegetarian patients' diets were too heavily based on dairy and soy and too little on whole grains and beans. Certainly, very few people I have met in my 35 years of teaching really consume their Five-A-Day of fruits and vegetable servings.

I don't have to repeat the statistics of obesity and degenerative diseases Americans suffer with. We only need to look around us and in our own medicine cabinet. Ninety percent of people over 50 years old are on at least one prescription drug. I know with absolute certainty that changing our diets to wholesome natural foods will improve our health and return to us our youthful vitality. It did for me, my family, friends and hundreds of students of mine who got back into the kitchen and started feeding themselves real food.

This book is written to gently encourage you to try more delicious vegetarian recipes, while slowly reducing your animal protein dependency. For all my readers and students, please enjoy exploring and tasting new recipes. As your diet changes so will your health, well-being and joy of life!

Suzanne Landry

The Birth of My Passion

"Without good health nothing else in life matters." That was one of the many truths my dad taught me when I was growing up. His seventeen years of recurring cancer taught him the value of good health. He died at the young age of forty-seven years. Soon after, I began a journey of my own healing. My dad's death at such young age, my own health challenges, and my children's chronic health problems were the catalysts to my journey. It's been fascinating to explore the connection between food and healing, and thirty years later, I'm still captivated by it.

When I was twenty-eight years old, I suffered from low energy, chronic back problems, digestive disorders, and painful ovarian cysts. My doctor recommended surgery to remove my ovary because of a lemon-sized cyst. At the same time, over an eighteen-month period, my five-year-old son had more than ten episodes of ear infections followed by several bouts of bronchitis. The "cure" offered was traditional antibiotics. Five pediatricians prescribed more than fourteen different antibiotics. At the same time, my eighteen-month old son was suffering from an irritating eczema that began when he was only six months old. The only "remedy" prescribed was hydrocortisone cream. I felt helpless, but unwilling to just treat the symptoms. I kept asking, "What's the cause?" My helplessness turned into stubborn determination as I searched for answers.

Even as a child I felt there was a cause for every effect and that nothing ever "just happened." I knew in my deepest self that there were reasons for everything. This deep searching for truth led me on many paths of study. I came to understand and believe that healing has to be holistic because it addresses the mind and body. True wellness includes both.

We, like most Americans, ate for pleasure and were totally unaware of the tremendous influence our food had on our energy levels, our sleep, our health and our overall sense of well-being. I had subscribed to the Standard American Diet (S.A.D.) which is excessively high in protein, salt and saturated fats, and dangerously low in fiber and complex carbohydrates. The S.A.D. diet is truly sad, and I wanted alternatives. My leisure time became study time. I read everything related to health and nutrition, and I implemented dietary changes that changed our lives. Our transition was slow and steady so these gradual changes were easily incorporated into our daily eating habits. Slow and steady progress is what I still recommend for my students today.

The first change to our diet was to reduce red meat and white sugar. Immediately I felt more energetic, especially in the mornings. I became less irritable and more patient. My family started appreciating the natural taste of fresh vegetables and whole grains. Since I had become bored cooking the S.A.D. diet for my family, I began experimenting with new foods, flavors and textures. Cooking immediately became an exciting and creative adventure. My boys joined me in chopping vegetables, making homemade breads and cookies. They began to feel a part of this new adventure.

The best news was that with every positive step we made, more of our symptoms disappeared.

After a few weeks, the eczema and ear infections that plagued my sons were gone, and after several months, my cysts disappeared! It seemed like a miracle then and it still does today.

Good health is within your reach. The road to good health is a joyous journey of learning. Our bodies gently teach us each step of the way. We need only to listen and learn. Our bodies tell us what makes us feel good, what gives us energy and what drains our energy. While it's not always easy to listen and respect these messages, every time we do, we enjoy a greater sense of awareness, self-love and vitality. My journey of good health has been the most important, interesting, rewarding, and yes, sometimes challenging journey in my life. And every step has been worth the effort. "Know thyself" echoes in my mind.

My efforts and commitment have rewarded us. For more than thirty years my family and I have been in good health. None of us have needed medication of any kind—not even aspirin. Even simple colds are very rare, as are most other commonly accepted ailments and doctor visits are seldom needed. Most importantly, we have an abundance of energy and good health.

My dad was right—good health is very important and without it nothing else matters very much. This fundamental belief guides my work as a health counselor, educator and speaker. Since 1987 I have been sharing my love of cooking healthy, delicious foods through classes, articles, newsletters, my website, television programs and now through this book. Whether you are just starting your journey, or looking for fresh ideas and innovative recipes, I hope you find the inspiration you are seeking within these pages.

To your health!

Suzanne

The Passionate Vegetable

1
True Food

YOU ARE WHAT YOU EAT

I have no doubt that health is directly related to diet. What we eat has far more influence upon our health than any other single factor in our lives. Food helps to fuel our body and build new cells, which in turn become tissue, then organ systems. Scientists say our bodies renew themselves every seven years and our brain every ten years. We are constantly replacing old cells. So we always have the opportunity to change the quality of our blood to create potential disease or vibrant health, and the opportunity to slow the aging process.

Our modern diet of overly processed, refined, and de-vitalized foods, further polluted with chemical additives, is far removed from our natural ancestral diet. Nutritional recommendations today remind us to increase our fiber, lower our refined carbohydrates and restrict foods high in trans-fats. It has turned many people into compulsive label readers. You don't have to read labels if you eat fresh foods—vegetables, fruits, whole grains, beans, free-range meats or organic dairy. Many of these items don't have ingredient labels. These foods are found along the periphery of a grocery store…shop there, it helps you to make healthier choices.

Over the years, I have been asked, "Well, what about my grandparents, they ate just about anything and they lived into their 90s?" My question to them was always, "What was the environment like when your grandparents were born? How much pollution was in the air, water, and food then?" Many of them grew their own food, raised their own chickens, had fresh eggs and drank milk from the local farmer, still often warm from the cow! The first 50 years our grandparents' lives, they built their *constitutions* with hearty wholesome food. If we look closer, processed food, pesticides and herbicides have only been around post-WWII. Sadly, each new generation is raised on more processed food and exposed to more pollution in the environment than ever before.

In 1935, there were 39 agricultural chemicals (mostly fertilizers) in use. In 1939, the pesticide DDT was released and was considered safe at that time but was eventually banned. Today there are over 20,000 pesticides registered with the Environmental Protection Agency (EPA) with a total application of over one billion tons per year. According to the EPA, 160 of these synthetic pesticides are considered possible carcinogens (cancer causing).

The term 'pesticides' used here includes: herbicides, fungicides, insecticides, and pesticides. A 2004 study by the Center for Disease Control (CDC) found 100% of subjects studied showed pesticide residue in their blood and urine. Perhaps this is because only an estimated 0.1% of pesticides applied reach the targeted bugs.

Of the 80,000 chemicals in commercial use in the U.S., only about 200 are assessed and approved as safe. The rest are on a GRAS list (Generally Regarded as Safe). GRAS means initial studies showed no adverse affects. The chemical is cautiously approved with a "let's wait and see" approach. Yes, we are all "wait and see" guinea pigs for the pharmaceutical and chemical industries. Environmental experts say we are exposed to over 65,000 chemicals in our environment, water, and food every year. Conventionally grown produce exposes us to an average of more than 50 different pesticide and herbicide residues still on our food. Peanuts and raisins, for example, can contain traces of more than 80 different chemicals.

Processed Foods

If spraying pesticides wasn't enough, we are next confronted by modern food processing. The number of chemical additives and preservatives used in prepared foods is staggering. Although the amounts are regulated to sub-toxic levels, what about accumulated amounts, or when chemicals interact with each other? Sadly, most chemical product safety testing does not address these issues. They are not required to! It's no wonder that daily, the typical American consumes in his/her food more than a hundred different chemical additives.

In fact, the current food safety standards set by the FDA are intended for *adults only*. Safe levels for children have never been established! The EPA reports that children are exposed to five times more environmental toxins than adults. The effect on children is much greater than on adults.

Although levels of toxic exposure to farm workers is regulated by the government, studies have shown that families who live on farms have a much greater chance of getting cancer than the general population in America! Usually, there is little or no enforcement of these regulations until it is too late and the workers have already developed health problems. Organic farming methods are safer for farm workers, rural residents, and you, the consumer.

Depleted Soil = Depleted Food

Large scale farming removes four inches of top soil, stripping vital nutrients, micro-organisms, worms, and soil culture. Synthetic fertilizers that are used replace only three major nutrients of the 42 needed to grow healthy nutritious food.

Chemical fertilizers consist of three primary nutrients: nitrogen (N), phosphorus (P), and potassium (K). These three are enough to produce *healthy looking crops*, but lack the other essential micro-nutrients that plants and our bodies need. Lack of proper nutrients results in weaker plants that are more vulnerable to pests and disease, necessitating *more* pesticide and herbicide use. Some herbicides actually function by preventing the uptake of key micronutrients, further reducing the nutritional value of our foods.

High crop yields forced through the use of chemical fertilizers often result in nutritionally degraded food. For example, at the turn of the century wheat contained 40% protein. Today wheat's protein content falls between 8–12%.

Our modern diet of refined food leaves our bodies with a continual yearning, a hunger that no amount of food seems to satisfy. We will eat greater quantities of food when quality in the food is lacking.

What About Organic?

What does the term "organic produce" really mean? The Food and Drug Administration (FDA) standard for organic produce requires that the soil in which organic seeds will be planted must be free of herbicides, pesticides, and fungicides for one year. Additional standards include no GMO seeds, no sewage sludge for fertilizer, and no food irradiation for preservation. California standards are stricter and require three years of clean soil. There are national and local reputable organizations that offer organic certification to farmers. They have set explicit standards which govern all areas of production. Look for the seal of organic certification on a package or label. For more information about organic labeling turn to my *To Meat or Not to Meat* chapter.

The organic food industry has grown in sales from $1 billion in 1990 to over $55 billion in 2010. Its annual growth is a steady 20% and it represents 4% of all food and beverage sales in the U.S. The amount of certified organic agricultural land increased from 914,800 acres in 1995 to now more than 91 million acres worldwide.

Healthy Soil = Healthy Food

Soil is a living creative mix of minerals and decaying organic material. Soil is being recycled by a multitude of living organisms, from microscopic to earthworms to larger burrowing animals. This soil community must be nourished like any living organism. Yet government farm subsidies actually discourage proven and sustainable farming practices such as crop rotation, allowing fields to lay fallow, and the planting of natural, nitrogen-fixed cover crops such as clover or soybean.

Organic farmers use soil-enriching natural methods such as crop rotations, utilizing natural compost created from organic matter. They integrate pest management and apply balanced minerals to keep conditions at their best for a natural growth cycle. Once harvested, organic produce is minimally processed, packaged, stored, and transported to retain maximum nutritional value. This is done without artificial preservatives, waxes, colorings, or other additives, irradiation, or synthetic pesticides.

Why wouldn't you want the safest and healthiest food for your family? This motivates me, as a mother, to buy organic food whenever and wherever I can. Is it more expensive? Some things are but others are comparable. However, when I compare the cost of getting sick, losing time from work or school, and medical bills to the cost of organic food it becomes a bargain. Nothing is more important to me than my health and my family's health. I had no medical bills for my children because I put my money and my time into nourishing them the best way I could and it paid off in prevention of illnesses. Without good health the quality of life is severely diminished.

No amount of vitamins or mineral supplements can substitute for nature's intricate balance of nutrients. Often, overeating and weight problems are the direct results of a diet lacking in essential nutrients.

Americans are some of the most overfed but undernourished people in the world. Every meal you prepare is an opportunity to improve you and your family's health.

Fruits and Vegetables

Eat organic, minimally processed fresh fruits and vegetables for a long and vibrant life. Fresh fruit and vegetables are essential to a healthy diet as they offers us the vitamins, minerals, and enzymes not found in cooked protein and fats. Include them in your lunch, dinner, and snack preparation every day. Frozen, canned or commercially available fruit or vegetable juices are not a substitute for freshly prepared organic produce.

Your diet should consist of 30–40% raw vegetables and fruits and 25% cooked vegetables. Enzymes are found in raw vegetables and fruits and are essential for optimal good health. However, enzymes are quickly destroyed within minutes of cooking. However, cooking more fibrous root vegetables softens the fiber and allows us to absorb more nutrients. So a balance of both is important.

When planning a meal, please include vegetables from each of these categories. They each offer a unique balance of minerals and vitamins necessary for optimum health.
- Under the ground: roots such as carrots, turnips, radish, parsnips, onions, etc.
- On the ground: broccoli, cabbage, cauliflower, winter squash, etc.
- Above the ground: leafy greens, peas, peppers, tomatoes, etc.

Color is essential in picking nourishing foods too. Fruits and vegetables will have a high amount of particular antioxidants based on their color. So choose some fruits and vegetables from each of these categories:

Red fruits and vegetables are colored by a red pigment called lycopene, an antioxidant that has been shown to reduce the risk of cancer and heart disease and improve memory. Red fruits and vegetables include cranberries, strawberries, red raspberries, watermelon, tomatoes, red peppers, beets, and red radishes.

Orange and yellow fruits and vegetables are colored by an orange pigment called beta carotene. These foods are abundant in antioxidants, vitamins, and phytonutrients that can help reduce your risk of cancer and delay aging. Orange and yellow fruits include mangos, oranges, peaches, winter squash, corn, sweet potatoes, and carrots.

Green fruits and vegetables get their color from chlorophyll. Chlorophyll molecules have a similarity to human blood. Chlorophyll aids in gastrointestinal issues, promotes formation of red blood cells, detoxifies cancer-causing toxins, treats bad breath, fights infections, and helps assimilate other minerals. Chlorophyll rich green vegetables include spinach, collard greens, green peas, kale, parsley, Swiss chard, turnip greens, broccoli, sea vegetables, bell peppers, Brussels sprouts, green cabbage, celery, and green beans.

Blue and purple fruits and vegetables are colored by purple pigments called anthocyanins, disease-fighting phytonutrients. Anthocyanins help to protect our brains as we age, and reduce the risk of diabetes, certain types of cancer, and heart disease. Purple fruits and vegetables include blood oranges, mangosteen (www.earthsjuice.com), blueberries, black raspberries, plums, red or purple grapes, eggplant, and radicchio.

White fruits and vegetables are colored by white pigments called flavonoids. These powerful phytochemicals can help reduce certain types of cancer, balance our hormones and activate natural immune cells. White fruits and vegetables include pears, bananas, dates, onions, garlic, potatoes, and cauliflower.

Free Range and Organic Meats

Free Range applies to poultry and simply means that the birds were allotted a specific amount of space to "roam" within the confines of their coops. There may be a small fenced-in area for some outdoor "pecking." This limits the number of birds a rancher can put in his hen house. By the way, an average hen house is the size of a football field and can house over 100,000 birds. Access to the outdoors is optional and allowed only during limited times.

One leading U.S. organic poultry brand affords their birds 5 square feet of outdoor area. The National Organic Standards Board Livestock Committee is proposing that USDA organic standards reduce the outdoor area to just 2 square feet layer and 1 square foot per broiler! This is no better than the current industry standard for factory farms, and certainly inadequate for organics.

Grass-fed meats are also referred to as free range and require the animals be allowed to graze outside the confines of the barn. This definition does not guarantee that the animals were fed organic feed or were spared antibiotics and growth hormones. Generally speaking, most ranchers who label grass-fed will also label hormone-free.

Organic standards for chicken or other meats have stricter guidelines. The animals must be free range or grass-fed, antibiotic-free and growth hormone-free and most importantly, they are fed organically grown feed, hay, etc. These are the "cleanest" choices for healthy protein.

Eggs from organic free range hens raised outdoors are far more nutritious than eggs from commercially raised hens. Compared to commercially produced eggs, organic eggs have:

- 4 to 6 times as much vitamin D
- ⅓ less cholesterol
- ¼ less saturated fat
- ⅔ more vitamin A
- 2 times more omega-3 fatty acids
- 3 times more vitamin E
- 7 times more beta carotene

Food Labels—Read Between the Lines

Many food labels are either unregulated or misleading. Federal regulations don't allow hormones in poultry or hogs. So the label stating hormone-free on a package of chicken is a standard industry practice. But growth hormones and antibiotics are permitted in the beef industry. So look for no antibiotics or growth hormones on meat labels.

Terms such as "all natural," or "lower in fat," or "good source of whole grains" aren't regulated and are considered volunteer labeling. Ad writers and marketers make sure the labels and packaging convince you, the consumer, to buy their products. "Natural" for meats and poultry means no artificial colors or ingredients were added to the raw product before packaging. For instance, a turkey labeled "natural" would not be allowed to have colored fat injected under the skin so it roasts more golden.

Not Milk?

You will find very few recipes in this book that include dairy ingredients for several reasons.

- Food can be delicious without added dairy.
- Most dairy available is pasteurized and devoid of beneficial enzymes.
- Most dairy comes from cows fed rBGH growth hormones.
- Reducing dairy consumption automatically reduces cholesterol and saturated fats.
- Many Americans suffer from health problems due to dairy consumption.

A balanced diet that includes calcium rich foods should give you enough calcium. I raised my now adult sons without dairy and they are 6'4", 6'3" and 6'1" in height. Clearly, they got enough calcium in the natural food diet I raised them on. Two thirds of the world's population doesn't eat dairy food and suffers no ill effects. However, I would recommend you seek the advice of a holistic practitioner or nutritionist before eliminating dairy completely out of you or your family's diet.

If you read my introduction you know that all my sons suffered from allergic reactions to cows' milk. Identifying food allergies or intolerances and then treating them through dietary changes is not the standard Western medical approach. The medical profession is primarily geared toward treating diseases and symptoms. After all, the American Dairy Association spends millions of advertising dollars convincing you and your doctor that milk is the best source of calcium and we need it to stay healthy.

The late Dr. Benjamin Spock discouraged parents from feeding their children what he referred to as "cow glue."

Casein, the protein of milk, is also used as a raw material in commercial glue, paint, plastics, and dental materials. Casein is one of two proteins found in milk and forms a ball in the stomach. It may 'gum up' the intestinal walls and may block nutrient absorption in some people. According to a study by the American Academy of Pediatricians, "Since cow's milk protein can irritate the lining of the stomach and intestine, leading to loss of blood into the stools, this can lead to iron deficiency anemia in children. In addition, cow's milk lacks the proper amounts of iron, vitamin C, and other nutrients that infants need. Cow's milk also does not contain the healthiest types of fat for growing babies. Human milk contains a natural balance of vitamins, especially C, E, and the B vitamins, so if you and your baby are both healthy, and you are well nourished, your child may not require any supplements of these vitamins."

Dairy Allergies

Lactose intolerance is the most common food allergy. Actually, it is less of an allergy and more of a food intolerance and malabsorption problem. Most of the world's population is not biologically designed to digest milk of an animal other than their own mother's milk. Pasteurization renders it further indigestible.

The biological purpose of cow's milk is to provide large amounts of energy and nutrients to grow a calf from 60 pounds to 800-1200 pounds within two years. To support that growth, cow's milk contains more protein and calcium than human milk. Human milk will contain a higher amount of carbohydrates for proper brain growth.

What we think of as common health problems are likely due to pasteurized milk intolerance.

Most people cannot digest cow's milk because it contains more than 25 different indigestible proteins. These can induce adverse reactions such as eczema, asthma, colds, allergies, ear infections, headaches, lethargy, fatigue, muscle pain, irritability, restlessness, hyperactivity, and mental depression. Worse yet, in some, it can contribute to diabetes, ovarian cancer, prostate cancer, osteoporosis, bone disease, Crohn's disease, constipation, and weight gain.

Got Hormones?

Most commercial dairy products come from farms that use a genetically engineered recombinant bovine growth hormone called rBGH. This hormone is produced by genetically engineered bacteria and can increase milk production by 3-5 times. A cow is injected every 14 days for 200 days of their 335 day lactation cycle, keeping the cow in a perpetual cycle of gestation and lactation, thus extending the length of milking time.

Cows are already overproducing milk. In 1930, the average cow produced 5 kilograms (kg) of milk per day, but by 1988, milk production was at 18 kg a day. With rBGH injections cows can produce and average of 22 kg per day! This is not the way nature intended cows to produce milk.

This kind of milk production wears out their bodies quicker, and an expected life span of 20-25 years is reduced to 5 years or less. Stress also causes mastitis (udder infection) necessitating the addition of even more antibiotics to their feed. Stress further reduces birth rates so fewer calves are born. It becomes a vicious cycle.

Are there hormones in your milk? You bet! Milk contains not only residues of rBGH as mentioned above, but also excessive amounts of estrogen. Cows treated with growth hormones (rBGH) require more energy-dense food. This is provided as meat and bone meal derived from rendered animals from slaughterhouses, increasing risk of mad cow disease. Add to this milk shake: antibiotics, rBGH hormone, pesticide residues, pus from the infections, and potential bacteria such as salmonella, staphylococci, listeria, and deadly E. coli. Now I ask you, does this sound like a safe and healthy food for you and your family?

The Center for Science in the Public Interest has reported that 38% of milk sampled in 10 U.S. cities are contaminated with antibiotic residues (30 to 60 different types) and sulfa drugs. This increases human tolerance to most antibiotics, which may lead to digestive problems and yeast overgrowth. So if you choose dairy, even occasionally, buy organic! Organic standards do not allow the use of rBGH, growth hormones, or antibiotics on cows.

Milk Substitutes

I don't recommend most of the many soy products that mimic dairy and meats on the market. To start with, 90% of soybeans are genetically modified. Additionally, soybeans go through some pretty extreme manufacturing to get them to the "just-like-meat" stage. Soybeans weren't eaten as a food until 1100 BC when fermenting soy came into use.

Some of the possible concerns are enzyme inhibitors, phytic acid and hemagglutinin, which are present in soybeans. The best forms of soy to eat are either fermented like miso, tempeh, or soy sauce, or sprouted soybeans. Tofu goes through very little processing and is fine for most people. Please always look for organic soy products to avoid GMO.

There are a variety of cheeses and milks made from rice and almond milk or grain milks that are delicious alternatives. Most of them, however, do not contain sufficient amounts of calcium so don't rely on them for your calcium needs.

Navigating the Carbohydrate Maze

Refined carbohydrate consumption has skyrocketed and saturated fat consumption has decreased, but Americans are still battling the bulge. If you are confused as to which carbohydrates are good for you (complex carbohydrates) and which are not (refined carbohydrates), it's time to clear the confusion. All carbohydrates (both refined and complex) are energy foods because they metabolize into blood sugar called glucose. Glucose circulates in our blood and provides energy to all our cells. Carbohydrates differ in their nutritional value and in how quickly they convert into blood sugar. This conversion of carbohydrate to blood glucose is measured by the glycemic index.

Refined carbohydrate sources include the more commonly eaten breads, pastas, cereals, crackers, cookies, desserts, sodas, sugars, candies, etc. Complex carbohydrates include whole grains, beans, vegetables, fruits, milk, and natural sweeteners. When excess sugar is eaten in the form of refined carbohydrates, it is stored as glycogen (fat) in the body.

At rest, our brain requires two-thirds of our body's total glucose needs! The brain cannot store fuel so it requires a constant supply of glucose. When glucose blood levels fall too low in the brain, some people may experience temporary mental fatigue or dizziness.

During exercise, our muscles use glucose for quick energy. Once limited glucose reserves are gone, the body will break down muscle to provide our brain and muscles with glucose. To meet our energy needs while preventing muscle loss, complex carbohydrates can be included in our diets to provide needed glucose.

The Glycemic Index and Carbohydrates

Before we can understand the value of complex carbohydrates over refined, we need to understand the glycemic index. Basically, the quicker a carbohydrate is converted into usable blood glucose, the higher its glycemic index. The slower a carbohydrate is digested and converted into blood glucose, the lower the glycemic index, which is more desirable.

A sudden rise in blood glucose (high glycemic reaction) from eating candy, for example, causes the pancreas to release insulin. Insulin is a storage hormone directly responsible for removing excess glucose from the bloodstream and storing it as glycogen and then later as fat. Eating only refined carbohydrates (see below) will cause insulin levels to rise and stimulate fat storage. When insulin levels in our blood rise, they block the release of fat-burning glucagon. Simply put, eating an excess of even fat-free carbohydrates will prevent your body from burning stored fat. This is not a formula for weight loss!

Refined Carbohydrates

Refined processed carbohydrates, the "bad" carbs, contribute to weight gain, obesity, insulin resistance, metabolic syndrome, type 2 diabetes, food addictions, overeating, and many diet related diseases.

Refined processed carbohydrates are the worst part of the Standard American Diet (S.A.D.). White flour products like breads, cookies, crackers, cereals, pastas, bagels, pastries, and donuts are downright addictive. These are all high glycemic carbs and will cause the undesirable blood sugar spike. However, fiber and protein both slow down the digestion of these carbohydrates, lessening the glycemic blood sugar. On the other hand, there is usually little to no fiber and very little protein in these refined carbohydrates.

So, for example, having a serving of white pasta with marinara sauce would be a high glycemic meal. Instead, choose whole grain pasta with at least 6 grams of fiber and 7 grams of protein per serving. For added protein and fat, serve with a meat sauce, or if you are a vegetarian, add chopped walnuts and sunflower seeds to your pasta sauce.

Complex Carbohydrates
Complex carbohydrates, the "good" carbs, will digest more slowly because they still contain their fiber and protein. Brown rice, a whole grain, contains carbohydrate starch, protein, fat and fiber, all of which helps to slow down a blood sugar rise. Perhaps an excess of brown rice could raise the blood sugar but it depends on what else is eaten in the meal. Did you ever try to overeat brown rice? It's so filling and delicious we are usually satisfied with ½ cup of it with our meals. White rice will cause a sudden blood sugar rise because it has been stripped of its fiber, fat, and protein (germ and bran). Sudden elevations of blood sugar can lead to fat storage.

Eliminating all carbohydrates from our diet is radical and unhealthy, but you can make smarter choices. I suggest you limit your consumption of refined carbohydrates and experiment with complex ones. Make whole grains an essential part of your healthy meal planning. You will find more than twenty-five recipes for whole grain cooking, plus a cooking chart, in my *Amber Waves of Grain* and *Salads that Satisfy* chapters.

THE IMPORTANCE OF PROTEIN
The word "protein" is derived from the Greek root word meaning "of first importance." Protein is the basic material of life. Excluding water, protein constitutes ¾ of our body tissues. Organs, muscles, some hormones, enzymes, and antibodies are largely composed of protein.

The basic structure of protein is a chain of amino acids. There are 22 amino acids identified as the building blocks of protein. Proteins are constantly being broken down, reused, replaced and rearranged with infinite possibilities. This process is known as protein turnover and goes on throughout life. However, there are only 13 of these amino acids that our bodies make. That leaves nine of them considered "essential" and necessary to obtain from our diets.

Foods that contain all the essential amino acids are considered complete proteins. Complete proteins will always be found in animal food and their by-products such as dairy or eggs. Those that don't contain all essential amino acids are considered incomplete proteins. Incomplete proteins found in grains, beans, vegetables, and fruits need to be combined with other proteins to help the body utilize all the amino acids. See my next section *Protein*

Combining for Vegetarians.

- Animal food is usually about 15–40% protein by weight. Excessive amounts of animal protein can decrease calcium in the body and put greater stress on the kidneys.
- The protein content of cooked grains and beans ranges from 3–10%.
- Most vegetable and fruit protein is lower than 3%.
- Soybeans and nuts have protein contents comparable to meat, but soybeans themselves are difficult to digest. This is why fermented soybean byproducts such as tempeh, miso, and soy sauce are more digestible and healthier.
- Although high in fat, nuts are a good source of essential fatty acids and protein. This fat is unsaturated and is considered a good fat.

Peanuts are not nuts but a legume and highest in protein. Commercial peanut butter contains hydrogenated oils that are added to increase the shelf life. Most commercial peanut butter is 47% fat! Almond butter, lower in fat than peanuts, contains some calcium, has an alkalizing effect on the body and is a delicious alternative.

Government estimates show that the typical American is consuming twice as much protein as the RDA (recommended daily allowance). Our protein needs are easily met with 20–35% of our total caloric intake.

Protein Combining for Vegetarians

Meat, milk, cheese, eggs, quinoa, and cooked soybeans are called complete proteins because they contain sufficient amounts of all nine essential amino acids. Whole grains, beans, legumes, nuts, seeds, vegetables, and fruit are foods that contain incomplete proteins. If you are a vegan or a

vegetarian, you should have a wide variety of these foods throughout the day. Combine the following in a meal or within a day's meal and you will increase the overall protein and nutrients:

Whole grains with any bean—Try chili over brown rice or with cornbread or tofu over brown rice, quinoa, or a whole grain tortilla with beans. See my *Black Bean and Garden Vegetable Enchiladas* or *Hot Tamale Pie with Red Beans* in the *Bean Cuisine* chapter.

Beans with any seed or nut—Hummus, a chickpea spread containing sesame tahini can be served with whole grain crackers or in a pita sandwich.

Whole grains with dairy—Try grated cheese over steamed vegetables or *Chicken Parmesan* in *To Meat or Not to Meat* chapter.

Whole grains with any seed or nut—Try *Rocky Road Rice* or *Bulgur Pilaf with Mushrooms* in *Amber Waves of Grain* chapter.

Beans with dairy—Add grated cheese over chili in my *Vegetarian Chili* in *Bean Cuisine* chapter.

Since many vegetables contain small amounts of protein, you can see it is quite easy to get protein in a vegetarian meal. It has been my experience that most vegetarians don't get enough protein and other vital nutrients to stay healthy because they haven't been as careful to combine protein foods in a wide enough variety. Many eventually return to a meat-based diet because they didn't feel as healthy as they expected. There are other factors, of course, including digestion and absorption problems,

Pick Your Protein

Food	Amount	Calories	Protein	Carbs	Fats	Saturated Fat	Cholesterol
Beef/Pork	8 oz	614	40	0	48	20	156
Chicken	4 oz	260	32.8		13.2	3.7	48
Bass	4 oz	141	26	0	2.9		
Cod	6.8 oz	377	25.9	0	29.5	95	
Shrimp	3 oz	90	17	1	1	0	129
Cream Cheese	1 oz	60	3	2	5	3	10
Yogurt	8 oz	100	13	13	0		
Almonds	1 cup	836	28	29	74		
Sunflower Seeds	1 cup	821	32.8	27	71		
Pinto Beans	1 cup	230	17	42	1		
Red Beans	½ cup	120	7.3	22	2.0		
Garbanzo Beans	½ cup	134	7.3	22	2.1		
Tofu	1 oz	22	2.3	.5	1		
Avocado	1 oz	46	1	2.1	4	1	
Soy milk	8.4 oz	140	10	14	4.6		
Rice	1 cup	232	4	.49	1.2		
Oatmeal	1 cup	87	7.9	25	2.3		
Egg	poached	74	6.2	.6	6.5		212
Quinoa	1 cup	222	8	39	4	*0*	

that can lead to low protein in vegetarians. Hopefully, you have found a health care practitioner that can guide you through a transitional diet. Take cooking classes too!!

Balance your vegetable, protein and carbohydrate dishes so they offer a variety of textures to your plate. You wouldn't want all your dishes to be soft like mashed potatoes or all chewy either. Whether you eat alone or with your family, attractive food presentation is important. Make sure your dishes have contrasting colors to create an eye appeal that can't be resisted. A little chopped parsley on top does a lot for a simple bowl of soup.

I recommend you keep a food journal to record your food choices each day. Recording quantity is less important unless you tend to overeat. You can also record your energy level and mental clarity for that day. I suggest you continue this for at least a month while you are transitioning your diet. After a month go back and read it to see if a pattern emerges between your food choices and how you feel. I guarantee that you will learn something from this practice that no doctor could possibly tell you!

Clarifying the Fat

Understanding healthy fats vs unhealthy fats can be less confusing if you remember that there are three major forms of dietary fat:

Unsaturated fats are liquid at room temperature and are considered healthy fats. High quality organic expeller pressed oils are your best choice and are found in health food stores. Unsaturated fats are mostly made up of polyunsaturated or monounsaturated fats. These oils are found in vegetable quality foods such as nuts, seeds, grains, and beans.

Monounsaturated fats include olive oil, peanut oil, almonds, avocados, sunflower oil, sunflower oil (high oleic), canola (rapeseed) oil and lard.

Polyunsaturated fats include soybean, corn, walnut, hemp, grape seed, safflower, sunflower (linoleic), and flax oils.

Saturated fats are solid at room temperature and should be eaten in moderation. They are found in animal proteins, tallow, suet, all dairy foods, butter, and tropical fats, such as palm kernel oil and coconut oil (more to follow on coconut oil and butter).

Saturated fats are stable and do not become rancid when subjected to high heat.

Trans fats and **hydrogenated fats** are the result of high heat specialized processing and are considered one of the unhealthiest fats. They rob oil of nutrition, leaving it virtually indigestible and carcinogenic, and it potentially raises blood cholesterol. Virtually all commercial oils, except olive oil, are processed this way. I strongly recommend you replace these oils with expeller pressed oils found in health food stores (refer to the section Trans Fats: The True Villain).

Unsaturated Fats

Omega-3 EFA (essential fatty acids) are essential to be obtained from our food. Research shows that Omega-3 is an anti-inflammatory that promotes blood flow. Additionally, it lowers the risk of heart disease, arthritis, and cancer. Many modern diseases begin with chronic inflammation. The best food sources for Omega-3 include salmon, sardine, herring, swordfish, green mussels, halibut, anchovy, mackerel, tuna, organ meats, egg yolks, flaxseed oil and flaxseeds, chia seeds, and hemp seeds.

Omega-6 EFA (essential fatty acids) promote blood clotting and reduced inflammation. Today, eggs and animal food contain more Omega-6 than Omega-3. When animals were grass fed, their meat contained a higher amount of Omega-3. It's interesting to note that the Alaskan Inuit people have a 1:1 ratio of Omega-3 to Omega-6. This is because they eat more seafood. They also have extremely low incidences of most modern diseases. In comparison, most Americans are getting a 1:15 ratio of Omega-3 to Omega-6. No wonder we have so many inflammatory-based diseases!

Flaxseeds are a great source of Omega-3. They are high in protein, soluble fiber, and alpha-linolenic acid (ALA). ALA is an Omega-3 fat that is a precursor to EFA, which is the fat found in fish oil. Flaxseeds are concentrated sources of lignans and phyto-nutrients that modulate hormone metabolism. They also have potential anti-cancer properties, especially for colon and breast cancers.

Flaxseed oil should not be heated. Instead use it in salad dressings or drizzle on vegetables or in oatmeal. It is best to grind flaxseeds at home yourself (using a coffee grinder) and store in the refrigerator for a few days. Always store flaxseeds and flaxseed oil in the refrigerator.

Extra virgin olive oil is the best of the best and the most nutritious grade. Light olive oils are refined and less nutritious. They are made from the same virgin green olives used for the extra virgin oil, but they are mixed with a chemical solvent to pull more oil out of the same olives. Then they are pressed again. This process is repeated three times! The combination of all these pressings results in light olive oil. Light olive oil is an inferior product in taste and nutritional value. When I want a lighter oil flavor in my dishes I use one of the other oils mentioned above.

Saturated Fats
Tropical oils are emerging as desirable, less-expensive alternatives to hydrogenated fats. In the late 1980s, tropical oils (palm, palm kernel, and coconut) were shunned because they are high in saturated fat. Now nutrition experts find that they may not be as bad as once thought.

Palm oil or *palm fruit oil* comes from the pulp of the palm fruit. It contains a significant amount of heart-healthy monounsaturated fats, vitamin E, and antioxidant compounds. Research now indicates that palm oil behaves like an unsaturated fat in the body—that is, it may help reduce blood cholesterol levels.

Palm kernel oil is more saturated than palm oil and contains little monounsaturated fat. Less is known about palm kernel oil; it is often further processed (fractionated) to reduce the liquid portion. This leaves behind more saturated solids. You may have noticed "fractionated palm kernel oil" as an ingredient in several energy bars and other reformulated products. This makes the coatings less likely to melt. It isn't known if this processed oil is any better for you than hydrogenated fats.

This doesn't mean these oils get a green light. How they're processed is still questionable and their quality is still debatable.

Coconut oil, although a saturated fat, more than half of it is lauric acid which has many health benefits. It has not been determined to have an effect on cholesterol. Coconut oil is considered to have antimicrobial, antioxidant, antifungal, and antibacterial properties.

Butter vs. Margarine
One tablespoon of butter contains 11 grams of total fat. A whopping 7 grams is saturated with 30 mg of cholesterol—10% of your recommended daily fat allowance! Butter has shortcomings but contains no trans fats. If it's made from organic, unpasteurized milk, it is even less processed.

Margarine was formulated in 1869 as a viable low-cost substitute for butter. Dubbed oleomargarine, it started with softened beef fat to which salty water,

milk, and margaric acid was added. By the turn of the century, the beef fat in the original recipe was replaced by vegetable oils. It was sold as a white spread and it wasn't until 1950 that the production of yellow margarine began.

Margarine is processed in a similar way to chemically extracted hydrogenated oils. To make margarine into a spreadable product, pulverized nickel is used as a catalyst to turn a liquid fat into a solid fat. As of this writing, most margarines still contain trans fats and have been hydrogenated. Read your labels! Almond or other nut butters are a better choice for your morning toast.

Trans Fats: The True Villain

For years the dietary fat villain had always been saturated fats. New evidence points to trans-fatty acids (trans fats) as the real villain.

Harvard University researchers reported that people who ate hydrogenated oils (high in trans fats) had nearly twice the heart attacks as those who did not. They reported that replacing trans fats with unsaturated vegetable oils could prevent at least 30,000 heart disease deaths in the U.S. each year.

Small amounts of trans fats are found naturally in meat and dairy foods. But trans fats found in processed foods contain partially hydrogenated oils. Processed foods include many baked goods, snack foods, margarines, microwave popcorns, frozen meals, and even some peanut butters.

Refined, bleached deodorized (RBD) vegetable oil contains unnatural polymers and carcinogens unfit for human consumption. It makes food crispy, creamy, moist, flavorful and shelf stable, the most important considerations in our profit-conscious food industry.

Fast food is often fried in partially hydrogenated oil, because the oil stands up well with repeated use. But the trans fats that result behave like saturated fats in your body. Trans fats raise both total cholesterol and LDL (bad) levels. Additionally, trans fats lower protective HDL (good) cholesterol. They may also increase triglycerides and inflammation and have been linked to an increased risk of diabetes.

Saturated fats and trans fats have been linked to elevated levels of cholesterol, so exercise caution with these foods. The standard recommendation is to reduce saturated fats by reducing portion sizes of meats and dairy or by choosing lowfat dairy.

All fats regardless of processing have about the same amount of calories, so use all fats in moderation, especially if you're concerned about weight gain.

Chemical Extraction vs. Expeller Pressed Oils

The way oil is extracted greatly affects its nutritional quality. Oils are either chemically extracted or expeller pressed. Chemically extracted oils are most commonly referred to as hydrogenated oils. These oils are the majority of the commercial oils typically found in your local grocery store.

Chemical Extraction

To extract oil from seeds, grains, or nuts (all having a hard coating) the commercial oil extractor first soaks these seeds in hexane, a petroleum solvent. The solution is then boiled at high temperatures to evaporate the hexane and release the oil. This damages the quality and taste of oil.

At high temperatures the oil converts from essential fatty acids into trans-fatty acids. Trans-fats have been shown to raise cholesterol levels and increase free radicals in the blood. Not healthy! Additionally, the high heat begins to spoil the oil giving it a shorter shelf life due to rancidity.

Under federal regulations, food-grade oils must be shelf stable for one and a half years. To prevent rancidity and to accomplish this, these oils are hydrogenated by passing oil through hydrogen gas, which leaves the oil gray, sticky and thick. The soluble materials are then removed with different processes including degumming (removing phosphatides), alkali refining (washing with alkaline solution to remove free fatty acids, colorants, insoluble matter, and gums) and bleaching (with activated carbon to remove color and other impurities.) Frankly, it sounds like a better oil for my car instead of my body!

None of this is clearly labeled, but is simply stated as "pure vegetable oil." How misleading! My teenage sons would break out in pimples within days after indulging in friends' potato chips. This oil is not digestible.

Expeller Pressed Oils
Expeller pressed oils (which I recommend) are mechanically pressed after soaking in a saline solution. They are superior in taste and quality. This method brings a smaller yield at a higher cost. However, it is a small price to pay for greater health. Since these oils are not hydrogenated, they have a shorter shelf life, usually three to six months. It is best to keep them refrigerated to retain freshness. You can leave a small oil bottle near your stove and refill as needed. Oils give rich flavor and moisture to dishes and shouldn't be eliminated. I recommend Spectrum Naturals oils as a superior alternative option to extra virgin olive oil. They can be found in most health food stores. Vegetable oils provide the essential fatty acids that many Americans lack in their diet.

SALT OF THE EARTH
Among the minerals our body needs are sodium, chloride, and potassium. They are essential in regulating body fluids and transmitting nerve impulses. So unless instructed by your health care professional, do not eliminate salt completely out of your diet. If you eat many meals at fast food restaurants, or consume snack or junk foods, you are getting more salt than you need for your daily dose. There is more salt on one potato chip than I use in an entire pot of rice for my family! In one can of store-bought soup, there is an entire day's recommended allowance of sodium! So, read your labels and limit salty snacks and processed foods.

I am frequently asked why I think sea salt is better than kosher or common table salt. All are at least 97.5% sodium chloride, but there are significant differences in the origin and processing of these salts. The textures are very different and professional cooks prefer one over the other depending on the dish prepared.

Sea salt is harvested from evaporated seawater and goes through little or no processing, leaving intact its minerals.

These minerals flavor and color the salt. Sea salt is not the best salt for canning or pickling as the minerals tend to cloud the water and discolor the food. Although the government requires that all salt sold for table use contains at least 97.5% sodium chloride, sea salt may contain trace minerals such as calcium .40%, potassium .12%, sulfur .11%, magnesium .10%, iron .06%, phosphorus .05%, iodine .002%, manganese .0015%, copper .001%, and zinc .0006%. These amounts are very small but the American diet is overly processed and deficient in trace minerals so I believe that whenever we can, no matter how small the amount, we should eat foods that contain trace minerals.

Common table salt is mined from underground salt deposits. In processing, a small amount of aluminum hydroxide or calcium silicate is added to prevent caking. This salt is flash-heated to over 1,200 degrees and then crystallized. Table salt is the name for sodium chloride. I don't consider this a healthy salt to consume on a daily basis. The RDA (recommended daily allowance) for sodium is 2,400 mg but most Americans are consuming two to three times that amount.

Iodized Salt is table salt that has iodine added. Added iodine is important in areas where a local diet is lacking in iodine-rich foods such as fish and seafood. Dextrose is added to stabilize the iodine and keep the iodine from evaporating. Otherwise, it is similar to common refined table salt.

The fine grains of a single teaspoon of table salt contains more salt than a tablespoon of kosher or sea salt.

Kosher salt is a coarse flake that takes its name from its use in the koshering process. Kosher salt is particularly useful in preserving because its large crystals draw moisture out of meats and other foods more effectively than other salts. Some brands of kosher salt contain yellow prussiate of soda, an anti-caking agent, but unlike the anti-caking additive in table salt, it doesn't cloud pickling liquids. It can be derived from either seawater or underground sources. Kosher salt is preferred in restaurants since its coarse texture is easier to use when seasoning dishes. Sea salt's cost prohibits its widespread use in most restaurants.

Salt Substitute is often used by people who are on a sodium-restricted diet. It's made from potassium chloride and contains no sodium. It may not be a healthy choice for people who have kidney problems or other ailments where excess potassium can be harmful. Always consult with your health care professional when making major changes in your diet.

Lite Salt is a sodium chloride and potassium chloride mixture. Lite salt has 50% less sodium than regular salt and may have iodine added.

How Sweet It Is!
The Real Scoop on Sugar

Who doesn't love sweets? I prefer fruit-based, homemade desserts occasionally over chocolate. Whenever I mention to people that I don't crave chocolate and I could do without, I get a startled response. We all have our preferences and being aware of the quality of sweeteners can help you choose healthier alternatives to the "addictive white poison."

Here are a few healthy substitutes:
- *Stevia* is an herb with highly concentrated sweetness.
- *Agave syrup* is made from agave cactus (same cactus used in tequila) and is similar to honey but is milder

and half as sweet.

- *Brown Rice Syrup* is a malted syrup from brown rice and is less sweet than honey.
- *Barley Malt* is a malted syrup from barley, similar to but milder than molasses.

These sweeteners can be purchased in health food stores. Most of these sweeteners have a low glycemic effect on your blood sugar. To learn more about the glycemic index and how it can affect our health and waistline refer to *Navigating the Carbohydrate Maze* in Chapter 1.

What is Sugar?

Sugar is a simple carbohydrate: a chemical compound composed of carbon, hydrogen, and oxygen atoms in a 1:2:1 ratio. Digestive enzymes reduce all carbohydrates to glucose (called blood sugar) for absorption. Whether we are eating brown rice or brown sugar, the end result will be blood glucose. So why eat brown rice when the end result is the same glucose? When we understand how our bodies process all carbohydrates, the answer becomes clear.

Whether carbohydrates are simple or complex, their main dietary function is to supply cells with energy. It is the speed at which carbohydrates turn into blood glucose that is important. Carbohydrates that convert quickly are referred to as high glycemic. Refined carbohydrates cause a sudden rise in blood glucose alerting the pancreas to release insulin to transport the sugar to the cells. This excess glucose is converted into fat energy for later use. The more refined a sweetener (such as white and brown sugar) the quicker and higher the glycemic effect on the blood and insulin levels.

Carbohydrates such as whole grains will digest more slowly causing a gradual rise in blood sugar without a "sugar rush" and the resulting insulin reaction. This gives us needed energy for hours without the "sugar blues" that often follow the use of refined sweeteners.

Sugar Blues

According to the U.S. Department of Agriculture (USDA), Americans are consuming 156 pounds of sugar and sweeteners per person, each year! Most of this excess sugar (60%) is in the form of high-fructose corn syrup (HFCS). According to the World Health Organization (WHO), consumption of the sweetener, which flavors everything from salad dressings to condiments, crackers, snacks and soda, has increased 3.5% per year in the last decade. That's twice the rate at which the use of refined sugar has grown.

- Soft drinks contain the greatest amount of HFCS. Our consumption of soft drinks has more than doubled since 1985 — from ten gallons per person a year to more than 25 gallons.
- Most of this HFCS is added to refined, processed, and junk food. You wouldn't imagine that yogurt, peanut butter, ketchup, and some types of crackers are loaded with hidden sugar, but they are. Always read labels.
- Between 1987 and 1997, sugar consumption increased another 20% during the low-fat and no-fat diet craze. Consumption of added sugar in processed baked goods replaced the fat for flavor and Americans gained an average of 8.5 pounds.
- Bone fractures in adolescents have increased by

34%. This is due, in part, to adolescent increased consumption of soda, decrease in milk, and very little water. Soda accounts for twice the volume of milk in an average child's diet. Soda contains phosphoric acid which can interfere with calcium absorption in the bones. Both the soda and lack of water can lead to a chronic acidosis condition which will further leach calcium from the bones and teeth.

The United Nations and the World Health Organization released guidelines in 2003 that said sugar should account for no more than 10% of daily calories. In a 2,000-calorie-a-day diet, that amounts to 200 calories, or only eight heaping teaspoons of table sugar! A single can of regular soda has the equivalent of 10 teaspoons! Check labels, because once you start paying attention, you will be shocked to learn that sugar and HFCS is everywhere!

High fructose corn syrup is made by an additional refining process using a GMO bacteria for fermentation. It is a very common ingredient in processed foods and beverages and has been recently linked to diabetes and obesity. HFCS will also be labeled as high fructose corn syrup, glucose syrup, corn syrup, and dextrose. HFCS has a glycemic index of 87, while white table sugar is 100! Avoid all high fructose corn syrup products.

Corn syrup is used in household baking and candy making. Corn syrup is chemically refined syrup made from GMO (genetically modified) corn and should be avoided.

White sugar lacks the vitamins, minerals, fiber, protein, and trace elements that were present in the natural plant from which it was processed. *Sugar is loaded with empty calories!* When you eat an excess

of sugar, your body must borrow vital nutrients such as calcium, sodium, potassium, and magnesium from healthy cells to metabolize this incomplete food. Over time, calcium loss can result in teeth decay and bone loss eventually leading to osteoporosis. Refined sugars cause a high glycemic reaction in the blood, setting off an insulin response that can lead to weight gain. Read more in my section *Glycemic Index and Carbohydrates* in Chapter 1.

White sugar is made from either sugar beets (30%) or sugar cane (70%) that has been refined and processed, resulting in 99.9% sucrose. By the way, sugar beets are one of the more recent patented GMO seeds (genetically modified) approved for planting by the FDA. Additionally, white sugar causes a very high glycemic reaction in the blood.

Brown sugar is white sugar with a bit of molasses added back in for color and texture.

Turbinado or raw sugar is made the same way as white sugar except for the last extraction of molasses. Still contains 96% sucrose with very little nutritional value.

Natural Sweeteners

Natural sweeteners can actually have some nutritive value, because they are made from natural whole food sources with very little processing. Natural sweeteners are digested more slowly and won't cause the glycemic spike and drop in our blood sugar ("sugar blues") like refined sweeteners. Natural sweeteners have varying degrees of sweetness and glycemic reactions, so experiment with them. Most are great for baking but depending on their liquidity, you might have to adjust your recipe for texture. Diabetics must be very cautious when using any type of sweetener. We are all familiar with honey, maple syrup, and molasses, but many others such as agave, date sugar, rapadura (evaporated cane sugar), rice syrup, barley malt, yucon, sorghum and fruit juices are all unrefined and so retain valuable nutrients.

HEALTHIEST WATER FOR COOKING AND DRINKING

No discussion of healthy living can be complete without a discussion of the quality of water you drink. The type and quality of water for drinking and to wash and cook your food is important because the contaminants and properties of water are absorbed into our foods. Tap water, depending on where we live, may contain chlorine, minerals, and undesirable contaminants such as rust, sediment, organochlorides like trihalomethanes, lead, hydrogen sulfide, barium, cadmium, arsenic, fluoride, nitrates, benzene, etc. Washing organic produce in chlorinated water simple contaminates your produce. That's not an ingredient in any of my recipes!

"Cancer risk among people drinking chlorinated water is as much as 93% higher than among those whose water does not contain chlorine."—U.S. Council of Environmental Quality

"Each day, millions of Americans turn on their taps and get water that exceeds the legal limits for dangerous contaminants."—USA Today-Special Report, "How Safe Is Your Water?"

Good water can help you achieve excellent health and vitality. If you are fortunate to have your own deep well water and live in a pristine, clean environment, you may want to skip this chapter. Apparently most of us don't, because bottled water sales have soared over the past few years. A more economical approach to better drinking and cooking water is to purchase a filter and do it yourself. Most good filters will remove some to all of the contaminants listed above. Please consider improving your water quality to be a top priority for a healthy lifestyle.

We are made up of 70% percent water! Our cells are bathed in, surrounded by, and made up of water. Doesn't it make sense to use the purest water possible?

Bottled Water—what you don't know

In March of 1999, the Natural Resources Defense Council (NRDC) released a report called "Bottled Water, Pure Drink or Pure Hype?" This report points out that 60% to 70% of all bottled water is completely exempt from the FDA's bottled water standards, because it is bottled and sold within the same state. Unless the water is transported across state lines, there are no federal regulations that govern its quality!

The Natural Resources Defense Council report concluded that, *"Therefore, while much tap water is indeed risky, having compared available data, we conclude that there is no assurance that bottled water is any safer than tap water."*

By the way, I have tested the pH of every bottled water we found and the majority of them are acidic from 4.5 to 6.5 pH, with a few that are a neutral 7.0 pH. Before I truly learned about the quality of water, I was drinking reverse osmosis water in which I added some trace minerals. I thought I was bringing up the pH by increasing the minerals but when we tested the water it was still very acidic at 5.5 pH!

The reality of bottled water is that you pay from $1 to $4 a gallon for the perception of higher quality, when in fact the quality of bottled water is at best an unknown. Quality home water treatment is by far the most economical (in the long run), the most convenient, and the best way to get and enjoy truly healthy, great-tasting water. It is also the right choice environmentally!

The other issue is that the plastics used in these disposable bottles are endocrine disruptors. Bisphenol A (BPA) and phthalates found in these plastics find their way into the water, especially when left in a hot car or in storage crates for too long. Some of this water was bottled over a year ago! These toxins have been found to cause fatigue, weight gain, and hormone imbalances. What about our landfills? It's estimated that 80% of the 28 billion petroleum-based plastic water bottles purchased every year land up in our landfills. Not to mention that bottled water manufacturing created more than 2.5 million tons of carbon dioxide. Oh, and biodegradable? Yes, but in about 1,000 years!

Are You Filtering Out Minerals?

Tap water can be purified by carbon filters, reverse osmosis, and distillation. However, the best water filtration method is electrolyzed (ionized) water. While filtration methods mentioned below may remove undesirable taste and most of the contaminants such as chlorine, detergents, parasites, pesticides, bacteria, viruses, and cancer-causing chemicals, some can also remove beneficial minerals such as magnesium, calcium, potassium, etc.

Water produced by these filtration methods is called "dead" water because the water produced tends to be acidic, has large water clusters and free radicals

(oxidizing) known to accelerate aging and cause disease. Drinking this water can cause the body to deplete minerals found in our bones, teeth, muscles, and other internal sources, to maintain an alkaline blood. This is counter-productive for optimal health, well-being, adequate hydration, and slower aging. Below are examples of some of the more common filters that are available.

Choosing a Filter

Granular Activated Carbon Filters create an increased surface area that can absorb many of the toxic chemicals and organisms found in tap water. Activated carbon filters can trap bacteria without destroying it. So solid carbon filters are preferred.

Reverse Osmosis (R.O.) will remove most of the remaining contaminants as stated by the manufacturer's specifications but, also removes essential minerals. R.O. uses pressure to push water through a membrane filter to remove contaminants. The resulting R.O. "dead" water is also acidic.

Distillation removes contaminants by boiling water to produce a vapor which is collected and cooled back into 99.9% pure liquid water. This "dead" water is also devoid of essential minerals and is acidic.

The Best Water

Electrolyzed (Ionized) Water is produced by a water ionizing machine. After water is filtered, it goes through the ionizer device. Unlike the above filters, the machine separates the water into acidic water and alkaline waters. The alkaline water contains minerals and is micro-clustered (groups of 5-6 water molecules per cluster) which brings out the flavor in the foods, cooks food faster and has a negative charge which means it has antioxidant properties. To read how important acid/alkaline pH is in our diet, see *Acid-Alkaline Balance*. Your water quality is just as important.

This sounded like the best choice for my family, so I researched different ionizers. I found and purchased a medical grade water ionizer device from Japan manufactured by a company called Enagic, Inc. The company was started in 1975 and is the only original equipment manufacturer (OEM) with an impressive list of industry certifications and awards unmatched by any other water ionizer company. The water produced by their machine is so unique that Enagic was granted a trademark by the U.S. government for Kangen Water™.

I bought their top selling model, the SD501, with a full 5 year warranty, and I expect it to last me 15–20 years. To learn more about Enagic machines and quality comparisons, visit www.LivingWaterForLife.com or go the link on www.SuzanneLandry.com. If you want to research, start by researching the international manufacturer's credentials and Gold Standards of Enagic, just as you would in choosing a board certified doctor. Choose quality over price when it comes to your health and getting results.

Improved Health

Do I feel an improvement with this water? Oh, yes! Always trying to drink more water to keep myself hydrated, it seemed I was also spending an equal amount of time in the ladies room, feeling like I wasn't absorbing it. Now, I feel hydrated and my skin and hands are soft and my nails are getting harder! I'm a chef with perpetually soft nails and dry skin. My husband's sinuses are clearing after years of childhood congestion and we are both sleeping better. Weight loss is happening for two friends of mine as they drink more alkalized water. I know personally three people had their psoriasis disappear after topically using this water for a few weeks.

How much water should we drink?

I recommend that you drink half your weight in water per day. So, if you weigh 150 lbs drink at least 75 oz or roughly 2.5 quarts of water. It is easier to drink this volume of ionized water because it tastes delicious. You can count fresh vegetable juices and herb teas in this volume of water but not caffeinated beverages, which are very acidic and dehydrating. For optimum health, drink 8.5 pH water, which is an option on these ionizers.

2
Getting the Nutrition You Need

ANTIOXIDANTS PROTECT YOUR HEALTH

Free radicals are basically incomplete and highly reactive molecules that attach themselves to cells and the genetic material inside them causing deterioration (called oxidation) leading to cell mutation or death. In turn, radicals released from these cells can start a damaging chain reaction to other tissues in the body. Free radicals are believed to play a role in heart disease, cancer, pre-mature aging and overall loss of health and vitality.

Free radicals are produced through the normal process of metabolism. Fortunately, the body is designed to handle a certain amount of oxidation and free radical activity. Today, we are exposed to a much larger amount of damaging free radicals from our environment, indoor and outdoor air pollution, radiation, home cleaning products, personal care products, and cigarette smoke. These place extra toxic loads on our bodies.

The current "standard American diet" consisting of fast foods, unhealthy fats, fried foods, processed foods, refined carbohydrates, sugars and excessive meat all contribute to free radical damage. The greatest control we have over limiting free radical damage is through the food choices we make. Antioxidants provide our body's protection against free radical oxidation by counteracting or neutralizing free radicals and their destructive effects.

Protective Antioxidants Rich Foods

Antioxidants found in fresh food can combat free radical damage. Although antioxidant supplements are widely available, it is most beneficial to obtain antioxidants through fresh food because your body can assimilate and use the antioxidants from fresh food much more efficiently. Organically grown foods have higher levels of vitamins, minerals and antioxidants than conventionally grown foods.

The antioxidants in foods, especially fruits and vegetables offer us some protection against free radical damage. Whole, fresh foods are abundant in antioxidant rich vitamins and minerals. There are hundreds of different substances that can act as antioxidants. The most familiar ones are vitamin C, vitamin A and E, beta-carotene, and other related carotenoids, along with the minerals selenium and manganese. They're joined by glutathione, coenzyme Q10, lipoic acid, flavonoids, lycopene, phenols, polyphenols, phytoestrogens, and many more.

Vitamins C and E are found in plentiful supply in fresh fruits and vegetables. However, at least 60% of vitamin C is destroyed after ten minutes of cooking. Nuts, whole grains, beans, some meats, poultry and fish also contain some antioxidants.

Here is a list of the top 20 sources of antioxidants in commonly consumed foods per the American Chemical Society. "Largest USDA Study Of Food Antioxidants Reveals Best Sources."

Starting with the richest source of antioxidants they are:

- *Small red beans*
- *Wild Blueberries*
- *Red kidney beans*
- *Pinto beans*
- *Blueberries (cultivated)*
- *Cranberries*
- *Artichokes (cooked)*
- *Prunes*
- *Raspberries*
- *Strawberries*
- *Red delicious apples*
- *Granny Smith Apples*
- *Pecans*
- *Sweet Cherries*
- *Black Plums*
- *Russet Potatoes (cooked)*
- *Black beans (dried)*
- *Plums*
- *Gala Apples*

Super-foods for Super Health
Some foods are called super foods because they are some of the most nutrient dense foods available and contain other phytochemicals that are found to be protective against disease. There are entire books devoted to super-foods. In fact, just about every brightly colored fruit and vegetable fits the category of a super-food, as do nuts, beans, seeds and aromatic and brightly colored herbs and spices. You can incorporate some in your meal planning while others would be taken as nutritional supplements. Here are some of the best.

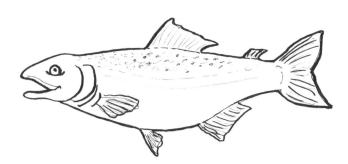

- Wild Caught Salmon—high in Omega 3
- Green super-foods have the highest concentration of digestible nutrients, vitamins and minerals. These include dark leafy greens like kale, collard greens, broccoli, spinach and super-greens such as wheatgrass and barley grass for example.
- Beans—chili beans are one of the best as well as lentils.
- Whole grains—quinoa which is highest in protein and gluten free. Barley and oats are among the others.
- Green and white teas are both high in antioxidants.
- Fruits—kiwi (highest in Vitamin C) berries (high in antioxidants), pomegranate and avocados. Super-fruits like mangosteen juice (www.earthsjuice.com) goji, acai and cacao are the highest in antioxidants.
- Nuts and seeds—almonds and walnuts are some of the best. Super-seeds include flaxseed, hemp and

chia seeds.

- Bee food (pollen, honey, jelly) The western world actually discovered the benefits of bee superfoods by accident during an investigation of native Russian Beekeepers who regularly lived past 100 years of age who ate raw honey, rich in bee pollen, every day.
- Seaweeds (sea vegetables)—hiziki, wakame, kombu (kelp), arame, nori, etc. are the most nutritionally dense plants on the planet containing up to 10 times more calcium than milk and eight times as much as beef. The chemical composition of seaweeds is so close to human blood plasma, that perhaps their greatest benefit is regulating and purifying our blood system.
- Herbs and Spices—turmeric, curcumin, rosemary, cinnamon, capsicum found in peppers, aloe vera, ginseng, Echinacea and nettle to name just a few. Herbs have been used for centuries as part of the wisdoms of natural healing methods. Herbs as medicine are essentially body balancers that work to heal and regulate itself.
- Fermented foods—yogurt, kefir, raw sauerkraut, pickles, sourdough breads, unpasteurized vinegars or acidophilus supplements for extra probiotic support.

THE VITAL ROLE OF ENZYMES IN DIGESTION

Proper digestion of your food along with the quality of the food you consume is essential. You may eat the highest quality of food available but if your digestion is weak, the assimilation of those nutrients will be incomplete and you will not derive the healthy energizing benefits of good food.

As we age, our digestion functions decrease. So eat more fresh fruits and raw or lightly cooked vegetables in your diet for their enzymes and be more aware of proper food combining. Consistent nourishment offers us consistent energy!

Before foods can be absorbed through the small intestines and transported to our cells via our bloodstream, they are broken down into simpler biochemical forms. The catalysts that break down the particles of our food into absorbable molecules are called enzymes. Without enzymes we would not be able to make use of the essential nutrients that we eat! Enzymes are vital to our life and without them our bodies would cease to function. Enzymes can be divided into three major categories:

Food or plant enzymes are present in all raw plants and are responsible for three functions: pre-digestion, nutritional support, and acute repair. Plant enzymes that are needed to digest food include protease (digests protein), amylase (digests carbohydrates), lipase (digests fat), disaccharidases (digest sugar), and cellulase (digests fiber).

Pancreatic enzymes are essentially digestive enzymes secreted by the pancreas, but are also found in our mouth, small intestine, and stomach. These enzymes play a vital role in the digestion of our food.

Metabolic enzymes are made by our body, and are responsible for running our body chemistry. These enzymes are involved in all body processes: breathing, thinking, talking, moving, and immunity. There are hundreds of thousands at work in our bodies at all times.

Early humans primarily consumed raw foods rich in plant enzymes. Our digestive systems are not designed to digest the assortment of processed foods that many people eat indiscriminately. Processed foods lack vital nutrients and enzymes which are found in fresh and raw vegetables and fruits. Less than 10% of adult Americans are getting their recommended "5-a-Day" of fruits and vegetables. Worse yet, less than 5% of children are getting the recommended amount! Of the few vegetables Americans do eat, they are often processed or overcooked, destroying vital nutrients (like french fries vs a baked potato).

Enzymes are destroyed by cooking temperatures above 118°F, pasteurization, canning, and microwaving. So you can see why it's essential to add raw vegetables and fruit to your daily diet. Eating a diet rich in raw foods and taking plant enzyme supplements will help replace those needed enzymes. Supplemental enzymes can be used to optimize digestion, absorption, and assimilation of food, which can reverse nutritional deficiencies, act as an anti-inflammatory and help detoxify. Speak to your natural health care provider if you are

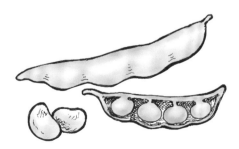

concerned about digestion. When any enzyme deficiency is left untreated, food cannot properly be digested and will inevitably result in many health problems. The most common disorders are food intolerances and allergies.

FOOD COMBINING FOR OPTIMAL DIGESTION

There are three macro-nutrients that need to be broken down into absorbable nutrients in the digestive system: proteins, fats, and carbohydrates. Each is digested by separate enzymes or acids and will take different times to digest along different areas of the digestive system.

Starches begin their digestion in our mouth and complete the metabolic breakdown in our small intestine. Therefore, starches pass quickly through our stomach for that purpose. Animal protein begins digesting in our stomach via hydrochloric acid and pepsin. It can take up to three hours for protein to break down in the stomach before continuing to the small intestine where the nutrients are absorbed. Fats digest later when bile is released by the gall bladder.

Because starches pass quickly through your stomach, proteins digest best without starches present. Eating starches with proteins encourages proteins to leave the stomach before they are completely broken down. Proteins may then *putrefy* in the small intestine! This can cause toxic by-products, gas and sometimes indigestion. A build-up of these by-products can result in anything from food allergies and tiredness, to assorted health problems. Don't combine proteins (which require an acid medium to digest) with carbohydrates, starches, sweets or fruits (which require an alkaline medium to digest). So avoid eating fruit for instance with a protein meal. Enjoy fruit (sweet carbohydrate) as an *in-between-meal snack* when you crave sweets or want a boost of energy.

The best carbohydrates to eat with animal protein are vegetables. A meal comprising of a small portion of chicken or other animal protein, cooked vegetables, and a small salad will digest easily and your body will feel better for it. If desserts are offered, it is best to wait an hour or more after a meal before eating them. Also, wait approximately 45 minutes to drink fruit juice or water after a protein meal.

Whole grains are a valuable part of a healthy diet. Whole grains, whole grain breads, and whole grain pastas are best eaten with vegetables or legumes. Heavy proteins, such as meat, should not be served with whole grains. The principles of food combining are biochemical facts of life and, if respected, will result in better digestion and a healthier you.

Although the efforts of changing your dietary habits can present a challenge, the rewards of health and vitality are definitely worth it.

In Summary:
- Avoid combining protein with carbohydrates, starches, or sweets.
- Eat your desert at least an hour after a heavy protein meal.
- Don't drink water or fruit juice or eat fruit with a protein meal. Instead, have fruit as a snack in between meals.

FOOD pH: ACIDITY AND ALKALINITY
A healthy body has many buffers that maintain the balance between the alkalinity and acidity of its fluids and tissues. Only a pH balanced internal environment allows normal body function and a strong immune system. Due to our modern lifestyle and the overconsumption of acid forming foods, we deplete our alkaline reserves. Tissue acid waste then increases, disturbs the pH balance, and leaves our body more vulnerable to disease. Additionally, most Americans do not drink enough water which can lead to acidosis. Refer to *The Healthiest Water for Cooking and Drinking*.

Acidosis (overly acid diet) can cause such problems as:
- Cardiovascular damage, including the constriction of blood vessels causing oxygen reduction.
- Weight gain, obesity, and diabetes.
- Slow digestion and sluggish elimination.
- Bladder and kidney conditions, including kidney stones. Yeast/fungal overgrowth.
- Acceleration of free radical damage, possibly contributing to cancerous mutations and immune deficiency.
- Premature aging, low energy, or chronic fatigue.
- Osteoporosis, weak, brittle bones, increasing the possibilities of hip fractures.
- Joint pain, aching muscles due to lactic acid buildup.

What is pH?
The pH is the potential of hydrogen. It is a measure of the acidity or alkalinity of a solution. It is measured on a scale of 0 to 14. When a solution is neither acid nor alkaline it has a neutral 7.0 pH. Under 7.0 pH is considered more acidic and above 7.0 pH is more alkaline. The body continually balances its

fluid and tissue pH, with exceptions such as stomach acid, which is measured at pH <2 for the proper breakdown of protein.

The body continually balances the blood pH to stay between 7.35 and 7.45. Most people who suffer from unbalanced pH are acidic. This condition forces the body to borrow minerals (such as calcium, sodium, potassium, and magnesium) from vital organs and bones to buffer (neutralize) the acid and safely remove it from the body. If this borrowing is prolonged, the body can suffer severe damage due to high acidity. Deficiency syndromes, such as osteoporosis, are caused by the body's ongoing attempts at buffering.

Our American diet is too heavy in acidifying foods: meats, poultry, fish, hard cheeses, coffee, alcohol, sodas, hydrogenated oils, desserts, sugars, and refined flour products, and not enough alkaline forming foods such as vegetables.

Your body is able to assimilate minerals and nutrients properly only when its pH is balanced. Without a balanced pH, it is possible for you to be taking healthy nutrients and yet be unable to absorb them. If you are not getting the results you expected from your nutritional, dietary or herbal program, please consult with a health care professional.

Bone Loss and pH
A seven-year study conducted on 9,000 women at the University of California San Francisco, showed that those with chronic acidosis were at greater risk for bone loss than those with normal pH levels. The authors believe that many hip fractures, common among middle-aged and older women are due to a high acid diet, rich in animal foods but low in vegetables (*American Journal of Clinical Nutrition*, 2001).

There has been a 34% bone fracture increase in adolescents due to the overconsumption of (highly acidic) sodas in their diet. Many kids today are drinking twice as much soda as milk and hardly any water. The phosphoric acid in the sodas prevents calcium from being absorbed into the bones. Less milk means less calcium to counteract the pH imbalance.

Keeping the Right Balance
Surprisingly, a food's acid or alkaline-forming tendency in the body is not directly related to the actual pH of the food itself. For example, lemons are very acidic, yet the end product they produce after digestion is alkaline. So lemons are actually alkaline-forming in the body. Likewise, meat will test alkaline before digestion but after digestion meat leaves a very acidic residue in the body. The most influential factors affecting your acid-alkaline pH balance are:
• Dietary choices
• Stress—emotional and physical
• Quality and amount of sleep
• Level of physical activity
• Changes in body temperature

In meal planning, it is important to remember to balance alkaline-forming foods with acid forming foods in a 3:1 ratio. If you fill your plate half-full with vegetables (some cooked, some raw) one quarter animal protein and one quarter complex carbohydrates you will maintain that 3:1 ratio. If you add fresh pressed vegetable juice, you balance your pH even better.

Eat a more balanced 3:1 ratio of alkaline to acid foods. You will become better nourished and feel more satisfied. An added bonus is that you won't experience food cravings and the need for excessive sweets.

If you desire weight loss, increase the vegetables and eliminate whole grains for a while. But if you are craving starches include vegetable starches such as potatoes, turnip, winter squash, carrots, beets, and peas along with other vegetables. The following is a brief and general list of alkalizing and acidifying foods that will help you with your meal planning.

Basic Acid-Forming Foods

It is impossible to eat a varied diet that doesn't include at least a few acid forming foods—you'd be eliminating all proteins! Acid-forming foods can be 25%–30% of your diet, depending upon lifestyle. These are general guidelines for relatively healthy individuals. If you are recovering from an illness or surgery, follow the recommendations of your health care practitioner.

Meats—all meats, poultry, fish, and shellfish.
Grains and Breads—rice, barley, wheat, oats, rye, and corn.
Nuts—cashews, walnuts, peanuts, pecans, macadamias, and filberts.
Dairy and Oils—pasteurized milk products, cream, cheese, egg whites, nut and corn oil.
Legumes and Vegetables—lentils, navy beans, kidney beans, adzuki beans, and cooked spinach.
Fruits—cranberries, blackberries, pomegranates, plums, prunes, and rhubarb.
Beverages—coffee (very acidifying), black tea, soft drinks, and alcoholic beverages.
Chocolate—in all varieties.
Soy products—tofu, soy sauce, and miso.
Sweeteners—white sugar and sugar substitutes, brown sugar, milk sugar, cane syrup, malt syrup, molasses, and processed honey.
Oils—flaxseed oil, olive oil, canola oil, evening primrose oil, and borage oil.
Nuts and Seeds—almonds, chestnuts, flaxseeds, sesame seeds, fennel, and caraway seeds.

Basic Alkalizing Foods

Alkaline-forming foods should make up 70–75% of your diet. Most of these should be vegetables and fruits. Eat at least 50% uncooked as salads and snacks. The following is a basic list of such foods.

Fruits—including citrus, apples, pears, peaches, blueberries, watermelon, papaya, mango, and cantaloupe.
Vegetables—sea vegetables (seaweed), mustard greens, asparagus, parsley, raw spinach, carrots, cabbage, broccoli, potatoes, sweet potatoes, lettuce, onions, garlic, and most other vegetables, and especially dark, leafy greens.
Grains—millet, amaranth, wild rice, quinoa, buckwheat, and sprouted grains (except wheat).
Fish—cold water fish, usually white meat fish.
Dairy—unpasteurized nonfat milk, goat's milk, cottage cheese, plain yogurt, butter, and egg yolks. Although I do not recommend dairy foods, they are generally neutralizing.
Beverages—clean or purified water, lemon water, green tea, ginger tea, and herb teas.
Legumes—peas, green beans, lima beans, and sprouted beans.

Sweeteners—raw honey, raw sugar, maple syrup, rice syrup, and stevia.

Food Cravings—Getting Off the Food Roller Coaster

Why do we crave certain foods? Whenever we experience a craving, our body is trying to maintain or restore balance. **When we eat excess salt or protein, we will desire sweets, sodas, alcohol.** For instance, the desire to have a dessert after a meal of animal protein or have a soda with salty popcorn is a natural response to an imbalance of pH. Our willpower has little to say when our body seeks to balance its blood pH and maintain homeostasis (state of whole-body balance). Please refer to the section

Food pH: Acidity and Alkalinity for more information.

Some foods create more "heat" while others are "cooling." The more protein and fat a food contains, the longer it takes to digest. The more energy that is used to digest it, the more heat it produces. Energy creates heat, so high protein and high fat foods create warmth in the body. That explains why we desire more meats, fats, and fried foods in winter seasons or colder climates.

Vegetables usually digest within one to two hours and fresh fruit within an hour. They produce very little heat during the digestion process. In addition, their higher vitamin, water, and sugar content have

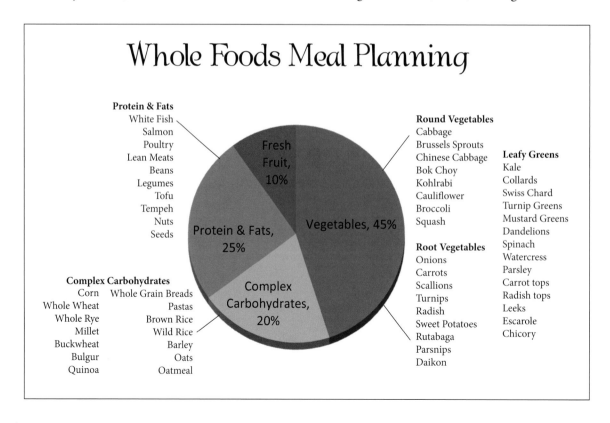

Whole Foods Meal Planning

Protein & Fats
White Fish
Salmon
Poultry
Lean Meats
Beans
Legumes
Tofu
Tempeh
Nuts
Seeds

Fresh Fruit, 10%

Protein & Fats, 25%

Vegetables, 45%

Complex Carbohydrates, 20%

Round Vegetables
Cabbage
Brussels Sprouts
Chinese Cabbage
Bok Choy
Kohlrabi
Cauliflower
Broccoli
Squash

Root Vegetables
Onions
Carrots
Scallions
Turnips
Radish
Sweet Potatoes
Rutabaga
Parsnips
Daikon

Leafy Greens
Kale
Collards
Swiss Chard
Turnip Greens
Mustard Greens
Dandelions
Spinach
Watercress
Parsley
Carrot tops
Radish tops
Leeks
Escarole
Chicory

Complex Carbohydrates
Corn   Whole Grain Breads
Whole Wheat   Pastas
Whole Rye   Brown Rice
Millet   Wild Rice
Buckwheat   Barley
Bulgur   Oats
Quinoa   Oatmeal

a cooling effect on our bodies. This explains why we desire more fruits, vegetables, ice cream, sweets, sugar, sodas, hot spices, and alcohol in summer and in warmer climates. When our diets are imbalanced with excess proteins and fats and not enough fruits and vegetables, we will crave these cooling foods.

Vegetables, especially dark leafy greens, are high in minerals. Yet when we are too acidic, the mineral we crave is salt. It's interesting how eggs taste so much better with a little salt, because eggs are acidifying and salt is alkalizing. A centered diet includes foods that are in a balanced ratio of proteins, carbohydrates, fats, vitamins, and minerals. An imbalanced meal leads to undesirable snacking which leads to further imbalances.

So keep a 3:1 ratio of plant foods to animal foods on your plate to prevent unwanted cravings. Plant foods include vegetables, fruits, whole grains, beans, nuts, and seeds. It's easier to maintain a healthful balanced lifestyle when each meal is balanced.

Food processing destroys nutrients making them empty-calorie foods which throws off our nutritional balance. Antibiotics in meat, artificial preservatives, herbicides, pesticides, and growth hormones further take the balance out of food. Is it any wonder that most people don't know what a balanced diet is? Many of my students comment on how well-nourished they feel after tasting the food in my cooking classes. Our shared meals consist of whole grains, beans, fresh vegetables, fruit-based desserts and perhaps sea vegetables. It's almost like our bodies want to say "YES" to healthy food!

To get off the food roller coaster, keep your meal balanced with a 3:1 ratio of plant food to animal foods.

Eat plenty of vegetables and fruits. Consistent good nourishment ensures us of consistent energy and health.

The secret is out—cooking is not a mystery. The way to be a good cook is…well…to cook—just plunge in! Even wholehearted efforts sometimes fall short and the best intentions don't always ensure success. There is no great secret, only the experience of doing it over and over again. The results don't have to be just right; some of my best dishes were the result of mistakes or substitutions I made in a recipe. Our cooking doesn't have to prove how talented we are or measure up to some imagined result. It's your unique way of nourishing yourself with food.

Our original worth is not something which can be measured, increased, or decreased by what we do… especially in the kitchen.

The more love you put in your cooking, the better your food will taste. Cooking for yourself or your family is an act of love because through food you create life. You give your life energy through cooking to create life again—what a beautiful circle of love. Love is the most powerful ingredient of all. I hope through my recipes I can encourage you to fall in love with creative cooking.

Approach cooking with abandonment and enjoy every morsel of the experience…just feed, satisfy, and nourish.

3
Making the Transition to Natural Foods

Food Budgets

Long ago I got the important message from my dad that good health was my wealth. The value of protecting my health was deeply instilled when he died at 47 years of age from a long battle with cancer. So I put my family's health first which meant I valued the quality of food that we consumed. As a single mom, the routine was to pay rent, make the car payment and insurance payment, and buy food. Everything else could be budgeted.

If I'm in the mood for asparagus or my son asks for red raspberries and the price is high, I buy them anyway. That desire is my body talking, needing certain nutrients, and when it talks healthy, I listen. Red raspberries are a good source of iron so my youngest son's love of raspberries was his body telling him he needs iron. I place my priorities on prevention of disease so we are never ill and don't have the need for doctor visits!

One of the ways I demonstrate love for myself and my children is through preparing and eating delicious healthy food… despite the cost.

I have worked closely with cancer patients for several years now. I have been blessed to have learned so much from them. One message that is driven home for me every time is that *prevention is so much cheaper than the high cost of recovering our health again.* We've been taught to ignore our bodies' desires—eat when we're not hungry, drink water to kill hunger, starve to loose weight, or follow someone else's schedule for meals. If we honor our body's language, feed and nourish it, our body tells us what we need and in turn rewards us with health and vitality.

Begin by Starting

Let's face it, we humans make transitions in our lives very slowly and sometimes kicking and screaming along the way. So don't expect your transition to good eating habits to happen overnight. You've had your present eating habits for a while so give yourself time to change those habits. After all, you may be changing the tide of ancestral eating habits, not to mention cooking with ingredients you may have never heard of before.

Step 1: Begin to read labels

The ingredients you use are crucial—choose the best! My rule of thumb was simple in the beginning of my transition: if I couldn't read it, I probably didn't want to eat it. Packaged Danish pastries (Entenmanns *was* my favorite occasional treat back then) are loaded with unpronounceable ingredients that do not enhance flavor, but just increase shelf life. Buy it freshly baked or bake it yourself and you'll know what goes into it. Ingredients are listed in order of volume first, so if sugar is the second ingredient, watch out! Most commercial cereals average 32–73% sugar!

Step 2: Substitute familiar ingredients

Start eliminating highly processed food from your diet and substitute natural alternatives. This change alone will affect the overall taste of your favorite recipes and will increase its nutritional value. For example, your favorite dessert recipe can be improved by substituting bleached white flour for unbleached or whole wheat flour. This way, you are improving the quality of the food you eat without eliminating all the family favorite dishes. For more substitution suggestions, please see *Food Substitution Chart* in this chapter. If your budget is limited, make this transition slowly as you replace pantry items.

Step 3: Stocking the Pantry

Fill your pantry with basic staples and always have lots of fresh vegetables and fruits on hand to make cooking easier and to be ready when the creative inspiration hits you! Except for buying fresh vegetables and fruits, we could probably live off of what's in our pantry for a month or more. I like it that way. Every grain and bean variety I cook with is in my pantry, along with a wide selection of herbs and spices, pastas, nuts, and some prepared condiments and canned foods. See *Pantry Essentials* in this chapter for a list of suggestions.

Step 4: Introduce vegetarian entrees

Throughout the week introduce a vegetarian entree instead of a meat or a dairy dish. Start by introducing a whole grain side dish a few times a week. If you are a vegetarian, whole grains are an important daily dish to include in your meal planning. You can start by preparing hot breakfast porridge such as cream of rice, cream of wheat, or oatmeal. Perhaps you'd like a cold, whole grain cereal instead. In my *Amber Waves of Grain* and *Salads that Satisfy* chapters, I show you how leftover grains can be turned into an international selection of new tastes. Whole grains are filling, nutritious, and will help you

get off the carbohydrate-craving rollercoaster.

Many of my students have, over the years, experienced a drastic drop in their cholesterol when they introduced whole grains in their diets.

For the first six months of our transition, I browsed vegetarian cookbooks for recipes that I then made for my family. If we all enjoyed it and it wasn't time consuming, I would prepare it again in two weeks. As my repertoire of recipes grew I eliminated more meat-centered meals. Before very long we were enjoying our new way of eating. Also, look for ways to present the meat entrees with more vegetables. Instead of steak or barbecued chicken, try beef stir fries or chicken stew with vegetables. This way the portion of animal protein is balanced with more vegetables and your food dollar will stretch serving more people. By the way, you probably won't miss the meat.

Step 5: Plan Ahead

Eating healthy can take a little more time in preparation, but planning ahead is the best advice I can give. Jot down some possible meal ideas and make a shopping list for the coming week. Having everything on hand makes a huge difference in time preparation for a meal. Having a wide assortment of ingredients doesn't necessarily mean you decide what you'll eat for dinner next Wednesday, but it does give you a general idea of what you can cook during the week.

Step 6: Saving Time in the Kitchen

This can mean soaking beans overnight (or a few days before) and cooking them in the morning while you are getting ready for work. Cooked beans keep for about five days.

You can add some vegetables, herbs or spices to them and in 15 minutes your beans are ready for dinner. Cooked grains will hold for three days refrigerated and so cook them anytime you're at home for an hour. For example, tomorrow's grain can be cooking on the stove while you are eating tonight's dinner.

If I am planning on making a chicken dish for tomorrow, I prepare the marinade tonight while I am making dinner. I will clean, chop, and bag enough kale or other greens for three dinner servings. While chopping carrots for tonight's stir-fry, I might chop extra for lunches or tomorrow's soup. Sometimes we cook a few more chicken breasts than we need for dinner and turn that leftover chicken into fajitas, tacos, or a Cobb salad for a few quick workday meals.

Try not to let a burner in your kitchen sit idle while you are at home. If you are good at juggling (if you have kids, you definitely are) then you can be cooking on the stove, roasting in the oven, stirring the soup, and chopping all at the same time. Okay, that's a bit much except for a passionate chef like me, but you can eventually learn to coordinate 3-4 dishes at once.

The point is, think on your feet, plan ahead, and when you are in the kitchen keep those hands moving and all those burners going! Just make sure you have all the ingredients on hand and begin prepping!

Step 7: Be Playful and Creative
As I said before, some of my best dishes are those that I had no idea what I was going to make when I started looking in the refrigerator and pantry. Once I see what's on hand, the creative juices of possibilities began to bubble in my mind. Experiment! You can always go out to dinner if it is a total disaster. Chances are you will discover a wonderful new dish that may become your new favorite. If you're like me, however, you will be enjoying the creative play so much that you forget to write down the quantities of the ingredients you used. Some of my masterpieces never quite got duplicated because of that.

SURVIVAL DINING FOR VEGETARIANS

Eating out can be challenging when you are transitioning your diet. But there are enjoyable dishes you can find to fit into your diet at the home of a friend, on airplanes, or in restaurants.

Visiting with families who eat differently from you does not have to be a stressful experience. If it is for one meal, ask them to prepare a pasta entrée (or bring it yourself). If their entree doesn't fit in to your diet, you can always eat the vegetable side dishes that are usually offered with an entree. The biggest challenge for some people is telling family members that they don't want to eat what has been served. You may feel you might hurt their feelings. An easy alternative, if you need one, is to explain you have allergies or you are doing a food elimination diet recommended by your doctor. If your visit is for several days, I recommend bringing some vegetarian protein sources to heat up without a lot of fuss. For example, frozen veggie burgers or canned beans travel easily and you can purchase tofu almost anywhere. Once your protein needs are taken care of, you can share and enjoy the vegetable and starch side dishes your family will be serving.

Another situation where you may feel your diet is challenged is during air travel. The few remaining airlines that offer meals at all usually have a vegetarian offering. Other healthier choices are the fish or kosher entree selections. It seems that airline caterers haven't caught up to the idea that whole grains and beans or tofu should be part of a vegetarian meal. If it is a long flight, I will carry on several snacks including nut mixes and fruit to tide me over.

An everyday challenge for some is eating in restaurants. If you're a vegetarian it is even more of a challenge. However, many ethnic restaurants serve vegetarian dishes that include acceptable protein entrees. Eating foods of a different culture can be both enjoyable and festive. My favorite is a Japanese restaurant where I get the sea vegetables and rice that I love (many of them serve brown rice). Chinese restaurants offer tofu entrees, and Mexican restaurants have bean entrees or soups. You'll also find bean entrees in Indian restaurants.

You can get a vegetable salad, cooked vegetables, or pasta anyplace in the world, but after a meal or two, you may need some protein to meet your nutritional needs. Carrying some mixed nuts along with you is a good way to add protein to your diet if beans, tofu, or fish are not available. If you eat out frequently, choose a restaurant that offers healthier choices of protein with lower fat content. When eating a fish entree at a restaurant, avoid deep fried entrees. Additionally, order a large salad and for a starch, order a side of rice or a baked potato instead of bread. Yes, and either skip the dessert or share with a friend. My husband and I will occasionally share a fruit based dessert when we eat out.

ADAPTING YOUR FAVORITE RECIPES

One of the easiest steps to transitioning your diet is to upgrade the quality of ingredients in your favorite recipes. In this way you are taking a step in a healthier direction without causing a mutiny at home. See my *Food Substitution Chart* below for exchanges.

USING HERBS AND SPICES

The transition to healthy eating can be a delicious experience if you learn to season with herbs and spices. Adding a few herbs and spices helps dishes pop with flavor while cutting down the need for salt. Even a simple dish becomes special and elegant with the addition of some favorite herbs and spices. The fine art of seasoning is not complicated when you use a few guidelines. As with many art forms, appreciate the process and you are more likely to appreciate the results.

Herbs: These are the flower buds and leaves of plants and the flavors are more delicate than spices. Herbs can be stored from six months to one year after which they lose their flavor and color. Basic keep-on-hand: basil, oregano, thyme, parsley, rosemary, dill or mint if you wish.

Spices: These are from the parts of the plant richest in flavor—stems, nuts, barks, seeds, and roots. Spices can be stored for up to three years before losing their flavor. Some spices are hot while others are sweet. Cinnamon, nutmeg, or cumin are considered sweet spices and cayenne, chili, ginger are hot. Basic keep-on-hand: ginger, cinnamon, cayenne or chili or hot red pepper flakes, cumin, black pepper. If you are wondering why I didn't mention garlic it is because it is technically not a spice or an herb but a bulb, which like onions, shallots and chives, is a member of the lily family.

Substitution: When substituting fresh herbs for dried you can increase the quantity by three. When substituting dried for fresh in a recipe, you should reduce by a third. You can be more generous with milder herbs such as basil because I don't think you

Food Substitution Chart

Reduce or Omit	Substitute	Other Changes/Notes
All-purpose flour	whole wheat flour or other whole grain flours	requires a little more liquid
Baking powder and soda	low-sodium, aluminum-free baking powder	
Bleached cake flour	whole wheat pastry flour or organic unbleached white flour	requires a little more liquid
Canned or frozen vegetables	fresh organic fruits and vegetables	at least 40% higher in nutrients
Chocolate	carob powder or organic chocolate	3 Tbs carob plus 2 Tbs milk powder equals 1 oz chocolate
Coffee/Tea	green or white tea, organic coffee, or herbal teas	Try it iced!
Common table salt	sea salt, kelp, or soy sauce	season to taste—may require less
Cornstarch	arrowroot powder, organic cornstarch, or kuzu	
Crackers or rice cakes	whole grain crackers	
Distilled vinegar	raw apple cider vinegar, unpasteurized vinegar, or lemon juice	adjust to taste
Eggs	organic and free range eggs	You can taste the difference!
High fat salad dressings	There are many good salad dressing on the market—avoid corn syrup, hydrogenated fats, and artificial preservatives.	or make your own—see *Fresh Garden Salads* chapter
Hydrogenated fats, oils & shortening	extra virgin olive oil or expeller pressed oils	using liquid fats instead of solid fats requires less liquid in recipe
Hydrogenated margarine	Earth Balance organic buttery spread	
Pasta - white flour	whole grain pastas, wheat free pastas, or organic flour pastas.	Needs to cook a little longer. Follow package directions.
Processed cereals	whole grain cereals, granola, or hot whole grain cereals	
Red meats and poultry	Natural beef, free range or organic chicken, or vegetable protein - beans, tofu, nuts, or seeds	
Sodas	natural fruit juice, natural flavored sodas, or sparkling water	
Sugar	natural sweeteners, pure maple syrup, evaporated cane syrup, barley malt, agave, raw honey, rice syrup, date sugar	Requires more dry ingredients or less liquid in recipe.
White bread	Whole grain breads or whole grain sprouted breads	Better nutrients and fiber. Will satisfy you with less.
White rice	brown or wild rice, or other whole grain	
Whole milk and dairy	Organic dairy or dairy substitutes—rice milk, coconut, almond, or nut milks	Please read *Not Milk?* in Chapter 1

can ever have too much basil or garlic for that matter!

Storage: Store dried herbs and spices at room temperature away from heat, light and moisture. Fresh herbs, such as parsley, cilantro and dill can last over a week when stored in the refrigerator. Place in a wide mouth glass jar, fill with water and place a loose bag over top. Change the water every two days and they will remain fresh.

Cooking Tips:
- Salt sometimes enhances flavor, but excessive salt can easily drown out delicate flavors and leach out important nutrients from vegetables.
- Add whole spices (such as a cinnamon stick) at the start of cooking to allow their flavor to permeate the food.
- Add ground spices midway through cooking; always start off with small amounts when using hot spices and build up to taste.
- When blending herbs with dressings or sauces that will not be cooked, add an hour before needed to let flavors meld.
- To increase the flavor of dried herbs, crumble them between your fingers to release their oil and aroma before adding them to your dish.
- To use fresh herbs, when the recipe calls for dried, you can use one tablespoon of chopped fresh herbs for every teaspoon of dried herbs.

Flavor Families
Some herbs and spices complement each other well. They form "flavor families" and can be used together to enhance dishes. Here are some winning flavor combinations:

Sweet—allspice, anise, cinnamon, cardamom, cumin, cloves, nutmeg. Use in breads and desserts, especially fruit based pies and fruit breads.

Hot—chili peppers, cayenne, garlic, radish, onion. Although fresh cilantro is not hot, it has a unique flavor and is used to cool down hot spices. These flavors are a must in Mexican, Cajun and Spanish dishes. Use in seafood, poultry, soups, salads, marinades and in bean dishes.

Spicy—cinnamon, ginger, pepper, star anise. These have a zing to them and are wonderful in Chinese stir fry, soups, poultry, meats, seafood dishes, and whole grain dishes such as "Chinese Fried Rice" in *Amber Waves of Grain* chapter.

Pungent—celery seed, cilantro, cumin, curry, ginger, black pepper. Curry blended here in America is less spicy. You can adjust the "heat" to your taste by increasing the amount of cayenne or ginger. Use these spices in poultry, shellfish, meats, beans, whole grains, and vegetable dishes.

Herbal—basil, parsley, dill, marjoram, rosemary, thyme and sage. These herbs are the basis for a great sauce. Use these herbs for flavoring sauces, gravies, poultry, soups, herb breads, stuffings and muffins.

Hot spices have a cooling affect on the body. That's why they are popular in countries with hotter climates.

PANTRY ESSENTIALS
My pantry is well stocked with a wide variety of ingredients so I always have on hand what I need when my creative culinary urge hits. It is certainly not necessary to have every one of these ingredients

in your kitchen! I am so well stocked I could whip up something for several unexpected guests at a moment's notice.

Condiments: sea salt, oils, soy sauce, vinegars, miso, organic mayonnaise and mustard, and ketchup to name a few. I have quite a large selection of dried herbs and spices. Most cooks can get by with twelve or so essential herbs and spices. I prefer mixing my own, so I purchase single herbs from the bulk section of a health food store as they are fresher and cheaper. Then I refill the empty store-bought jars or label my own.

Sea Salt: Use only natural sea salt. Natural sea salt contains trace elements and minerals. You will find that you may need less in a recipe. Read more in *Salt of the Earth* in Chapter 1.

Oils: I keep a variety of oils in my pantry, including extra virgin olive oil (for almost everything except frying), light sesame oil for light pan frying and some salad dressings when I don't want an olive flavor; toasted sesame oil for Asian dishes; hot chili oil for a touch of heat in just about anything; and corn oil for baked goods. Unrefined corn oil is thick and rich like melted butter. Every oil imparts a unique flavor and consistency, and some recipes do better with one over the other. When I refer to expeller pressed oils in my recipes, it is Spectrum Naturals brand that I am using. Spectrum Naturals is a high quality oil found in health food stores.

If a recipe calls for a solid fat like butter, margarine, or shortening and you want to substitute with oil, you must compensate for the liquid. Either add a tablespoon or two of flour to bring it up to its original consistency or reduce the oil. Oil is 100%

fat, and butter is a combination of fat, water and whey, so don't use the same measurement or it will be too oily. If a recipe calls for ½ cup of butter, use ⅓ oil to achieve the same richness. There are also "prune pureed with flaxseed butters" available that are meant to be used instead of oil or eggs. Spectrum Naturals makes a vegetable shortening that is non-hydrogenated and can be found in health food stores. A non-hydrogenated margarine free of trans fats is Earth Balance. Again, it is found in health food stores.

The quality of oils you use in your cooking will greatly affect the flavor of your dish! Look for unrefined expeller pressed oils found in health food stores. For more information on fats and oils refer to Clarifying the Fat *in Chapter 1.*

Soy Sauce or Tamari: Traditionally, tamari was the name given to soy sauce that was aged without wheat. That's no longer the case today. Soy sauce and tamari are essentially the same except that tamari tends to have a less salty taste. Be sure to get authentic soy sauce, without artificial ingredients and preservatives. If you are allergic to wheat, do read the labels.

Vinegars: I keep a variety of vinegars in my kitchen. My favorite brand is Spectrum Natural vinegars because they are unpasteurized. Similar in health value to the bacteria in yogurt, unpasteurized vinegars continue to ferment and age in the bottle. If you purchase one of these vinegars you may want to keep them refrigerated. If they get cloudy, that is a good sign and you should continue to use it in your recipes. They are many varieties available. Braggs Apple Cider vinegar is the best and perhaps the only raw unpasteurized apple cider vinegar available. White distilled vinegar is too acidic and too processed to be used for food but is great for cleaning carpet stains! Occasionally I'll purchase or make herb or fruit infused specialty vinegars.

Herbs and Spices: I stock a wide variety of dried herbs and spices and I also keep some fresh ones on hand. To keep them fresh, place fresh herbs such as parsley, dill and cilantro in a glass jar, with a few inches of water, and cover with a plastic bag. Keep refrigerated up to 10 days and change water every few days. For more information read Using Spices and Herbs.

Whole Grains: These are the staple carbohydrates in our house, replacing the pasta and breads of my childhood diet. Although we still enjoy good whole grain breads or pasta, it is not our daily fare. I keep a variety of rice on hand that includes brown basmati, short grain brown rice, and wild rice. I always stock millet, quinoa, barley, and whole oats. You can include bulgur wheat, couscous, and buckwheat too. If you are new to cooking whole grains, there are some mixes available on the market.

Baking Ingredients: I keep a typical selection of baking ingredients in my pantry except that all my ingredients are organic and whole grain based. You will find unbleached flour, whole wheat flour, and aluminum-free baking powder among my vanilla extract, spices, and natural sweeteners.

Pasta: The pastas I frequently use in my recipes are whole grain pastas, rice noodles for Thai cooking, udon, somen, or soba (buckwheat pasta) for Asian dishes. Whole grain pastas will have more fiber and protein than conventional white pastas but not as much as the whole grain itself. Look for whole grain pastas with at least 7g of protein and 6g of fiber per serving. It is a light, easy to digest occasional meal. I serve pasta once a week during hot weather.

Beans: Keep a variety of dried beans and some canned beans on hand such as adzuki, black beans, great northern, navy, pinto, garbanzo (chickpeas), red or green lentils, as well as split green peas. I always prepare more than I need and freeze the remainder in dinner size portions for later use. See my *Bean Cuisine* chapter for helpful hints on how to successfully cook beans.

Extras in a Can: Some extras that come in handy and can be kept in your pantry are a variety of canned organic tomatoes, capers, sun-dried tomatoes, olives, and light coconut milk. These ingredients sometimes show up in my recipes, so they are always good to keep on hand. I also stock organic frozen corn and peas year round in the freezer.

Extras: Additional pantry items would include hot and cold cereals and non-dairy milks.

Sweeteners: For flavor and nutrition, I prefer using pure maple syrup, as well as raw honey, brown rice syrup, barley malt, or agave syrup. In a recipe, if you are exchanging a dry ingredient (white or brown sugar) for a wet one, you can use the same amount but add a little flour to the recipe to bring it back to its original consistency. See *How Sweet It Is* in Chapter 1.

Sea Vegetables: Not your common "beach seaweed," sea vegetables are cultivated and harvested specifically for food consumption. They have been a major part of Asian diets and coastal cultures since ancient times. Very alkalizing and full of minerals, you will find sea vegetables quite flavorful. Hiziki, for instance, contains fourteen times more calcium than a glass of milk! I keep kombu, wakame flakes, dulse, nori, hiziki, and arame in my pantry. My kids and I love them all!

Nuts and Seeds: Using nuts and seeds in whole grain dishes adds protein, good quality fat and makes for a surprising texture. I always stock almonds, walnuts, peanuts, pecans, and pine nuts as I never know when the urge to snack or throw a handful in a recipe might stir me. Keep them in the refrigerator or freezer to extend their freshness.

Dried Fruit: Use organic or sulfur-free dried fruits whenever possible. Most conventionally grown produce will have pesticide residuals and drying the fruit only concentrates these chemicals. Mostly for baking, I keep organic dried cranberries, raisins, currants, figs, apricots, and apples in my refrigerator. Sometimes they find their way into salads or into whole grain dishes. My kids like to snack on them as well. They are a nutritious sweet alternative.

Onions and Garlic: These are staples in my house because I'm not sure I would know how to cook without them! See Bites of Insight for easy peeling of both onions and garlic. Check my website www.SuzanneLandry.com for helpful video tutorials on how to chop an onion without crying.

ESSENTIAL EQUIPMENT AND COOKING TECHNIQUES

Although I don't believe it is necessary to buy special equipment for natural foods cooking, there are some tools that I find essential for whatever cooking I am doing.

Stove: I mention this because I believe strongly that healthy food cannot be prepared on electric stoves. Food tastes better and is better cooked with natural gas. Gas flames are easier to control. Electric burners are harder to control and can easily overcook or dry out food.

Cookware: All metal weakens with repeated heating and cooling, which expands and contracts the metal, allowing leaching of the metal into your food. Though it will take a few years, even stainless steel will leach eventually. Most health-oriented professional chefs use heavy clad stainless steel, cast iron, or baked enamel cookware. Aluminum, a weaker metal, leaches quickly into our food and is absorbed into our bodies. Please replace aluminum cookware as soon as you can. Nonstick cookware also leaches even when it hasn't been scratched. You can purchase nonstick cookware that is non-toxic. Look for "green pans" or eco cookware in your local kitchen department store.

Cutting Boards: Yes, wood is best! Acrylic boards dull knives quickly. Further, bacteria lives on wet surfaces and moisture stays on acrylic boards longer; whereas wooden boards absorb the moisture. However, I do recommend acrylic boards for meat and chicken. Sterilize them in the dishwasher after each use. Some cooks like to have a separate small board for onion and garlic chopping. I use a wooden board that is at least 1–2 inches thick and pieced together. A solid piece of wood will warp. A board 12 x 14 inches is a good size. You can ask at a wood furniture store or hobby shop if they will custom make your board from scrap wood or you can purchase one at a good kitchen shop.

Monthly, I sterilize my boards by wiping the surface with a solution of 50% water and 50% vinegar. The following day I oil the surface thoroughly with light cooking oil. My boards have lasted for many years and don't show signs of wear. By the way, never put a wooden board in the dishwasher or wash it in soapy water or with a soapy sponge. If you use a wood board for vegetables and fruits, wipe it down with a hot sponge without soap. I have a designated cutting board sponge that never gets used for washing dishes or for general cleanup. Your board will last for many years when you take proper care of it.

Egg Slicer: It can multi-task beyond boiled eggs. Use it for slicing hulled strawberries or firm mushrooms.

Essentials: Small essentials can include measuring cups, garlic press, spatulas, citrus juicer, storage containers, a variety of small kitchen knives and of course, your favorite gadgets.

Knives: If you want to cut vegetables with ease and speed, invest in a good knife and keep it sharp. You don't have to spend a lot of money on a knife but there are some features to look for. One of my favorite, yet inexpensive knives is a Santoku style from Cuisinart. Stainless steel is easier to clean but doesn't stay sharp as long as carbon steel. Ceramic blades stay sharp much longer but are brittle when dropped. Additionally, a couple of very good paring knives are all you'll need. Knife sharpening can be done with a wet stone, steel rod or an electric

sharpener, whichever you are most comfortable with. Note: you can sustain a more serious injury with a dull knife than a sharp one. Sharpen your knives once a week. Invest in a good knife, buy it at a kitchenware shop and ask them to give you a demonstration on knife sharpening. Add for a video tutorial on knives go to www.SuzanneLandry.com.

Food Processor: Every kitchen should have a processor because it can be used for blending soups, chopping nuts and vegetables, and mixing just about everything. You don't need an expensive processor with many attachments. Most of those extra gadgets you won't use anyway. The high powered blenders available are great for vegetable and fruit smoothies and protein breakfast drinks.

Ginger Grater: This is an easy and inexpensive tool if you frequently use fresh ginger as I do. A small handheld cheese grater can also work.

Juicer: If you are serious about stepping up your health and vitality a notch or more, then a juicer is a necessity. For those who work, it is nearly impossible to get the 5 servings of fruits and vegetables in our daily diet. The easiest way to sneak in more of these veggies and fruit and the antioxidant protection they bring, is to juice. I will bring 16 oz of fresh squeezed vegetable and fruit juice with me most workdays. I can see a difference in my skin when I do. It looks smoother and softer and more youthful. The juicer I have now is a Green Star. It is a low speed twin gear juicer that gently crushes and squeezed my veggies so they don't heat up, which destroys nutrients, antioxidants, and enzymes. I prefer this style of juicer to the basket type that shreds and spins the produce at high speed. It's faster than mine but the pulp comes out wetter and you get less juice for your money with these styles.

Immersion Blender: Also known as a handheld blender. I love this tool! These blenders are designed to blend soup, gravies, and sauces without removing them from pot. It saves time and mess. They are available in most kitchen department stores. Hold it down in your pot of soup and blend away without dirtying any other equipment!

Microwave: I don't use it...not even for heating foods. There are other methods of reheating and cooking food that are far more healthful.

Pressure Cooker: While not an essential piece of equipment, a pressure cooker does cut cooking time in half when cooking beans. Rice tastes sweeter when cooked in a pressure cooker. Use only stainless steel or enamel, not an aluminum pressure cooker. Aluminum, as mentioned before, will leach easier into food than stainless steel.

Salad Spinner: I use mine everyday. Easy to wash, drain and spin your salad. You can even store it in the bowl. I like the Zyliss style because it is easy to use and nearly indestructible.

Scissors: Get kitchen shears meant for cutting chicken bones and skin. Scissors are an invaluable tool to keep in the kitchen for snipping herbs, cutting up dried fruit or whole tomatoes in a can, and trimming fat from meats.

Toaster Oven: This is another frequently used item in my kitchen. I use it for toasting nuts or seeds, melting cheese on tortillas, and reheating food. It saves energy and time. Why heat a whole oven (and the whole house) to cook one small dish?

Vegetable Peeler: Unless a vegetable has been waxed,

I recommend not peeling most vegetables. The most versatile peeler is the one that looks like a sling shot. The blade is placed horizontally and you simply pull the peeler along the surface of the vegetable. It saves your knuckles and is the best tool for hard-to-peel vegetables like squash. It is one of my most frequently used tools. My favorite is the Kuhn from Sweden.

Water Ionizer: Drinking ionized, clustered (restructured) water everyday can improve your health and overall well being. We chose the Kangen Water Ionizer because of its quality and versatility. The machine gives an option of pH drinking water from 7 to 9.5 pH. It can also create strong acid water which I use for disinfecting everything from my countertops to my chopping blocks. Most importantly, this 2.5 pH is acidic enough to kill most salmonella, E. coli and other pathogens within 30 seconds. I soak my vegetables and salad in this water for 30 seconds and then put them in an alkaline water of 11.5 pH. This pH will help to remove pesticide residue from all my produce (even organic vegetables get rained on). Meats and chicken will also get a quick rinse in the 2.5 pH water. My fresh food is squeaky clean by the time I'm ready to prepare it. We cook with this water and drink it exclusively at a 8.5 pH. For more information go to www.LivingWaterforLife. com or return to Chapter 1, *Healthiest Water for Cooking and Drinking.* Every cook has her/his own special way of doing things, so I'll define my favorite cooking methods. Remember: cooking destroys most enzymes, so be sure that you include raw vegetables and fruits everyday. This insures that you will get a well balanced diet that includes enzymes, vitamins, and minerals.

Steaming: Most vegetables are best when steamed as it retains moisture, flavor, and nutrients. In steaming, the water should never touch the vegetables and should boil gently. A handy tool for steaming is an expandable steamer basket which adjusts to fit different size pots. You can buy one just about anywhere these days. It takes only a little bit longer to steam on the stove than to microwave with better nutrient retention.

Blanching: This is a very quick way to cook vegetables. This is the method used prior to freezing vegetables. The water remains boiling while vegetables are placed in the water for a very brief period of time. The vegetables are then immediately plunged into iced cold water for several seconds to stop the cooking and then drained. Vegetables should be brightly colored and still have a fresh crisp taste without sacrificing nutrients. I use this method for some vegetables that will go in salads but are difficult to digest raw such as broccoli and cauliflower. I've blanched the vegetables that will go in my *Cauliflower and String Bean Dijon Salad* recipe in the *Fresh Garden Salads* chapter.

Boiling: This technique is most often used for whole grains, beans, soups, stews, and some vegetables. First the water is brought to a high boil, vegetables are added and then the temperature is lowered to a low boil for the remaining cooking time. Cover the pot to prevent evaporation and to have better control over cooking time.

Sauté: This method of cooking uses low heat and a small amount of oil. Sautéing is usually used for vegetables that have high moisture content, like onions and mushrooms.

Stir-Fry: Stir-fried vegetables are crispier and tastier than boiled or steamed. In this method of cooking, high heat and oil is used to quickly sear vegetables. Add vegetables according to their cooking time. Usually a small quantity of water or stock is added, the pot is covered and the vegetables cook in the steam. See my *Easy Stir-Fry with Teriyaki Sauce* in my *Vegetables—Nature's Bounty* chapter.

Baking: Is an alternative way to cook grains, meats, beans, and vegetables. Sweet vegetables such as onions, carrots, squash, and parsnips become sweeter when they are baked. Always preheat your oven for 15 minutes before baking to ensure even heat and consistent cooking time. Vegetables can also be wrapped in foil and then baked or grilled. See *Golden Squash Casserole* recipes in *Vegetables–Nature's Bounty*.

Pressure Cooking: A pressure cooker can reduce the cooking time of beans by almost half. However, lentils, black-eye peas, soybeans, and split peas should never be cooked in a pressure cooker. The foam that is created when cooking these beans will clog the vent of the pressure cooker. Also, be careful to not overfill a pressure cooker; filling to two thirds of capacity allows for expansion of beans and grains. Grains cooked this way retain their flavor better too. I prefer the taste of pressure cooked rice over boiled.

Deep Frying or Pan Frying—I never deep fry anymore and would recommend pan frying instead. Deep frying is very high in fat calories, so use it rarely. The difference is depth of oil. Deep frying is usually done in a pot with several inches of oil. Pan frying may only be enough oil to cover the bottom of the frying pan. For deep frying or pan frying use an oil that is stable at higher temperatures. Good options for high heat are grape seed, sesame seed, and canola or sunflower oils. Very Important—make sure oil is hot enough before adding food. Food placed in oil should begin to sizzle immediately. If it does not, the oil is not hot enough and it will absorb an excessive amount of oil, making the food soggy. Also, do not crowd the pan with too much food. The more food, the quicker the oil temperature will cool and the soggier the dish will be. Fill only half the surface of the pan with food to be fried.

Roasting—There is nothing tastier than a roasted root vegetable dish. Root vegetables like parsnips, sweet potatoes, leeks, turnips and onions become sweet and chewy. Roasting differs from baking in that the oven temperature is usually 400–450 degrees. The pan is usually uncovered resulting in a caramelized intensely flavored vegetable. See *Roasted Winter Vegetables* recipe in *Vegetable—Nature's Bounty* chapter.

Reheating Food: Avoid using the microwave so you can retain more nutrients. If you enjoyed a great meal, and want to reheat leftovers another day, you can make a plate of food and put the plate inside a bamboo steamer basket, cover and set it inside a skillet of water and bring water to boil. Food will steam-heat in 5 minutes and you only have one plate to wash. Bamboo steamer baskets are very inexpensive and found in Asian food markets or kitchen specialty stores. Or reheat the leftovers in an inexpensive stainless steel steamer basket placed inside a covered pot. Or wrap the plate in aluminum foil and place in a preheated 325°F toaster oven for 15 minutes. Careful, the plate will be hot!

MEASUREMENTS

I use standard American measuring cups. You can use the same measuring cup for both wet and dry ingredients. The weight differs from dry to weight ingredients but not the volume. For your information, I never refer to weight in my recipes.

Equivalents to Liquid Ounces:
1 cup = 8 oz
2 cups = 1 pint (16 oz)
2 pints = 1 quart (32 oz)
4 quarts = 1 gallon (64 oz)

Measuring Spoons: Use whatever spoons or measuring gadget you have that indicates fractions of teaspoons or tablespoons. Oval deep spoons are better than round shallow spoons, as it is easier to scoop out the ingredients. My recipes will refer to tablespoon by using the abbreviation of Tbs and teaspoons as tsp. I believe most cooking measurements are standard and well understood with the possible exception of the pinch/dash (see below).

Pinch/Dash: This usually refers to salt or pepper. A pinch is the very smallest amount that you can pick up between two fingers; you probably could count the grains of salt. Dash is as much as you can quickly pick up between two fingers or one quick shake from the container.

KNIFE SKILLS

All vegetables should be washed or scrubbed thoroughly before cutting. You should cut vegetables appropriate for the method of cooking you will be doing. For example, if you are creating a winter casserole of root vegetables which includes carrots, and it will cook for 30 minutes, cut carrots in large stew size pieces. On the other hand, if you are stir-

Minced Cut

Diced Cut

Chopped Cut

Round Cut

Half Moon Cut

Roll or Stew Cut

Diagonal Cut

Small Matchstick

frying carrots, cut them in thin diagonal slices or matchsticks so they cook quickly.

When cutting vegetables, it is easiest to use a knife with a rectangular cutting blade. Hold the knife by the handle close to the blade, with your thumb firmly placed on the side of the handle. You should feel you have a very good grip on the knife blade. Hold the vegetable with your other hand, with your fingers tucked under, using your knuckles to guide the vegetable toward the knife. The hand holding the vegetable should be cupped as if you were holding an egg in the palm of your hand. The front end of the knife should remain on the board in front of the vegetable you are cutting. As you lift the back end of the blade just high enough over the vegetables to slice it, move the vegetable toward the knife while you continue to raise the back end of the knife and slice again, creating a rocking action. For a short demonstration video go to my website www.ThePassionateVegetable.com

The following cuts are most frequently used:
Minced—about ¼-inch cube
Diced—about ⅓-inch cube
Chopped—about ½-inch cube
Rounds—cut across a round vegetable such as a carrot
Half Moon Cut– slice in half lengthwise once and then crosswise in desired width.
Roll/Stew Cut—very thick diagonal cut—roll vegetable toward you and cut through the flat face of the vegetable and diagonally cut again. Keep rolling and cutting across diagonally. You should end up with triangular cut vegetables.
Diagonal—cut a vegetable at an angle (on the diagonal)
Matchstick—cut diagonally, then into thin strips about 1 inch long
Quarter Cut—As in a tomato or onion. Cut in half and half again ending up with four quarters.

Healthy Start Breakfasts

• • •

Opposite: Very Berry Fruit Salad and Salmon Asparagus Quiche,
see pages 68 and 64

Healthy Start Breakfasts

Students in my cooking classes are always asking for healthy breakfast ideas. I remind them, "Your choice of foods in the morning will influence how you feel and think the rest of the day." Breakfasts that are wholesome and nourishing are the best choice. There are other important variables such as how much to eat and when. Some students will inquire if breakfast is really necessary. It is, though not everyone does well on a big breakfast. Many prefer a lighter meal while others do better by delaying breakfast until mid-morning.

The necessity of breakfast varies from person to person. From my own personal experience, as an O blood type and a moderate metabolizer, I prefer not to eat first thing in the morning. In fact, the thought of food is quite unpleasant. My energy is great in the morning, and I don't require coffee or even a piece of toast to get me going. However, by 10:30 a.m., my appetite kicks in and I am ready for a hearty and healthy breakfast. If I don't have the opportunity to eat at that time, as soon as noon approaches, I start to lose my early morning pep.

Start your day off with a balanced breakfast that includes both complex carbohydrates and protein. Give your body and brain the energy you need to tackle your day. For a quick, on-the-run breakfast, choose a healthy whole grain cold cereal. Be sure it has a fair amount of protein (more than 4 grams per serving—check ingredients) and a low amount of sugar. If you enjoy hot cereal such as oatmeal, be sure to add some chopped nuts, flaxseeds or sunflower seeds, and almond milk. Read *Not Milk?* in the beginning of this book for more information on milk.

Other easy-to-fix breakfast ideas include a premade frittata, which is an egg and vegetable pie. When sliced, it is quick to heat in the toaster oven. Occasionally, I enjoy having smoked, wild-caught salmon on whole grain toast with capers, fresh tomatoes, and some organic mayonnaise. It takes only a few minutes to prepare a slice of toast with a fried or boiled egg.

Metabolism plays an important role in what food is best for you and when.
Some people do fine on two meals per day, and others need to eat four or more small meals to keep fueled. The latter are usually fast metabolizers who burn lots fuel (food) very quickly. (Hint: they were always slim in high school no matter how much they ate.) If you are a moderate metabolizer, as 75% of us are, it's best to have at least some protein in the morning, but don't make breakfast the biggest meal of the day. Remember: always consider your physical needs for the entire day. For instance, a breakfast bar will not give you the energy and calories needed for a physically strenuous day. On those days, choose a well-balanced breakfast such as eggs, whole grain toast with slices of tomato and avocado.

Stay away from refined carbohydrates for breakfast.
Avoid bagels, donuts, pastries, white bread, cookies, cereal bars, and sugared cereals. These carbohydrates are high glycemic (which turn into blood sugar very fast) and although supply a quick surge of energy, they will leave you feeling tired shortly after. If you rush out in the morning without a morsel or a plan, I can almost guarantee that you will find yourself at

your favorite coffee shop succumbing to a muffin and latte. You will likely regret it later on, as will your waistline, mental focus, and energy level. Essentially, your get-up-and-go will have got-up-and-gone without you. For more information, refer to *Energy Robbers* at the beginning of this book. Consider making your own breakfast muffins (recipe in this chapter). You can also improve your own favorite muffin recipe by adding one tablespoon of wheat bran, wheat germ, oat bran, or flaxseeds to the mix to increase the protein and fiber. Using a healthier lower glycemic sweetener, such as stevia, instead of refined sugar would make it that much better for you!

Are you hungry … or thirsty?
After teaching to thousands of students, I've discovered that most people (especially women) don't really know when they are truly hungry. Most Americans are dehydrated. Thirst is often mistaken for hunger and hunger is often mistaken for thirst. Are you drinking a half ounce of good filtered water per pound of your body weight every day? Drink alkalized water to help flush toxins and excess fat from your tissues. Please read more on water quality and filters in the beginning of this book. An overly acidic diet prevents us from having the energy, vitality and clear mind that we all want. The traditional American breakfast of coffee, eggs, bacon, and sweet jam is very acidic. Don't be surprised if you crave sweets by mid-morning after such a breakfast. Please read more on *Acid/Alkaline Balance* in the beginning of this book.

Does skipping breakfast equal weight loss?
No! Meal-skipping causes your metabolism to slow down, therefore burning calories more slowly throughout the day. You don't want that if you want to lose weight. To burn calories and excess fat, keep your metabolism humming consistently all day long. The very best way to do this is by exercising first thing in the morning. Then have a light breakfast. Eat lean protein, vegetables, fruits and only complex carbohydrates such as whole grain toast. Again, refer to beginning of this book for more helpful information. Researchers from the National Weight Control Registry collected a database of more than 3,000 people who lost at least 60 pounds and were able to keep it off for an average of 6 years. They found that 78% of the successful dieters had been eating breakfast everyday as part of their weight loss strategy. These people also followed a low-fat diet and exercised an hour or more each day.

Why eat breakfast?
Many studies have been done around this question especially regarding children. A Tufts University research study showed that children who eat healthy breakfasts score better on tests. They have less incidences of hyperactivity, are able to focus better and have better overall attitudes. This is true for adults as well. Improved concentration and mental clarity can have a positive effect on overall cognitive performance.

What is a grown-up breakfast?
Not your typical breakfast food, adult breakfasts can include egg frittatas or leftover bean soups with whole grain bread for example. Let go of your childhood breakfast choices of pancakes, waffles, French toast dripping with sweet syrup, or fried bacon. It's time to experiment with sophisticated adult breakfast options. So enjoy experimenting and try a bowl of hot Minestrone soup for breakfast….it's good and you may be pleasantly surprised at how tasty your grown up breakfast can be.

Breakfast Fruit Muffins

(Makes 8)

Dry Ingredients:
1 cup whole wheat pastry flour
1 cup unbleached white flour
⅓ cup wheat germ
1 tsp baking powder
¼ cup organic cane sugar
½ tsp sea salt
½ cup fresh blueberries

Wet Ingredients:
1 large egg
¼ cup natural vegetable oil
1 cup milk (cow's, almond, or rice)
½ tsp vanilla extract

1. Preheat oven to 350°F. Combine dry ingredients, except blueberries, and mix well. Gently fold in blueberries. If blueberries are added to wet ingredients, or if they are overmixed with the dry ingredients, they will begin to "bleed" their juice into the batter making purple muffins. This is also good to know when making blueberry pancakes.

2. Combine wet ingredients in a separate bowl and mix well. Now combine both dry and wet ingredients and mix only long enough that no pockets of dry ingredients remain. Do not overmix!

3. Oil muffin pan, pour batter into muffin cups, filling them to the top of the rim. Put on middle oven rack and bake for 20–25 minutes. Cool and remove.

Alternative Muffins—Flours, salt, and eggs remain the same but adjust the following:

Cranberry Raisin:
¾ cup organic cane sugar
½ cup raisins
½ cup fresh cranberries
        (add to dry)
2 tsp baking powder (increase
 from 1 tsp)
2 cups orange juice
½ cup corn oil
½ Tbs orange zest

Banana Nut: (add to basic
 muffin mix)
1 cup crushed banana
1 tsp cinnamon
½ tsp nutmeg

Breakfast Smoothie

(Serves 1)

This will get your day off to a good start and yet is light, easy to digest, and low fat.

1 ripe banana (overripe is better)
6 plump strawberries
½ cup ice
½ cup milk (cow's, almond, rice, or soy)
1 cup low-fat plain yogurt

Optional nutritional boosters:
1 Tbs wheat germ
1 Tbs brewer's yeast
1 Tbs protein powder
1 Tbs hemp seeds
1 Tbs chia seeds

1. Use in-season fruit. Any combination of your favorite fruit is fine, but it is best if you include one starchy fruit like bananas to give the smoothie its creaminess.

Bites of Insight

When choosing yogurt look for organic labels. Organic standards do not allow the use of rBGH hormone in dairy cattle. Additionally, organic standards should insure that you have a yogurt that contains more of the beneficial lactobacillus acidophilus that is good for our digestion.

Chunky Apple Oatmeal Pancakes

(Serves 2)

These sweet cake-like pancakes are full of nuts, fruit, and flavor! Forget the chocolate chip pancakes!

Dry Ingredients:
¾ cup organic whole wheat flour
½ cup rolled quick cooking oats
2 Tbs oat bran
½ tsp ground cinnamon
2 tsp baking powder
¼ tsp sea salt

Wet Ingredients:
1 cup apple juice
1 egg, beaten
¼ cup chopped walnuts or
    sunflower seeds
¼ cup organic raisins
½ cup peeled and chopped
    apple (½ apple)

1. Combine dry ingredients in bowl: flours, oats, oat bran, cinnamon, baking powder, and sea salt.

2. Combine wet ingredients: apple juice and egg, mix thoroughly.

3. Combine wet with dry ingredients and mix again. Fold in nuts and fruit to the batter.

4. Preheat frying pan with oil or vegetable shortening (Spectrum Naturals is the only acceptable product at this writing). If the oil is hot enough a drop of batter should start sizzling right away.

5. Keeping heat on medium-high, pour ¼ cup of batter in the frying pan. When bubbles appear around the edges, turn over and brown other side. Continue until all the batter is used.

Bites of Insight

For porridge the best oats are whole oats or oat groats. Quick cooking oats have been processed and will have lost some nutritional value. However, they are best in recipes such as this one. See Grandpa's Oatmeal Porridge.

Eggless Egg Salad

(Serves 4–6)

Fool just about anybody. I was asked to present a lecture to a group of cardiologists and I provided this as a snack among other dishes and no one knew the difference!

12 oz package organic tofu, firm
    or extra firm, drained
½ tsp ground turmeric
½ cup chopped celery (2 stalks)
¼ cup minced onion
3 Tbs organic mayonnaise
½ tsp sea salt
⅛ tsp ground black pepper

Optional: ¼ cup of pickle relish
and/or ¼ tsp dry mustard

1. Slice tofu into four slabs. Place tofu on paper towel and putting another piece of paper towel on top, press to remove as much moisture as possible. Crumble between your fingers into a colander and press again with paper towel on top of tofu to remove excess liquid. Tofu should resemble scrambled eggs. Place tofu in medium-sized bowl.

2. Slice celery down the rib twice so that you have four long pieces. Cut across the celery into small pieces. Toss celery and minced onion with tofu and add turmeric, salt, and pepper. Add mayonnaise and mix all together. Add more if necessary to help bind it together.

3. Refrigerate covered at least one hour before serving so flavors blend and the turmeric spice will begin to yellow the egg salad. Initially, the spice does not seem to change the color of the salad, but it will after a few minutes. Do not keep adding more turmeric, or you will end up with neon yellow egg salad!

Serving Suggestion: This is a great dip for crackers or a filling for a pita sandwich with lettuce leaves or sprouts and shredded carrots. Tofu is high in protein and a ½ cup serving is sufficient protein for a light lunch or snack if it is served with whole grain bread or crackers.

Bites of Insight

You can also make your favorite egg salad, just use fewer eggs, and extend it with 6 ounces of crumbled tofu and turmeric to increase protein without increasing cholesterol. You can also add 6 ounces of crumbled tofu to tuna fish or chicken salad to extend the protein as well. Add it to your meatloaf! The possibilities are endless!

Golden Home Fried Potatoes

(Serves 4)

*Another use for my **Rosemary Roasted Red Potatoes** found in the **Vegetables, Nature's Bounty** chapter or below. I always make more roasted potatoes knowing that I will want leftovers for weekend brunches.*

2	Tbs extra-virgin olive oil
½	cup chopped onion (1 small)
½	cup chopped red bell pepper
½	cup chopped green bell pepper
2	cups leftover roasted potatoes (see below)
1	tsp ground paprika

1. Preheat large frying pan with olive oil. Add onions and sauté for 2–3 minutes until they become a little tender.

2. Add red and green peppers and continue to sauté for another 2–3 minutes. Now add leftover potatoes and sprinkle with paprika. The potatoes were salted in the original recipe so they may not need any salt now but check for your liking.

3. Keep turning the potatoes over and over as they mix with the paprika and peppers. They will soften a little and the paprika will give a golden color to the potatoes.

Rosemary Roasted Red Potatoes

(Serves 3–4)

8	baby red potatoes, sliced into quarters or wedges
2	Tbs extra-virgin olive oil
½	tsp dried rosemary leaves, crushed
⅛	tsp ground black pepper
¼	tsp sea salt

1. Preheat oven to 400°F. Wash red potatoes thoroughly. Cut into halves or quarters depending on the size of potatoes.

2. Place potatoes in a large bowl and toss with oil. Sprinkle with salt, pepper, and rosemary to taste and toss again. Put in a large flat baking pan so that you can spread your potatoes in a single layer.

3. Bake for 40 minutes depending on the size of the cut you made. The smaller the size the quicker they will cook.

Grandpa's Oatmeal Porridge

(Serves 4)

You would have to eat 7 bowls of oatmeal today to get the same nutrition as grandpa got in one bowl!! Organic oats will have more nutrition than non-organic. Once you try real oatmeal from oat groats, you will think the quick and instant oatmeal tastes like wallpaper paste! Seriously, it would probably work too!

1 cup oat groats or whole oats (found in health food stores only)
½ tsp sea salt
1 cinnamon stick or 1 tsp ground cinnamon

The finishing:
  Maple syrup
  Milk (cow's, almond, or rice)
  Fresh berries, raisins, or roasted walnuts, pecans, or sunflower seeds

1. Rinse groats in colander and drain. Place groats in a large pot (the one you will use to cook the oats in) and turn the heat to medium high. Stir slowly while groats begin to dry and emit a fresh-baked-bread aroma. Don't roast them until they are brown or they will become bitter. Add 4 cups of water (5 cups if you like creamy oatmeal), salt, and cinnamon stick; cover and bring to a boil. Oats will foam and make a mess on your stove if you use too small a pot. Now reduce heat to medium and cook for one hour. Since there is a lot of water in the pot there is no need to stir frequently.

2. If you have a slow cooker, place all ingredients roasting in the slow cooker, cover and place medium for suggested time according to manufacturer to cook whole grains. Slow cookers a great way to cook oat groats. Wake up to sweet, creamy breakfast cereal. Add roasted nuts seeds, milk, or sweetener to taste.

Serving Suggestion: This will make four cups finished oatmeal. This keeps in the refrigerator fo several days. Just spoon out of your container the amount you want for breakfast, add more milk an reheat for 5 minutes. Top off with nuts or berries if you wish.

Bites of Insight

Whole oats (also called oat groats) are the natural form of oatmeal before it is "rolled" or cut as in steel-cut oats. They contain more vitamins and minerals than their processed versions. They also haven't oxidized because they are still whole. Of all the varieties available for oatmeal this is the king of nutrition.

Mom's Lemon Crepes

(Serves 2–3)

My English mum's crepes were always a treat to have on weekends when breakfast could be special. They take a little more time but are well worth the wait.

Dry Ingredients:
1   cup whole wheat pastry flour
1   tsp baking soda
½   tsp sea salt

Wet Ingredients:
2   large eggs
1   cup milk (cow's, almond, or rice)

2   Tbs Spectrum Natural Vegetable Shortening

Topping:
2   lemons, halved
¼   cup pure maple syrup (warmed)

1. In a large bowl, combine dry ingredients first: flour, baking soda, and salt. In a separate bowl, beat eggs and milk with a fork or whisk. Combine with flour mixture. Wisk until lumps are smooth.

2. In a large 8-inch frying pan, melt shortening over medium-high heat. When shortening is very hot, batter should sizzle immediately when you drop a little in the oil. Pour ¼ cup of batter in a circular direction into the pan. Quickly lift the pan and holding it at an angle turn the pan around so that the batter spreads evenly on the bottom of the pan, making sure to fill in all the holes. Seasoned cast iron pans work best.

Turn crepe over when underside browns in spots and on the edges and sides begin to curl. Brown again on that side and serve immediately. This takes less than 2 minutes on each side. Repeat with rest of batter. You can keep them warm on a plate with a clean linen towel over the top and in a preheated oven at 250°F while you prepare the entire batch.

3. Serve by buttering the crepe and squeezing fresh lemon juice on the inside of the crepe. Roll up into a tube and drizzle warmed maple syrup over the crepe. You can also garnish with fresh fruit and serve with cashew cream (see this chapter). My mom used white sugar, lemon, and butter but pure maple syrup is a healthier step up.

Bites of Insight

To juice a lemon without a juicer, roll lemon on a cutting board by pressing down with the palm of your hand to soften. Slice in half and hold this half in one hand while you push a fork into the center of the lemon with the other hand. Now, twist in opposite directions with your hands. Squeeze the lemon at the same time and the juice will come pouring out.

Mediterranean Egg Salad

(Serves 3–4)

The inspiration for this egg salad came from an old friend, Danny, who lived in Israel for many years. Lettuce salads are not common, but vegetable salads are, and this is a big hit with everyone I serve it to.

4 large eggs
2 small tomatoes, chopped
¼ cup pumpkin seeds, toasted (called pepitas)
¼ cup diced celery (1 stalk)
½ small cucumber, peeled and cubed
¼ cup chopped scallions (2 scallions)
¼ cup minced red onion
½ avocado, diced
½ lemon, juiced

Dressing:
3 Tbs extra-virgin olive oil
1 Tbs red wine vinegar
¼ tsp sea salt
⅛ tsp ground black pepper (or to taste)

1. Boil eggs for 8 minutes, drain, and run under cold water to cool. When cool enough to handle, peel eggs and chop in eighths. Don't mince the eggs as you would for an egg salad as this salad is supposed to have a chunkier texture.

2. Chop tomatoes and celery into ½-inch pieces and add to eggs. Slice a cucumber in half, peel, and cut into ½-inch cubes, add to eggs. Mince scallions and add to mixture.

3. Slice onion in half, and make very thin slices across the length of the onion, from stem to root. Holding the onion together, turn, and slice very small ¼-inch pieces. This is a minced cut. Add to eggs.

4. Cut avocado into small ½-inch pieces. Toss with a little lemon juice to prevent browning. Mix with eggs.

5. Toss vegetables and eggs together. In a separate bowl, combine oil, vinegar, salt, and pepper. Add to egg and mix; it will begin to "cream." It will appear and taste as though you added mayonnaise. Gently add in avocado and toss again.

Serving Suggestion: Serve it with whole grain crackers or bread for a snack or in a sandwich. I have served this for lunch as well as breakfast and everyone loves it.

Bites of Insight

If you presoak an onion for 10 minutes before you peel and chop, you will avoid irritated eyes, and the onion will peel much easier. Sorry, should have told you earlier.

Melt-in-Your-Mouth Granola

(Serves 4)

Very difficult not to eat a bowl as soon as it comes out of the oven. Like crumbled oatmeal cookies… yum.

Dry Ingredients:
- 2 cups old fashioned rolled oats
- ¼ cup sunflower seeds
- ½ tsp ground cinnamon
- ¼ cup unsweetened coconut
- ½ cup chopped walnuts

Wet Ingredients:
- ¼ cup natural vegetable oil
- 1 tsp vanilla extract
- ¼ cup honey or pure maple syrup

1. Preheat oven to 325°F. Combine dry ingredients and toss well.

2. In a separate bowl, combine oil, vanilla, and honey or maple syrup. Mix this thoroughly with the oats until all oats are coated.

3. Spread on a cooking sheet or jelly roll pan and bake for a total of 25 minutes. Check every 10 minutes to turn granola away from edges of sheet (it burns faster in the corners). Alternatively, granola can also be placed in a casserole pan and checked every 15 minutes, stirring granola with each check. Granola should be a little damp. It dries out as it cools. The color should be light golden brown.

4. Add chopped dried fruit if you wish, but do this just before serving as the granola will become too moist if it is stored with fruit. Dried fruit choices include raisins, date pieces, cranberries, peaches, and apples.

Bites of Insight

This is certainly a guilt-free healthy cereal for your family but not a calorie-free cereal. Most granolas, wherever they are purchased, will be higher in calories per cup than other cereals so read your labels!

The Passionate Breakfast Cookie

(Makes 1½ dozen 4-inch cookies)

Why passionate? I'm passionate about oatmeal-raisin-walnut cookies—always have been my favorite. This is better than oatmeal in a bowl. Loaded with fiber and protein, these are the ultimate breakfast-on-the-run cookies. These have a lower glycemic index than a bowl of oatmeal.

Dry Ingredients:
- 2 cups old fashioned rolled oats
- ¼ cup whole flaxseeds
- ¼ cup ground flaxseeds
- ¼ cup wheat germ
- 1 cup coconut, flaked and unsweetened
- 1 cup chopped walnuts
- ¼ cup whole wheat flour
- ¾ cup raisins
- 2 Tbs ground cinnamon
- 2 tsp ground nutmeg
- 1 tsp ground turmeric
- 1 tsp ground cloves
- 1 tsp sea salt

Wet Ingredients:
- 4 large eggs, beaten
- ½ cup butter, melted
- 1 cup brown sugar

Optional: 2 Tbs hemp seeds or substitute whole wheat flour for teff flour

1. Preheat oven to 325°F. Combine all dry ingredients in a large bowl.

2. In a small saucepan, melt butter and add sugar. Stir to combine. When cooled slightly, add beaten eggs.

3. Add wet ingredients to dry ingredients and mix thoroughly. Spoon approximately ½ cup of cookie mix onto a parchment lined cookie sheet. Using slightly damp hands, press the mix down and form a round cookie approximately 4 inches wide. I usually fit six cookies per cookie sheet. Place cookie sheets on separate racks in the oven. Bake for 10 minutes, then switch cookie sheets and bake again for another 10 minutes.

4. When cookies have cooled after about 5 minutes, remove them to a plastic container. They will stay crispy when kept air tight. You can store extras in an airtight container for up to two weeks or freeze them for up to a month.

Bites of Insight

Teff grain or flour contains high levels of calcium, phosphorous, iron, copper, and thiamin. Teff is high in protein, carbohydrates, and fiber. It contains no gluten so it is appropriate for those with gluten intolerance. For added nutrition, replace whole wheat flour in this recipe with teff flour found in any health food store.

Smoked Salmon on Rye

(Serves 2)

In many European countries, pickled or smoked fish is served with fresh crusty breads and a few vegetables for breakfast. I have to agree it is one of my favorite ways to start the day.

2	slices rye toast
4	slices wild-caught smoked salmon
2	Tbs organic mayonnaise or cream cheese
2	small vine-ripened tomatoes
2	tsp capers
2	slices red onion (optional)

1. Toast bread slices. I use a variety that is 100% rye purchased from health food stores. It has a great texture and a hearty European bread taste.

2. Spread organic cream cheese or mayonnaise on the toast and layer salmon on top of that in one thin layer.

3. Slice tomatoes in thin slices and layer again on top of salmon. Sprinkle on thinly sliced red onion and capers. Yum!!

Bites of Insight

Wild-caught salmon is the only salmon I recommend. Salmon that have lived a natural existence spawning upstream in cold waters develop Omega-3 essential fatty acids in their tissue which is why we want to eat them in our diet. Farm-raised do not develop this. Additionally, the orange color of the salmon is from their diet of tiny crustaceans such as krill. Farm-raised salmon are fed food pellets with food coloring to enhance their color. Wild caught costs more because it is worth it!!!

Southwest Fiesta Scramble

(Serves 2)

This is a makeover from my **California Fiesta Quinoa Salad** *which you will find in the* **Salads that Satisfy** *chapter and it is one of my favorite ways to have scrambled eggs in the morning.*

2 large eggs, beaten
1 cup leftover *California Fiesta Quinoa Salad*
1 Tbs butter or extra-virgin olive oil
¼ cup cheddar cheese, shredded (cow's, rice, or almond)
salt and pepper to taste

Optional: Salsa (for garnish)

1. Beat eggs until foamy, add salt and pepper to taste.

2. Preheat frying pan with butter or olive oil and pour in eggs. Begin to turn eggs with a spatula so they do not brown but become light and fluffy.

3. Just before the eggs set and while they are still wet but beginning to hold together, add the quinoa salad and toss again to mix.

4. Sprinkle cheese over top and cover with a lid. Reduce heat to low and cook for 2–3 minutes while cheese melts. Serve with whole grain toast for a very yummy, satisfying breakfast.

Bites of Insight

For those who need to avoid dairy, there are a few good cheese alternatives at health food stores. Rice cheddar cheese comes in a block or shredded, which melts faster. Almond cheese comes in several flavor varieties as well and is a tasty alternative.

Salmon Asparagus Quiche

(Serves 6–8)

Dairy-free and gluten-free and yummy! I make this on the weekend so we can have a quick workday breakfast that's hardy and delicious!

1   8-inch premade gluten-free pie crust
¼   lb wild-caught salmon
¼   fresh lemon, juiced
     dash of garlic powder
½   cup asparagus, blanched, cut into ½-inch pieces
½   cup green peas
1   Tbs extra-virgin olive oil or butter
½   cup minced red onion
6   large eggs, beaten
⅓   cup original unsweetened almond milk
½   tsp dried dill
½   tsp dried thyme
¼   tsp sea salt
¼   tsp ground black pepper
2   Tbs fresh minced parsley
1   cup shredded rice mozzarella cheese

1. Preheat oven to 350°F and bake pie shell for 15 minutes. Set aside to cool. Reduce oven to 325°F.

2. Drizzle salmon with lemon juice and sprinkle with garlic powder. Place in a baking pan and bake in the oven for 8–10 minutes or until salmon just begins to flake. Salmon should still be very moist. Remove and set aside to cool. Flake into small bite-size pieces.

3. In a small saucepan, bring water to boil and blanch asparagus pieces for 1 minute. Remove, drain and cool. Do the same for green peas and set aside to cool.

4. In a small frying pan, preheat 1 Tbs of butter or olive oil and sauté onion for 2–3 minutes on medium heat.

5. In a medium sized bowl, combine eggs, milk, dill, thyme, salt, pepper, parsley, and onion. Now add peas and asparagus. Slowly pour this mixture into the pie shell. Sprinkle top with mozzarella cheese.

6. Bake at 325°F for 40 minutes. Increase heat to 375°F and bake for 10 minutes more. Remove and cool for at least 10 minutes before serving.

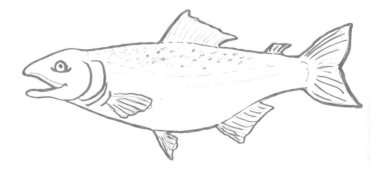

HOT!
CHILIS
25¢ EACH
OR
5 FOR $1⁰⁰

Spanish Style Quiche

(Serves 6)

This is an inspiration from Katie, a friend who assisted me in many of my cooking classes and is a terrific cook herself!

1   8-inch premade pie shell, unbaked (or homemade)
1   Tbs extra-virgin olive oil
¼   cup diced red onion
¼   cup diced bell pepper
2   tsp minced jalapeño (½ pepper) or ½ tsp chili powder
½   cup corn, fresh or frozen
¼   cup precooked black beans, rinsed and drained
¾   cup grated Mexican cheese blend (or rice cheddar cheese)
5   large eggs
½   cup almond milk or half and half
½   tsp sea salt
¼   cup chopped fresh cilantro

1. Preheat oven to 350°F. Place dry beans or pie weights into bottom of pie shell to keep shell from puffing up. Bake pie shell without filling for 15 minutes.

2. Heat olive oil in a frying pan and sauté red onion and bell pepper until onion is translucent, about 3 minutes. Add corn and jalapeño and sauté 2 minutes. Turn off heat, add black beans, stir to combine and set aside.

3. Remove pie shell from oven and spoon the corn and bean mixture on the bottom of the pie shell and spread evenly. Sprinkle ½ cup of shredded cheese on top.

4. Beat eggs, milk or half and half, and salt together; add chopped cilantro. Gently pour cream and egg mixture into pie shell. Sprinkle the remaining ¼ cup of shredded cheese over top.

5. Using either aluminum foil folded into a strip or a pie wedge saver, cover the edges of the pie to prevent the crust from overcooking. Place pie on middle rack of oven and bake for 15 minutes and then remove foil or pie saver. Return to oven and continue to bake for another 20 minutes. Eggs should be set by now. This quiche should be just a little puffy and golden on top.

Serving Suggestion: Serve with salsa and avocado slices. This is great as a quick breakfast leftover. Just heat a slice in the toaster oven for 5 minutes for a quick and hearty breakfast.

Bites of Insight

If you presoak an onion for 10 minutes before you peel and chop, you will avoid irritated eyes, and the onion will peel much easier. Sorry, should have told you earlier.

Very Berry Fruit Salad

(Serves 2)

The deep rich colors of these berries shout healthy antioxidants that are good for you and luscious too!

½   cup strawberries, hulled and halved
½   cup blueberries
½   cup red raspberries
½   cup blackberries

1. Prepare fruit, toss with lemon juice, and top with cashew cream.

Cashew Cream

(Makes 1 ½ cups)

Such a yummy creamy topping! Tastes so much like soft cream, rich and velvety.

1   cup presoaked raw cashews
1   cup almond milk (vanilla or plain)
½   tsp vanilla extract
1   Tbs agave syrup or honey

Optional: Exchange ¼ cup cashews for macadamia nuts for more fat calories and a richer flavor

1. You can presoak cashews overnight or for a few hours to make them easier to blend. Drain your presoaked nuts and put in blender with remaining ingredients and blend on high until very creamy (this takes several minutes depending on the speed and motor of your blender). Add a little more almond milk if necessary. This will store in the refrigerator for up to 5 days.

Serving Suggestion: This is a wonderful cream topping for fruit salad, berries and cream, oatmeal and any dessert that needs a creamy topping. Good for those avoiding dairy.

Fresh Garden Salads

Apple-Fennel Salad with Arugula 74

Beets and Tangerine Salad 76

Broccoli and Red Grapes Salad 78

California Waldorf Celery Salad 79

Cauliflower and String Bean Dijon Salad 80

Fresh Figs, Spring Greens, and Bleu Cheese Salad with Raspberry Vinaigrette 81

Crunchy Jicama Cabbage Salad with Dill Dressing 82

Hawaiian Cole Slaw 84

Mandarin Orange and Bibb Lettuce Salad 85

Shrimp and Sugar Snap Pea Salad 86

Spinach Salad with Turkey Sausage and Buttermilk Mustard Dressing 87

Tuscan Tomato and Bread Salad 88

Dressings:

Balsamic Salad Dressing 89

Buttery Flaxseed Dressing 89

Miso Ginger Salad Dressing 90

Fresh Raspberry Vinaigrette 91

. . .

Opposite: Crunchy Jicama Cabbage Salad with Dill Dressing, see page 82

Fresh Garden Salads

Light, delicious, crisp, colorful and refreshing—the essence of fresh salads. A fresh salad is nature's gift in its simplest form.

Fruits and uncooked vegetables are essential for a healthy diet. They provide us with vitamins, minerals, and enzymes not found in other food groups. Enzymes are essential to digestion, but cooking destroys most enzymes found in vegetables. Many vitamins are also lost in cooking. For example, more than 60% of vitamin C is lost after just ten minutes of cooking. Therefore, the importance and need for fresh, raw vegetables in our daily meal planning can't be overstated. Your diet will be the healthiest when vegetables make up the largest portion of your daily meals.

Fresh salads add color, texture, and variety to our meals. With the influence of so many ethnic cuisines in our culture, salads can reflect a wide variety of flavors and textures. Beans are often added to salads in Italian cuisine and noodles are often added in Asian cuisine, combining the savory flavors of the west and the exotic intense flavors of the east.

Create your salads to be a simple appetizer or a hearty meal.

When I started making salads for my family, I made the mistake of adding every vegetable I had on hand. At first, the salads were great, hearty, and full of crunch, but they quickly became boring, because each day the salad was the same. I wondered what was so tasty about the salads I ate at fine restaurants. I realized that a gourmet salad will often have a simple theme of three or four vegetables. So I began to create simpler salads by choosing vegetables that complemented each other. The results were delicious! With fewer ingredients, our salads had more flavor. I didn't buy fewer vegetables—I just didn't use them all in one salad.

Serve fresh salads all year long, especially when serving a meal centered on animal protein.

Preparing and Storing Salad Greens
Organic vegetables are free of pesticides and chemicals, so just rinse before eating. Dry your salad greens thoroughly, preferably in a salad spinner. These inexpensive spinners help remove excess moisture and are well worth the modest price. Make sure leaves are dry before adding them to your salad bowl. Dressing won't adhere to wet leaves, and this excess moisture will dilute your dressing.

Pre-washed bagged spring greens and cut salads are convenient and available most everywhere. They are intentionally very dry, however, to prevent the salad from spoiling in the bag. To remedy this, I soak these greens in filtered water for five minutes. This allows the leaves to "refresh" and become crispier and moister. Drain and spin dry as usual.

There are several varieties of vegetable sprays intended to remove pesticides and herbicides from vegetables. Although they do remove the superficial residue, they cannot remove what the plant absorbed from the soil by its roots. The most nutritious and safest way is to purchase organic vegetables and fruit whenever you can.

For storage and to prevent wilting, keep salad greens in a closed plastic bag in the vegetable crisper section of your refrigerator. Frost-free refrigerators constantly remove moisture, so a plastic bag helps avoid moisture loss. Check out the new "green" bags available at health food stores. They're made from plant cellulose, which helps keep veggies fresher for a longer time, and they are reusable!

Homemade Salad Dressing
Bottled salad dressings are very convenient but homemade dressings are so easy to make. They are more flavorful and fresher tasting.

Make your salad dressing right before you add your salad, and make only enough for that salad.

Have fun experimenting with all the available oils, vinegars, herbs and spices. Someone recently gifted us an artisan bottle of balsamic raspberry vinegar and I loved making dressings with it. Surprisingly, it was wonderful drizzled over ice cream and strawberries too!

Keep a variety of vinegars on hand: red wine vinegar, organic apple cider vinegar, balsamic vinegar, rice wine vinegar, and specialty vinegars. For your dressing base, use extra-virgin olive oil, expeller pressed sesame oil or walnut oil. If desired, you can add a sweetener like honey, agave, maple syrup, or organic cane sugar. Sometimes adding a little prepared mustard or fresh garlic is nice too. Fresh herbs or dried herbs are necessary to make your vinaigrette special. Remember if you exchange dried herbs for fresh you can increase the amount by three times. I grind my own Himalayan salt and black peppercorns that are available in most supermarkets, but you can use any sea salt and ground black pepper to finish off your salad.

Make your own salad dressing:
1. Use the bowl in which you will serve the salad and add 1 Tbs oil for each serving of salad.
2. Vinegar is a 1:3 ratio to oil. Drizzle vinegar into oil.
3. If you want to add sweetener, make it half the amount of the vinegar. Drizzle that into the oil.
4. Next add salt and pepper to taste. Always start with a pinch and work from there.
5. Dried herbs can be ½ tsp and spices ¼ tsp or less depending on how much heat you like. Fresh herbs can start with 1 Tbs and up.
6. Mix together with a spoon and taste. Adjust flavors to your preference.
7. Now add all of the chopped vegetables but not the leaf lettuce you will be using. Don't toss or mix yet. Then add your washed lettuce to the top, so that it sits above the dressing until you are ready to toss. You can make a salad ahead of time this way.
8. When ready to serve, toss vegetables and lettuce with the dressing. Consume immediately.

Now Enjoy Experimenting!

Apple-Fennel Salad with Arugula

(Serves 4)

2 cups arugula salad
2 cups spinach, torn into
   bite-size pieces
1 small fennel bulb
¼ cup walnut pieces, toasted
1 Fuji or Pink Lady apple, sliced

Dressing:
4 Tbs walnut oil
2 Tbs apple cider vinegar
4 Tbs apple juice
2 shallots, minced
¼ tsp sea salt

1. Prepare salad dressing by whisking together walnut oil, vinegar, apple juice, shallots, and sea salt. Place dressing in salad bowl.

2. Remove any course stems from the spinach. Rinse and dry arugula and spinach. Place in salad bowl and toss.

3. Discard outer leaves of bulb if it is "pithy" or looks scarred. Cut bulb lengthwise in quarter slices. Then slice again crosswise into ½ -inch pieces. Wash green tender fennel leaves, chop and add ¼ cup of leaves to the spinach and save the rest for garnish.

4. Sprinkle toasted walnuts and apple slices on top of salad and serve (sliced Chioggia beets shown with salad on opposite page).

Bites of Insight

Walnuts are an excellent source of manganese and copper. They also contain good levels of magnesium and phosphorous, zinc, iron, calcium and selenium and traces of iodine can also be found in walnuts. Walnuts contain excellent levels of vitamin B6, thiamin (B1) and pantothenic acid. They also contain very good levels of vitamin E, niacin (B3) and riboflavin (B2).

Walnuts contain unsaturated fats and little cholesterol, significant amount of omega-3 and antioxidant properties. Use in dressings rather than heating as it can remove some of the oil's flavor and nutrition and produce a slight bitterness.

Beets and Tangerine Salad

(Serves 4)

3 beets, cooked, peeled and cubed
6 seedless tangerines, peeled and sectioned
½ cup crumbled feta cheese

Dressing:
⅓ cup extra-virgin olive oil
3 Tbs balsamic vinegar
2 Tbs minced fresh mint

1. If using fresh beets, scrub well but do not peel. Cut stem off to within one inch of beet. Immerse in water, cover and bring to a boil then reduce heat to medium. Depending on the size of the beets, cooking will take about 30 minutes or longer. They are cooked when the beet feels tender when a fork is pushed into the center. Drain and cool. Remove skin and stem by rubbing off with your fingers under running water. Cut beets into ½-inch bite size pieces and keep in a separate bowl.

2. Peel tangerines and separate wedges. Remove any white membrane. Keep tangerines and beets separate until right before serving. Before combining toss tangerines with a little oil. This will help keep the tangerines from absorbing the beet juice.

3. Combine dressing ingredients in a separate bowl. This recipe will make more dressing than you need for this salad. It's a favorite in our house and I'm sure you'll want to have extra. For this amount of salad,

place ½ cup of finished dressing in a salad bowl. Add cooked beets and tangerines and toss. Sprinkle with feta cheese.

Bites of Insight

Beets are available at our local farmer's market in three varieties: the standard red, yellow, and candy striped (or Chioggia). The candy stripped beet is a variety from a small coastal town in Italy called Chioggia. This "peppermint candy" beet looks beautiful grated in salads. However, it loses its candy stripe once cooked and becomes pale pink. It is milder in flavor and requires less cooking.

Broccoli and Red Grapes Salad

(Serves 4)

This was adapted from a Weight Watchers salad that I made for a client of mine and it is quite yummy.

2   cups broccoli florets, stems removed
¾   cup halved seedless red grapes
½   cup chopped celery (2 stalks)
½   cup dark raisins
¼   cup sunflower seeds, roasted and salted

Dressing:
¼   cup fat free plain yogurt
1   tsp white wine vinegar
1   Tbs organic cane sugar, agave, or honey

1. In a pot big enough to hold a steamer basket, bring water to a boil. Place broccoli pieces in basket, then cover and steam for approximately 3 minutes, until the broccoli is crunchy but not raw-tasting. Immediately remove broccoli to a colander and rinse with cold water. Or, transfer broccoli to a bowl of iced water to stop the cooking process (even warm food will continue to cook).

2. Combine remaining ingredients. In a separate bowl, combine dressing ingredients and whisk. Add to salad and toss. It is best if you refrigerate salad for 1 hour before serving.

Bites of Insight

Broccoli, string beans, snow and sugar peas and green peas will lose their bright green color after a while when mixed with vinegar or lemon juice. To avoid discoloring, keep the dressing on the side or toss with dressing a half hour or less before serving.

Broccoli stems have a wonderful flavor and remain crunchy for stir-fries and salads or can be used as a base for a broccoli soup. Remove outer peel carefully with a knife. Then slice or chop into smaller pieces. You can add the stems to any recipe that calls for broccoli, or just use them as a vegetable for dipping.

California Waldorf Celery Salad

(Serves 4)

This is a great crunchy salad for picnics and BBQ dinners! Simple, quick and easy, and one of my favorites!

2   cups chopped celery
    (8 stalks)
1   apple, cored and chopped
    (your favorite red apple)
½   cup chopped walnuts
½   cup dried cranberries
¼   cup mayonnaise
1   Tbs lemon juice (½ lemon)

1. Clean celery. Slice celery stalks down the middle lengthwise and then crosswise into ¼-inch pieces and place in large bowl.

2. Core unpeeled apple and chop into 1-inch chunks. Squeeze lemon juice over the apples as you toss them. The red color in this salad adds to its attractiveness. Add to celery.

3. You can roast the walnuts in the oven or toaster oven at 350° for about 5 minutes. Roasted walnuts are much tastier and worth the effort. Chop into coarse pieces and toss with celery and apple mixture. Or you can just add raw, chopped walnuts.

4. Add dried cranberries and toss. Add mayonnaise, toss, and adjust seasoning to taste. This salad is best served a little chilled, so refrigerate for 1 hour before serving.

Bites of Insight

Celery is on the "dirty dozen" list of foods most heavily sprayed with pesticides and herbicides. I always buy celery organically grown to avoid these sprays. You can go to www.ewg.org for their "dirty dozen" list of foods to avoid. Walnuts contain omega-3, an essential fatty acid that has an anti-inflammatory effect in our bodies. Dried cranberries are high in antioxidants that fight free radical damage. This salad is really good for your health!

Cauliflower & String Bean Dijon Salad

(Serves 4)

A tangy mustard dressing livens up this unique cold salad.

½ head cauliflower, cut into bite-size pieces
¼ lb string beans, cleaned and trimmed
¼ cup watercress, washed, stems removed
¼ cup thinly sliced red onion
½ small red bell pepper, sliced thin

Optional: Add 1 small shallot, minced

Dressing:
3 Tbs extra-virgin olive oil
2 tsp prepared Dijon mustard
1 tsp apple cider vinegar (preferably raw and organic)
2 Tbs lemon juice
1 tsp honey
2 Tbs water
¼ tsp sea salt
1 clove garlic, minced

1. In a large enough pot to hold a steamer basket, bring water to a boil. Place cauliflower pieces in basket and cover. On medium heat, steam for approximately 3–4 minutes until the cauliflower is crunchy but not raw-tasting. Immediately remove to a colander and rinse with cold water, or transfer cauliflower to a bowl of iced water to stop the cooking process (even warm food will continue to cook).

2. Bring water back to a boil in the same pot with the steamer basket. Remove woody stems from string beans and cut beans once or twice on a diagonal. Steam in basket for 3–4 minutes or until bright green and crisp. Immediately remove to a colander and rinse as instructed in step 1 for cauliflower. Toss string beans, cauliflower, watercress, onion, and red bell pepper together. If using shallots, add them now.

3. Combine dressing ingredients in a blender and process until smooth, or mix vigorously by hand. Pour dressing over vegetables and toss lightly. Serve immediately.

Bites of Insight

Shallots are a small root vegetable common in French cooking and taste like a combination of garlic and onion. The first appearance of mustard-makers dates back to 1292. Dijon, France, became a recognized center for mustard-making by the 13th-century. One of the most famous Dijon mustard makers was Grey-Poupon.

Fresh Figs, Spring Greens, & Bleu Cheese Salad

(Serves 4)

If you love fresh figs, you will love this salad!

1   bag fresh spring greens or baby mixed greens (4 cups)
¼   pomegranate, seeds removed
4   fresh figs (when in season)
4   oz bleu cheese, Gorgonzola, or Stilton

Dressing:
⅓   cup red raspberries
2   Tbs raspberry vinegar
⅓   cup natural vegetable oil
1   Tbs honey or agave syrup
⅓   tsp sea salt

1. Rinse raspberries and remove any overripe and moldy ones. In a small saucepan, combine raspberries and vinegar. Cover and simmer on very low for 2–3 minutes until raspberries have "juiced." Crush raspberries with a spoon to help release juice. If you plan to use fresh raspberries to toss in the salad, reserve some of them before cooking the rest.

2. Strain cooked raspberries in a small mesh strainer to remove seeds. Add this raspberry juice to the rest of the dressing ingredients and mix well. Put aside to cool. You can make the dressing up to a week ahead if necessary. This will give a pink hue to some of your vegetables in the salad.

3. To prepare the pomegranate, slice in quarters and break open the pieces by bending back the skin of the fruit. Clusters of seeds will emerge. You can peel back the thin membrane to expose more of the seeds. Pull some of those out to sprinkle on the salad and eat the rest! Discard remainder of pomegranate.

4. Wash figs and gently pat dry with a paper towel. Quarter them after removing stems. Place salad on 4 plates, top with pomegranate seeds, bleu cheese and figs. Drizzle raspberry dressing on salads and serve immediately.

Bites of Insight

Pomegranate seeds are available seasonally already packaged. They are an antioxidant powerhouse. In this recipe you can use balsamic vinegar if you do not have raspberry vinegar. Adding almost any fresh fruit to a salad is a great way to liven up the ordinary. Peaches, strawberries, and apples are some of my favorites.

Crunchy Jicama Cabbage Salad with Dill Dressing

(Serves 4)

Once you try jicama, a crunchy sweet root vegetable, you will love it!

1   cup peeled and julienned jicama
1   cup thinly sliced green cabbage
¼   cup thinly sliced red cabbage
½   cup julienned carrots (1 medium)
¼   cup fresh minced dill or 2 tsp dried dill

Optional: Use daikon radish instead of jicama for a spicier salad

Dressing:
⅓   cup natural vegetable oil
¼   cup rice vinegar
1   Tbs honey, agave, or organic cane sugar

1. Peel and slice jicama into thin slabs. Stack 2–3 slabs on top of each other and slice very thin cuts into julienne (matchstick) slices.

2. Cut cabbage into quarters. Using one quarter, hold at an angle with cut side toward you. Slice very thin long slices on the diagonal. Do the same with red cabbage. Toss with jicama.

3. Prepare carrots into julienne cut by following the same instructions for jicama and add this to the cabbage with minced dill.

4. Combine dressing ingredients in a separate bowl and process until smooth, or mix vigorously by hand. Pour dressing over vegetables and toss lightly. Serve immediately.

Bites of Insight

Jicama (pronounced hick-a-ma) is a round root vegetable from Mexico that has a fresh, juicy, and crunchy texture. It tastes like a cross between an apple and a potato. Rice vinegar can be found at health food stores and most supermarkets in the Asian food section, or you can use white balsamic vinegar instead.

Hawaiian Cole Slaw

(Serves 4)

Cabbage, a cruciferous vegetable, is very high in vitamin C and antioxidant rich nutrients!

2   cups shredded green cabbage
½   cup shredded red cabbage
½   cup shredded carrots
     (1 medium)
⅓   cup golden raisins
1   tsp poppy seeds
½   cup chopped pineapple
     (fresh or canned)

Dressing:
2   Tbs mayonnaise
1   Tbs nonfat sour cream
     or plain yogurt
1   Tbs rice vinegar
2   Tbs pineapple juice
½   tsp sea salt

1. Shred cabbages and carrots and place in bowl. Toss with poppy seeds. Drain pineapple and reserve juice.

2. Soften raisins by soaking in a bowl of hot water for 5 minutes. Drain and toss with cabbage mixture.

3. Combine dressing ingredients in a separate bowl and mix vigorously by hand. Combine dressing with vegetables and mix. This is better if it sits for a few hours in the refrigerator and best the next day. This will hold in the refrigerator for 3–4 days.

Bites of Insight

Rice vinegar is found in most stores and is less acidic that white vinegar. Distilled white vinegar is very acidic and distilling kills the beneficial bacteria that good vinegar offers to our digestion.

Mandarin Orange & Bibb Lettuce Salad

(Serves 4)

This is a light summery salad. Fresh mandarins are best in this salad!

1 head Bibb, Boston, or Butter lettuce
5 oz can mandarin oranges (or 2 tangerines)
¼ cup thinly sliced red onion
¼ cup thinly sliced red bell pepper
⅓ cup pine nuts or raw hazelnuts

Dressing:
⅓ cup reserved mandarin juice
2 Tbs fresh orange juice
2 Tbs rice vinegar
⅓ cup canola oil or other natural vegetable oil
1 tsp honey or agave
¼ tsp sea salt

1. Rinse and dry lettuce, tear into bite-size pieces.

2. Drain mandarin oranges and reserve liquid for dressing. If using fresh tangerines, increase orange juice in salad dressing to ½ cup.

3. Combine dressing ingredients in a small bowl and mix thoroughly before drizzling on salad.

4. Roast pine nuts or hazelnuts in a pan in the oven at 350°F for 5 minutes. Be careful not to burn; they should be light brown.

5. Place salad on 4 plates; garnish each salad plate with mandarin orange slices, red onion, red pepper, and nuts. Drizzle dressing over salad immediately before serving.

Bites of Insight

Bibb lettuce was so named after Jack Bibb, a 19th-century American vegetable grower and typically has soft, sweet leaves. Tangerine oranges are a broad class of oranges that include mandarin and clementine. They have a distinct thin, loose peel and have been dubbed "kid-glove" oranges.

Shrimp and Sugar Snap Pea Salad

(Serves 4)

One of our favorite "picnic on the sailboat" salads. Sometimes I substitute pasta for quinoa and it works great!

4   cups precooked ziti or bowtie
     pasta or 2 cups precooked
     quinoa
12 large shelled shrimp
1   cup sugar snap peas,
     strings removed
½   cup chopped celery (2 stalks)
½   cup chopped red bell pepper
½   cup chopped fresh basil
     leaves

Optional: Add 1 cup chopped ripe
tomatoes or ¼ cup sliced sun-
dried tomatoes

Dressing:
½   cup extra-virgin olive oil
3   Tbs red wine vinegar
½   tsp prepared mustard
1   Tbs honey
2   Tbs water
1   tsp dried thyme
¼   tsp sea salt
⅛   tsp ground black pepper

Optional: Add jalapeno pepper or
other fresh herbs such as mint
or dill

1. Cook pasta according to package directions. Drain, cool and set aside.

2. If shrimp are not precooked, place in boiling water for 3 minutes. Remove to colander and drain immediately. Cool with cold water and set aside.

3. Remove string from sugar snap peas by pinching at the top end of the pea and pulling string down and off. Blanch peas by dropping in boiling water for 10 seconds, drain immediately. Plunge into ice cold water. When cooled, drain and place in large bowl.

4. Slice celery stalks down the middle lengthwise and then crosswise into ¼-inch pieces, and add to the sugar snap peas. Add the red bell pepper and basil leaves to the mixture.

5. Toss vegetables with cooled pasta. In a separate bowl, mix dressing ingredients together and toss with pasta, shrimp, and veggies.

Spinach Salad with Turkey Sausage and Buttermilk Mustard Dressing

(Serves 4)

4   cups baby spinach leaves
¼   cup each chopped yellow and red bell peppers
½   cup sliced cucumber (½ medium)
2   fresh tomatoes, sliced into wedges
2   precooked turkey sausage links, any variety

Dressing:
3   Tbs extra-virgin olive oil
2   Tbs lemon juice (1 lemon)
5   Tbs organic buttermilk
1   tsp prepared Dijon mustard
2   tsp chopped fresh parsley

1. Wash spinach and spin or dry with a paper towel. Place on individual plates.

2. Chop peppers, slice cucumbers, and cut tomatoes into six wedges. Add vegetables to spinach salad plates.

3. Simmer sausage in a covered skilled with a little water to heat thoroughly for 5 minutes. Slice on a diagonal. Place several pieces of sausage around each salad.

4. Prepare dressing by whisking olive oil and lemon juice together. Add in buttermilk, mustard, and parsley. Whisk again and spoon over salad. Serve immediately.

Note: There are many gourmet flavored precooked turkey dinner sausages now widely available in most grocery and health food stores. Almost any flavor would be great with this salad. Experiment!

Bites of Insight

Commercial buttermilk is made by adding a lactic acid bacteria culture to pasteurized whole, skim or nonfat milk. After the addition of the culture, the milk is left to ferment for 12 to 14 hours at a low temperature (optimum 69 degrees F.). It is usually labeled cultured buttermilk and may be salted or unsalted. Yogurt can be substituted for buttermilk in this recipe.

Tuscan Tomato and Bread Salad

(Serves 6)

Fresh heirloom tomatoes from the farmer's market are the best! Pick a variety of yellow, green, red, and purple tomatoes for a colorful dish! If heirlooms are not available…use sun-ripened tomatoes to get the full juicy flavor of this "can't stop eating" salad.

3   lbs fresh heirloom tomatoes
1   small red onion, sliced thin
¼   cup chopped scallions
      (2 scallions)
¼   cup chopped green bell
      pepper
¼   cup chopped fresh Italian
      parsley
½   cup chopped fresh basil
1   Tbs chopped fresh oregano

Day old crusty bread such as a
      French loaf or prepared large
      croutons

Dressing:
⅓   cup extra-virgin olive oil
2   Tbs balsamic vinegar
½   tsp sea salt
¼   tsp fresh ground black
      pepper (it's the best)

1. Slice bread loaf crosswise into 2-inch slices. Place on cookie sheet and brush with olive oil. Bake in oven at 350°F until slightly brown on edges and dry, approximately 3–5 minutes each side. Cut into cubes and toss with salad immediately before serving, otherwise it will get soggy quickly.

2. Slice tomatoes into quarters, then into bite-size pieces about 2 inches thick. (If tomatoes are cut too small the salad will resemble a salsa).

3. Chop remaining vegetables and fresh herbs; toss together with tomatoes.

4. Combine dressing in a small bowl and set aside until a half hour before serving. If allowed to sit too long with the tomatoes, it will darken the salad and make the dish soupy. Add bread croutons into salad immediately before serving.

Bites of Insight

Always store tomatoes at room temperature, unless it is a cut leftover piece. Tomatoes are a fruit and refrigeration will spoil their delicate texture and sweetness. Leave them in a basket on the counter out of direct sunlight and they can last up to a week or more.

Balsamic Salad Dressing

(Yields 1½ cups)

This is by far our favorite salad dressing and the most popular with my clients and students.

⅓ cup extra-virgin olive oil
¼ cup balsamic vinegar
¼ cup water
¼ tsp ground black pepper
1 Tbs maple syrup
1 tsp dried basil
2 cloves garlic, minced
½ tsp sea salt

1. Blend all ingredients in blender. Store in glass jar in refrigerator for up to 3 months.

Buttery Flaxseed Dressing

(Yields 1¼ cups)

*Flaxseed is high in Omega-3 essential fatty acids. This is a nutritious, rich, and very satisfying salad dressing! Please refer to the chapter on **Good Fats vs. Bad Fats** for more information.*

½ cup flaxseed oil
   (always keep refrigerated)
½ cup extra-virgin olive oil
4 Tbs lemon juice (2 lemons)
2 tsp prepared Dijon mustard
1 clove garlic, minced
¼ tsp ground black pepper
1 tsp Herbamare (health food store) or ½ tsp sea salt

1. Combine in a blender or shake thoroughly in a sealed container to blend. Store in refrigerator up to two months.

Miso Ginger Salad Dressing

(Yields 1 cup)

For those cooks who have these unusual ingredients on hand this is a yummy creamy dressing. I use the miso in my soups, tahini in salad dressings and sauces.

½ cup light sesame oil
⅛ cup toasted sesame oil
2 Tbs light miso
1 Tbs sesame tahini
1 tsp prepared Dijon mustard
1 ½ Tbs fresh ginger juice
1 Tbs lemon juice (½ lemon)
3 Tbs rice vinegar
1 Tbs agave syrup
2 Tbs water
2 cloves garlic, minced
½ tsp dried basil
¼ tsp ground black pepper

1. Combine oils, miso, tahini, mustard, lemon juice, vinegar, agave, water, garlic, basil, and black pepper in a blender.

2. Using a handheld cheese grater with small holes, grate fresh unpeeled ginger onto your cutting board until you get a small ball of ginger pulp. Take this ginger in your hand and squeeze the juice into the blender with remaining ingredients.

3. Blend for 1–2 minutes until mixed thoroughly.

Bites of Insight

Miso is a paste made from fermented soybeans and is the base for miso soups. It is found in health food stores or Asian markets. Agave is the syrup from the agave cactus and is found in health food stores. Tahini is a nut butter made from ground sesame seeds and is a delicious substitute for dairy in dressings. It is found in health food stores and most grocery stores.

Fresh Raspberry Vinaigrette

(Yields ¾ cup)

This is such a refreshing dressing, especially accompanied by a sharp cheese with the salad. It is best with fresh raspberries but frozen would work too.

⅓ cup canola oil or extra-virgin olive oil
1 Tbs honey
2 Tbs raspberry vinegar, white wine, or rice wine vinegar
⅓ cup fresh raspberries
⅛ tsp sea salt

1. Rinse raspberries gently and pick out any overripe and moldy ones. Place raspberries and vinegar in small saucepan and cover. Simmer on very low heat for 2-3 minutes. Wait until raspberries have "juiced." You can help the process along by crushing the raspberries with the back of a spoon to get more juice.

2. Pour raspberries in a strainer and push the juice out with the back of a spoon until only seeds are left. Add this pure raspberry juice to the remaining dressing ingredients and shake well. When cooled, toss with salad. This dressing can be made a week ahead if necessary. This will add a pink hue to some of your vegetables in the salad.

Note: This dressing is especially dynamic with my *Fresh Figs, Spring Greens, and Bleu Cheese Salad,* as well as my *Fruited Quinoa Salad* recipe in the *Salads that Satisfy* chapter. You'll find new ways to use this dressing too!

Salads that Satisfy

•   •   •

Opposite: California Fiesta Quinoa Salad, see page 98

Salads that Satisfy

This chapter has more of my favorite whole grain recipes. You might want to begin your journey of whole grains with this chapter. Serving whole grains in salads with lots of fresh vegetables and herbs is a great way to excite people about eating good carbohydrates. You'll find you'll be serving these substantial salads often.

When we think of salad, we think of crisp green lettuce, juicy tomatoes, and an array of garden fresh vegetables. What also comes to mind is: "It's a nice side dish, but what about the entree?" Vegetable salads are a nutritious necessity in our diets, but they are not always filling. After all, most vegetables are composed of 80% water. No wonder we still feel hungry after eating them! Yet, fat-laden pasta salads that might fill us up can cause unwanted weight gain. So what are the healthy, satisfying salads that are a meal in themselves?

Picnic salads have not changed since I was a kid. Despite warnings of fat, most picnics offer soggy macaroni salad with too much mayo, potato salad, or variations on pasta, coleslaw and canned baked beans. I once received a call from one of the den moms at school asking me what I would like to contribute to the end-of-year BBQ. My choices were hamburgers, hot dogs, buns, potato chips, or paper products. I must have sounded indignant when I asked her, "Is that all we are serving the kids? I want to bring something healthy." She suggested I bring the paper plates! After several minutes of conversation, she commented that she and the other adults would love to have a healthy salad, but she could not think of anything else besides a pasta salad. A week later, I went to a baseball picnic for my son that had the same offerings. I brought my

California Fiesta Quinoa Salad and my *Lentil and Wild Rice Salad with Cilantro*. The parents were surprised and delighted. Both salads were the talk of the picnic and the recipes were happily passed around.

Why do we feel adults are the only ones who like healthy food? Perhaps if more of us brought healthier alternatives to our summer picnics and our kids saw the adults eat them, we might find that our kids would eat a whole lot healthier.

Basic Ingredients

What ingredients could be included in a vegetable salad that would give us the protein and carbohydrates that our bodies need to feel satisfied as a main meal? Whole grains, beans, and nuts! Whole grains are high in energy-giving complex carbohydrates, and important vitamins and minerals that are lacking in our diet. Combined with beans, whole grains offer a substantial serving of protein. On hot summer days, do you need a better reason to offer a cooling main meal salad using these wholesome ingredients?

Starting with leftover cooked grains such as barley, brown rice, wild rice, quinoa or bulgur and perhaps some precooked beans, a dinner "salad" can be made in 15–20 minutes. I always make sure I have leftover cooked grains by cooking more than I need for the evening's meal. Refrigerated whole grains can last 4–5 days. Whole grain cooking is as simple as boiling water. Most grains cook in a 2 to 1 ratio of water to grain, most of them needing 20–40 minutes of simmering. For specific cooking times, see the *Amber Waves of Grain* chapter for a cooking chart. I will have enough leftover brown rice, for example, that would give me a foundation for 3–4 other dishes such as veggie burgers, soups, salads, loaves, casseroles, and yummy *Chinese Fried Rice.*

Add fresh chopped vegetables such as carrots, green or red bell pepper, peas, tomatoes, corn, string beans, celery, cucumbers, scallions, broccoli, or whatever else you have on hand. Don't use leftover cooked vegetables. They lack flavor and crispness and have lost nutritional value. Blanch vegetables lightly for whole grain salads, or keep them raw to still maintain that fresh, crisp flavor and maximum nutrition.

When using herbs, use fresh herbs for best results in these salads. Dried herbs can be used, but their flavors take longer to be released unless they are cooked with the dish. Some of my favorite fresh herbs to use in *Salads that Satisfy* are dill, parsley, cilantro, chives, scallions, and mint. I enjoy using lemon thyme and sorrel when my herb garden is growing.

If you are adding beans to the salad, make sure you drain the broth and rinse the beans well. When you add nuts or beans to a whole grain, you are increasing the protein in the dish. Salads that have both would be appropriate for a vegetarian entrée, but would also work well as a side dish to a grilled entree of choice. There are a variety of organic canned beans that are quite good to keep on hand for quick meals.

The preferred dressing is usually a vinaigrette. My favorite dressing other than a prepared vinaigrette uses a lemon base. I have used raspberry vinegar, balsamic or red wine vinegar, brown rice vinegar or lemon and lime base with of course good quality oils. Keep in mind, vinegars and citrus juices can "bleach the green" out of green vegetables, especially peas, string beans, and broccoli. If you've made a salad that has one of these vegetables in it, keep the dressing separate and toss it with your salad an hour before serving it.

Use unrefined oils or expeller pressed oils which are minimally processed without chemicals. These are the best to use in these salads and in your cooking. I always use the most nutritious organic extra-virgin olive oil. I also use expeller pressed sesame oil (or sunflower oil) when I want a lighter vinaigrette in my recipes. Please note that whenever I mention expeller pressed oil or natural vegetable oil in my recipes, I am referring to one of these oils. Whole grain salads are naturally moist and require less oil to flavor them. Sea salt is the best to use because it contains additional trace minerals that are often missing in our diet. Sea salt can be purchased in health food stores.

Maybe if we all try to introduce one new whole grain salad at a picnic, then we might start a picnic revolution. Wouldn't that be great?! Try these salads at your next picnic and watch them disappear.

Barley Confetti Salad with Fresh Dill

(Serves 4)

With its lighter dill flavor, this is a delicious and refreshing summertime salad for picnics and family gatherings.

3 cups precooked hulled barley or 1 cup uncooked (see Whole Grain Cooking Chart)
½ cup fresh or frozen corn
1 cup precooked kidney beans, drained and rinsed
½ cup chopped celery (2 stalks)
¾ cup seeded and chopped red bell pepper
½ cup sliced scallions (4 scallions)
½ cup minced fresh dill or 2 Tbs dried dill

Dressing:
⅓ cup red wine vinegar
½ cup extra-virgin olive oil
2 tsp sea salt

1. To cook barley, add 1 cup uncooked barley to a large pot with 3 cups of water, cover, and bring to boil. Decrease heat to medium and cook for 1 hour without stirring. It is best to precook barley ahead of time and keep refrigerated up to 3-5 days. You can substitute precooked rice for barley in this recipe.

2. In a medium pot, bring water to boil and blanch corn for 2 minutes. Remove, drain, and rinse with cold water.

3. Prepare vegetables and add them to the barley with the beans. Mix in corn, scallions, and dill.

4. Combine dressing ingredients and toss with salad. Let salad stand for 30 minutes before serving.

Bites of Insight

Hulled barley is the natural unpolished whole grain. It's a little chewier and more flavorful than pearled barley. It contains protein, vitamins and minerals. Pearled barley is polished and has had the bran/fiber and the germ removed which results in an 80% nutrition loss. Pearled barley is like white rice and hulled barley is like brown rice...big difference!

California Fiesta Quinoa Salad

(Serves 6)

Absolutely one of the most loved salads by my clients, students, family, and friends!

1   cup uncooked quinoa
¼   tsp sea salt
¾   cup chopped tomato
     (1 medium)
¼   cup chopped celery (1 stalk)
½   cup seeded and chopped
     cucumber (1 medium)
½   cup chopped scallions
     (4 scallions)
½   cup chopped fresh cilantro
½   cup blanched fresh corn
½   cup precooked black beans,
     rinsed and drained
¼   cup pitted and diced black
     olives (Kalamata are the
     best!)

Dressing:
⅓   cup extra-virgin olive oil
1   tsp hot red pepper flakes
     (or more to taste)
2   Tbs red wine vinegar or
     ¼ cup lemon juice
½   tsp sea salt

1. Boil 2 cups water and add salt. Thoroughly rinse quinoa in strainer. Place in boiling water, cover, and reduce heat to medium-low. Cook for 15-20 minutes or until grain is fluffed and water is absorbed. Remove from pot into a large bowl and allow to cool before adding vegetables.

2. To cut tomatoes into cubes, slice tomatoes into ½-inch slabs and remove most of the seeds. Then cut tomatoes into sticks and crosswise into ½-inch cubes. This will give you evenly sized tomato pieces that won't get mushy if the salad isn't eaten right away.

3. Cut celery by slicing down the rib in the center of the stalk. If the stalk is large you might want to cut it in thirds. Then cut crosswise into ½-inch pieces.

4. Slice cucumber lengthwise into 4 strips and then remove center seeds. Chop these strips into ½-inch pieces. Remove root ends of scallions and cross chop into ¼-inch pieces. In a large bowl, toss cooled quinoa with all remaining vegetables, beans, and olives.

5. Mix vinegar, oil, hot pepper flakes, and salt together in a bowl. Toss lightly with salad. Refrigerate for an hour before serving. This will last 5 days in the refrigerator.

Serving Suggestion: My favorite way of enjoying this as a leftover is in scrambled eggs! Just before the eggs set hard, I add ¼ cup or so of this salad and give it a stir. Very yummy breakfast!

Chinese Chicken Salad

(Serves 4)

A quick and easy weeknight dinner if you have cooked chicken on hand.

½ cup julienned carrots
    (1 medium)
2   stalks of bok choy, chopped
    with leaves
¼   cup each chopped red and
    green cabbage
¼   cup chopped red bell pepper
    (½ medium)
1   cup mung bean sprouts
½   cup snow or snap peas
¼   cup slivered almonds

Marinade for chicken:
2   large boneless, skinless
    chicken breasts
¼   cup soy sauce
1   Tbs water plus 1 Tbs honey
1   Tbs toasted sesame oil
1   Tbs light sesame oil
1   tsp ginger juice
1   tsp prepared mustard

Dressing:
2   Tbs orange juice
2   Tbs soy sauce
2   Tbs light sesame oil
1   tsp toasted sesame oil
½   tsp ginger juice

1. To juice ginger, use a handheld parmesan grater and grate ginger with skin until you get a small ball size. Squeeze this ball in the palm of your hand into a small bowl. Measure out from there. If the ginger is old or dehydrated this will not work well. If you don't have a grater, then peel, thinly slice and mince ginger and add to dressing and marinade.

2. Marinate chicken for at least ½ hour or longer if possible. You can also marinate overnight. Remove, drain marinade, and discard. Grill or panfry chicken until no longer pink, about 4-5 minutes on each side. Once chicken has cooled, cut into bite-size pieces.

3. Clean, slice or chop, and toss vegetables together and add to chicken.

4. Combine dressing ingredients and toss with chicken and vegetables and top with almonds.

Bites of Insight

To avoid contamination, don't use the marinade for a dressing if it had raw chicken soaking in it.

Cajun Turkey Salad

(Serves 2)

This is my version of a salad I once enjoyed at a gourmet deli in New Jersey. Spicy with a hint of sweet.

8   oz cooked white turkey breast
⅓   cup chopped celery
½   cup halved firm cherry tomatoes
⅓   cup chopped scallions (3 scallions)
6   sun-dried tomatoes packed in oil, sliced

Dressing:
1   Tbs extra-virgin olive oil
2   cloves garlic, minced
⅛   tsp ground cloves
½   tsp ground cayenne pepper
½   tsp sea salt
2   Tbs chicken broth
1   Tbs rice vinegar or white vinegar

Optional: ¼ cup chopped cilantro; Or replace turkey with cooked chicken breast

1. Shred or slice turkey breast into 1-inch cubes and place in medium sized bowl. Slice celery stalk down the middle lengthwise and then crosswise into ¼-inch pieces. Add celery, tomatoes, and scallions to turkey.

2. Drain and pat sun-dried tomatoes with paper towel to remove excess oil, slice thin, and add to turkey.

3. In a small pot, heat olive oil and add garlic, sauté for 5 seconds. Add spices and salt, and simmer again for 30 seconds. The cayenne will start turning brown; remove from heat before it burns. Browning the spices brings out their richness.

4. When the spiced oil cools slightly, add chicken broth and vinegar and stir. Add this dressing to turkey mixture and toss. Garnish with cilantro if you are using. When the turkey marinates in these flavors for a few hours it tastes even better.

Serving Suggestion: Add ½ cup of kidney beans to this salad. Serve it on a bed of salad greens for a light lunch or dinner on a hot summer day.

Dilled Rice and Green Pea Salad

(Serves 6)

A quick-to-make simple refreshing summer grain salad. You can also use precooked rice if it is still moist.

1   cup uncooked long grain or
    brown basmati rice
⅛ tsp sea salt
½ cup fresh or frozen peas
½ cup chopped red bell pepper,
    (½ medium)
¼ cup finely chopped fresh dill
    or 1 Tbs dried dill

Dressing:
2   Tbs extra-virgin olive oil
2   Tbs brown rice vinegar or
    red wine vinegar
¼ tsp sea salt

1. Rinse and drain rice. Place in a small pot; add 1 ½ cups water and salt. Cover and bring to boil. Reduce to medium heat and cook for 35 minutes; don't stir. Fluff with a spoon and transfer to a large bowl. Cool rice in refrigerator for 15 minutes. You may substitute 2 cups of precooked rice.

2. Bring 1 cup of water to a boil. If using fresh peas, blanch for 4 minutes, if frozen, blanch for 2 minutes. Remove, drain, and cool. Toss together rice, peas, red bell pepper, and dill.

3. For dressing, combine oil, vinegar, and salt in a small bowl. Mix thoroughly. Combine with rice mixture. Refrigerate for at least 1 hour to blend flavors.

Serving Suggestion: To create a complete protein entrée, increase the protein by adding garbanzo beans, chopped walnuts, or roasted almonds.

Bites of Insight

The vinegar in this recipe will bleach the green out of the peas within a day or two so it is best to toss this salad with the dressing right before you will serve it. Rice dries out quickly in the refrigerator so only make enough for one day of leftovers.

Fruited Quinoa Salad

(Serves 4–6)

This is a beautiful and unusual salad blending sweet with savory and added crunch.

1   cup uncooked quinoa (can
    prepare up to two days
    before)
¼   tsp sea salt
⅓   cup chopped roasted
    cashews
½   cup chopped celery (2 stalks)
⅓   cup dried cranberries or
    1 cup fresh red grapes
¼   cup chopped fresh cilantro

Dressing:
2   Tbs fresh lemon juice
2   Tbs raspberry vinegar
2   Tbs extra-virgin olive oil
1   Tbs water
1   Tbs honey
⅛   tsp sea salt

Or use ⅓ cup prepared
Raspberry Vinaigrette

1. Rinse and drain quinoa thoroughly. Bring 2 cups water to boil, add salt and quinoa. Cover, reduce heat to medium-low and simmer 20 minutes or until quinoa has absorbed all liquid. It will be fluffy. Remove to bowl and refrigerate to cool. Don't add raw vegetables to hot grain.

2. If using raw cashews, place cashews in a preheated toaster oven tray at 325°F. Roast for 5 minutes until a nutty aroma is present. Chop coarsely. Skip this if you have roasted unsalted cashews. If you have salted cashews then omit the salt in the dressing and the quinoa.

3. If using fresh red grapes instead of cranberries, slice them in half or quarters. Toss together cashews, quinoa, celery, grapes or cranberries, and cilantro.

4. Prepare dressing by combining lemon juice, vinegar, oil, water, honey, and salt. Stir thoroughly and toss with the quinoa salad. Adjust seasoning and chill several hours to allow flavors to mingle.

Greek Quinoa Salad with Feta

(Serves 4)

A light salad with a dynamic Greek influence.

1 cup uncooked quinoa
⅓ cup chopped artichoke
   hearts, marinated in oil
½ cup pitted and chopped
   Kalamata olives
⅓ cup sliced sun-dried tomatoes
   or 1 cup chopped fresh
   tomatoes
¼ cup finely chopped celery
   (1 stalk)
⅓ cup chopped fresh Italian
   parsley
1 Tbs fresh oregano or
   1 tsp dried oregano
⅓ cup diced red onion
¾ cup crumbled feta cheese
¼ cup finely chopped scallions
   (2 scallions)

Dressing:
½ cup extra-virgin olive oil
2 Tbs red wine vinegar
¼ tsp sea salt
2 cloves garlic, minced

1. Rinse quinoa and drain. Bring 2 cups water to boil. Add quinoa to water, cover, and reduce heat to medium-low. Simmer for 20 minutes or until water is absorbed. Fluff with a fork. Transfer to a large bowl to cool.

2. While quinoa is cooking, begin preparing your vegetables. For celery, slice first down the rib twice to give you 3 long pieces. Then cut crosswise into smaller pieces. Toss all vegetables and herbs with quinoa.

3. Combine dressing ingredients, mix well and stir into quinoa salad. Add feta cheese and toss again.

Serving Suggestion: For best results, make salad an hour before serving and leave at room temperature so the olive oil can infuse into the grain. Salad will keep up to 5 days in the refrigerator. You can also substitute couscous instead of quinoa.

Bites of Insight

The quinoa germ separates after cooking and looks like a white piece of string attached to the grain. Quinoa is the only whole grain that is a complete protein and is gluten free!

Italian Pasta Salad with Sun-Dried Tomatoes

(Serves 6–8)

I sold this salad to fitness centers and health food stores and it always sold out!

1½ cups uncooked mini cheese ravioli or pasta

¼ cup sliced marinated sun-dried tomatoes, drained

¼ cup chopped flat Italian parsley

¼ cup sliced black olives (Kalamata are the best)

¼ cup chopped fresh basil (fresh is a necessary essential for maximum flavor)

¼ cup grated zucchini (½ medium)

Dressing:

⅓ cup extra-virgin olive oil

2–3 Tbs red wine vinegar

½ tsp dried oregano or 2 tsp minced fresh oregano

2 cloves garlic, minced

¼ tsp sea salt

Optional: Spice Hunter Italian Seasoning mix is very flavorful. If you can find it use 1 Tbs instead of oregano.

1. Bring 6 cups of water to boil and add ravioli or pasta, reduce heat, and simmer according to package directions. Drain and run cold water over pasta to stop cooking.

2. In a small bowl, combine dressing ingredients thoroughly and allow to sit for 5 minutes. This allows the seasonings to soak up some of the dressing.

3. In a large bowl, combine cooked pasta and remaining ingredients. Add in dressing only if you are serving right away. To give it a better "shelf life," toss dressing only with the portion you plan on eating within a day or two, and store remaining dressing on the side in the refrigerator. Pasta continues to absorb liquid (dressing in this case) and when refrigerated for more than a day, it will become pasty.

Serving Suggestion: This is a rich and delicious salad, and can be served as the main protein entree with side dishes of vegetables or salad. This is nutritious enough to substitute for a meat or bean entree.

Lentil and Wild Rice Salad with Cilantro

(Serves 4)

My absolute favorite whole grain salad after the **California Fiesta Quinoa Salad.** *Great picnic, potluck, or party salad!*

¼ cup uncooked wild rice
1 cup precooked brown rice
¼ cup uncooked green lentils
¼ cup finely chopped scallions
(2 scallions)
½ cup chopped fresh cilantro
¼ cup chopped celery (1 stalk)
½ cup shredded carrots
(1 medium)

Dressing:
⅓ cup extra-virgin olive oil
¼ cup lime juice, preferably
fresh
¼ tsp hot red pepper flakes
(or to taste)
¼ tsp ground cumin
½ tsp sea salt

1. Rinse and drain wild rice. Place wild rice in medium-size pot with 1 ½ cups of water. Bring to a boil, cover, and reduce heat to medium. Cook for one hour (option below). Wild rice is cooked when most of the grains are split open and curled back. At this point, they will be tender enough for a salad. Drain any remaining water. Set aside to cool.

2. While rice is cooking, rinse and drain lentils. Place in 1 cup of water, cover, and bring to boil. Reduce heat to low and simmer for 15 minutes. Drain any remaining water and quickly rinse cooked lentils in a strainer. Set aside to cool.

3. Chop scallions, cilantro, and celery. Shred carrots on a grater or using a food processor. Toss with lentils, wild rice, and brown rice.

4. Combine olive oil, lime juice, red pepper flakes, cumin, and sea salt. Toss with salad and either serve immediately or refrigerate. This tastes even better the next day and will last up to 3–4 days in the refrigerator.

Bites of Insight

To shorten cooking time, cook wild rice for 30 minutes and then let it sit for a half hour or longer while you are away. It will continue to absorb water. Most wild rice I have ever tried is undercooked. If the grain is not split open, it will be chewy and starchy and will not absorb any dressing. Rice dishes can become dry and hard in the refrigerator so start with rice that is cooked on the soft side.

Herbed Couscous Salad with Garbanzo Beans

(Serves 4–6)

Aaron, my oldest son, created this dish and it is one of the most popular in my cooking classes. I invite you to make it for your family and friends at your next gathering.

1   cup uncooked couscous
¼   tsp sea salt
⅓   cup chopped red onion
½   cup diced carrots
    (1 medium)
⅓   cup green peas, blanched
½   cup diced cucumber, peeled
    and seeded (½ medium)
¼   cup minced fresh dill or
    1 Tbs dried dill
¼   cup minced fresh parsley
½   cup precooked garbanzo
    beans, drained

Dressing:
2   Tbs extra-virgin olive oil
1   Tbs red wine vinegar
½   tsp sea salt

1. Bring 1 ½ cups water to a boil, add salt and couscous. Cover, remove from heat, and allow to stand for 5 minutes. Do not let it stand for much longer. Hold the pot over a large bowl and remove couscous by pulling a fork lightly through the grain to release the individual grains into the bowl.

2. Blanch carrots for 30 seconds in boiling water, strain, and place in ice-cold water to stop cooking for 2 minutes and drain again. Add chopped vegetables and garbanzo beans to couscous.

3. For dressing, combine oil, vinegar, and salt. Add dressing and herbs to couscous and mix well.

4. Serve immediately or refrigerate for an hour before serving to improve flavors. This tastes even better the next day. The green peas will be bleached light green because of the vinegar. If you don't want that to happen, keep the dressing separate and toss with the couscous an hour before you serve.

Serving Suggestion: You can use this to stuff salmon or flounder or serve it as a side. Couscous is semolina pasta and not a whole grain. It is a wonderful, light carbohydrate side dish.

Mexican Black Bean and Corn Salad

(Serves 4)

A great side salad with meats, seafood, chicken, or vegetarian only!!

2   cups precooked black beans, rinsed and drained
½   cup fresh or frozen corn
½   cup chopped red bell pepper (1 medium)
½   cup chopped scallions (4 scallions)
½   tsp hot red pepper flakes

Optional: ⅓ cup chopped cilantro

Dressing:
¼   cup extra-virgin olive oil
2   Tbs balsamic vinegar
½   tsp sea salt

1. Bring 1 cup of water to a boil and add corn; blanch fresh corn 4 minutes or frozen corn 2 minutes. Remove from heat, drain, and rinse with cold water.

2. Combine beans, corn, red bell pepper, scallions, and red pepper flakes in a medium bowl.

3. In a separate bowl, mix dressing ingredients. Toss dressing with bean mixture. Add cilantro if using and toss again. You can serve immediately or allow to cool in the refrigerator for 30 minutes to allow the flavors to blend. Good for 4–5 days refrigerated.

Serving Suggestion: This is a hearty protein dish. It is a fantastic side dish for my *Best Fish Tacos, Crunchy Corn Crusted Picnic Chicken* or my *Spicy Salmon* entrées. This would also do well as a vegetarian entrée served with a green salad.

Bites of Insight

Fresh bell peppers are on the "dirty dozen" list of foods most heavily sprayed with pesticides and herbicides. I always buy organic bell peppers to avoid these sprays. Visit www.ewg.org for their "dirty dozen" list of foods to avoid and foods that are safe.

Quinoa Tabbouleh Salad

(Serves 4)

This is a lighter version than the traditional bulgur tabbouleh salad with fresh mint and parsley. It will become one of your favorites.

1   cup uncooked quinoa
½   cup peeled and chopped
    cucumber (1 medium)
½   cup quartered cherry
    tomatoes
½   cup minced fresh mint
½   cup minced fresh parsley
⅓   cup finely chopped scallions
    (3 scallions)

Dressing:
½   cup extra-virgin olive oil or
    natural vegetable oil
2   Tbs lemon juice (1 lemon)
½   tsp powdered mustard or
    1 tsp prepared mustard
½   tsp ground cumin
½   tsp sea salt
¼   tsp ground black pepper

Optional: Add ½ cup cooked garbanzo beans or lentils for a dish with more protein.

1. Rinse and drain quinoa. Bring 1 ¾ cups water to boil; add quinoa, reduce heat to medium-low and simmer covered for 20 minutes or until all water has been absorbed. Do not stir. Transfer to bowl and allow to cool.

2. Add cut vegetables: cucumber, cherry tomatoes, mint, parsley, and scallions.

3. Combine all dressing ingredients. Whisk or mix vigorously before tossing with salad. If using garbanzo or lentil beans you can add them now. Serve immediately or allow flavors to blend for about one hour at room temperature.

Note: Fresh herbs in cold salads take time for their flavors to "open." Whole grain salads taste best when they have been able to rest to let all the flavors blend.

Bites of Insight

Quinoa is the only whole grain that is a complete protein and it is also gluten free! The quinoa germ separates after cooking and looks like a white piece of string attached to the grain.

For the Love of Soups

• • •

Opposite: Marvelous Minestrone, see page 129

For the Love of Soups

Who can resist a steaming bowl of homemade soup on a cool fall or winter day? If your family is like mine, they will love coming home to the wonderful aromas of fresh home-cooked soup. There is no better way to add vitamins, minerals, and fiber to everyone's diet than with a warm, hearty bowl of homemade soup. Soups are a favorite low-calorie meal for weight watchers. Use them to sneak vegetables in your kids' diet, too, as most kids love soup.

Soups are great make-ahead meals for the working person. When made in larger quantities, soups can be frozen to provide wholesome meals that can be ready in minutes. Soups are a great way to use vegetable, bean, or whole grain leftovers. Small quantities of leftover pasta, grains, or beans can be the inspiration for a new vegetable soup. By simply changing the herbs, spices, and vegetables, you can create an incredible variety of soups from the same basic recipe!

Fresh vegetables are crucial for delicious soups. Combined with herbs, spices, whole grains, beans, pasta, and fresh organic poultry, you can create easy make-ahead meals everyone will enjoy.

Building Soup vs. Making Soup

A great soup is built slowly by adding vegetables in layer by layer. Never add all your vegetables at the same time. Let each vegetable have a chance to simmer in the bottom of the pot to allow it to release its flavors. The hardest vegetables such as onion and carrots go in first as they will be closer to the heat and will cook longer. The next layer of vegetables have more water in them such as peppers and celery. The quickest cooking ones go in next such as zucchini and string beans. Finally, parsley, cilantro, or green peas are added in the last few minutes because they only need to cook 1–2 minutes. There is no need to stir a soup that has been layered in this manner. By the time you have finished chopping and adding your last vegetables, the soup is minutes away from being done.

Soup Broths

Traditionally, broths are made with meat and vegetables. Stocks are made with just the bones of the meat so broth and stocks are interchangeable unless you are a vegetarian.

Keeping homemade vegetable broth on hand and in the freezer is easy and convenient. Put together a broth while you are doing other things in the kitchen. Accumulate several days' worth of vegetable scraps and keep them refrigerated until ready to use. Vegetable pieces you might normally throw away are perfect for creating a soup broth, such as:

- Onions (not too many of the dark outer skins as they can be bitter), leeks, green onions, chives, scallions.
- Root vegetables such as carrots, parsnip, turnips, rutabaga.
- Green vegetables: zucchini, green beans, parsley stems, kale stems, broccoli stems, celery leaves, and hearts.
- Sweet vegetables: cabbage, winter squash, cauliflower, etc.
- Miscellaneous: mushroom stems, pepper pieces (not the seeds).

To ensure that the broth has a sweeter flavor, add the following to your vegetable scraps:
- 1 medium onion, chopped;
- 3 large carrots, chopped;
- 2 cups green cabbage, chopped; and
- 2 cups winter squash (if you have it on hand), chopped.

For every four cups (1 quart) of total vegetable scraps, add 3 quarts of water to a covered pot, bring to a boil, reduce heat, and simmer for 30 minutes. Strain out and discard scraps, then store this soup broth in freezable containers. Freeze up to 3 months or refrigerate up to a week. You can also use this broth instead of water when cooking grains or beans to add more flavor.

Other ideas for enhancing soup broths:
Miso (fermented soybean paste) is my favorite ingredient for soups. I keep a variety of light and dark miso on hand. Miso adds flavor and nutrients and healthful digestive enzymes. I use light miso when I want to add a subtle but salty flavor to a soup, as in my *Curried Split Pea Soup*. Dark miso is stronger and is good for *Hot and Sour Miso Soup*. Never boil miso after it is added to soup, as this will destroy its helpful digestive enzymes. If eliminating miso from a recipe, then replace each 1 Tbs of miso with ½ tsp sea salt.

Sea salt can be added to soup while it is cooking to enhance its flavors. Sea salt helps to draw out the juices of the vegetables into the broth improving overall flavor. Never use sea salt on food once it has been cooked and brought to the table. You will consume more salt than necessary if you do.

Sea vegetables enhance the flavor and add important minerals to soup. These include kombu (kelp), wakame, wakame flakes, and dulse. Add kombu at the beginning of the soup, others during the last 15 minutes of cooking time.

Soup Broth
If you have not mastered the art of soup broth yet, don't let that stop you. There are several healthy and nutritious broths available in fat free and low sodium forms. Remember, the fun in cooking is experimenting with food and different flavors, so don't be afraid to follow your creative urge and try some new combinations and seasonings you haven't tried before.

Thickening Soups
In this chapter, I offer several creamed soup (non-dairy) recipes. Experiment on your own. If you need to avoid dairy cream in a recipe that calls for it, you can substitute one of the following:

- Add oat bran to thicken soup—usually ¼ cup is sufficient for a large pot.
- Use canned light coconut milk (available in organic too!) for a creamy texture without a noticeable coconut flavor. Found in grocery and health food stores.
- Use one of the non-dairy milks available: soy, rice, or almond milk (unsweetened original flavor is my favorite).
- Add oatmeal or precooked leftover grains, such as quinoa, that has been blended with a little soup broth to produce a "cream."
- Add silken or soft tofu that has been blended with a little soup broth. Add to soup near the end as high heat may curdle the tofu.
- Simply take out and blend some of the ingredients, as in *Potato Leek Soup* or *Creamed Winter Squash Soup* and then return it to the pot to thicken and "cream" the soup.

Soup as a "One Pot Meal"

Transforming a pot of soup into a one-pot-meal requires only a minimal knowledge of balancing nutrients. Protein is usually the focal point of a balanced meal. If the soup contains beans or tofu, you are halfway there. To increase the protein, add a whole grain side dish or whole grain bread or whole grain pasta. For more vegetarian protein complements, see the index.

Serve a soup that contains beans and pasta, like my *Marvelous Minestrone Soup*, and you have a hearty soup that needs only a salad or a cooked green vegetable to complete a light meal. Serve my *Herbed Lentil Soup* with a piece of whole grain bread and a salad for a hearty, protein-complemented meal. For a complete meal, serve my *Mushroom Barley Soup with Dill* with hummus (bean and seed), pita bread, and a side dish of vegetables. Alternatively, soup can simply be an enjoyable, low-calorie appetizer.

Bites of Insight

It's important not to eat heavy food late at night, so if you find yourself preparing dinner and eating late, it's better to fill up on food that is quickly and easily digested so it won't interfere with your sleep. Stir-fried veggies, potatoes, pasta, and soups are good choices for a light dinner. Many soups in this chapter are filling enough to have for a light dinner with a salad.

Weight Loss and Soups

Soups can help make a good meal into a great meal by satisfying the appetite without filling up on excess fats and proteins. Even one small serving can help reduce your appetite for heavier, more calorie-rich dishes. A weight loss soup will have a delicious broth and many veggies for fiber, vitamins, minerals, and enzymes. The soups in this chapter are very satisfying, filling, and low in calories. I am not referring to a cream of cheddar soup, which you will not find in this cookbook! Soups can also make a wonderful light breakfast choice with a piece of whole grain toast.

Weight Gain and Soups

Not a contradiction, just different soups. Certain soups add more calories, more fat, protein, or carbohydrates than others. Adding beans (legumes), and/or cooked whole grains (such as wild rice or barley) can thicken soup while adding healthy calories and fiber. Although I do not advocate a lot of pasta because many nutrients are lost in processing, it can be good filler for soups. Adding chicken and beef will increase calories as well. If someone is underweight, having a hearty soup as a snack between meals can increase their overall daily caloric intake and help them regain needed weight.

Soup Tip #1: Add vegetables according to their cooking time. Putting all the vegetables in at the same time might result in a fair tasting broth but soggy and tasteless vegetables. Begin with root vegetables, like onions and carrots, and sauté until onions are tender, usually about 2 minutes. As you add other ingredients, keep in mind how long the soup needs to cook. For instance, if the soup is almost ready, add green vegetables like broccoli, string beans, or zucchini in the last five minutes. Green vegetables will lose their healthy complexion if cooked longer than 5 minutes. Vegetables high in vitamin C will be depleted if cooked longer than ten minutes.

Soup Tip #2: Add only a little water in the

beginning or you will drown the flavors. When simmering vegetables, add enough water to cover the veggies by two inches or so. By keeping the volume of water low, it helps to build a tasty soup broth without having to rely on canned broth and bouillon. Adding dried herbs and spices helps improve the flavor. You may then add more water to get the right consistency of your soup *after* the vegetables are cooked. Remember, you can always add more water, but you cannot take away what has already been added.

Never add cooked pasta until soup is ready to be served. Pasta will absorb broth and get soggy. Keep the pasta separate if there is leftover soup and add as you are warming up the servings.

Soup Tip #3: When to add dried herbs and spices. Dried herbs and spices should always be added at the start of cooking so the flavors have a chance to meld with the soup broth. To help release their flavors, place dried herbs in the palm of one hand and rub with your other fingers and let them sprinkle into the soup pot.

When adding fresh herbs such as cilantro, oregano, parsley, dill, or basil, add half of them in the beginning to help flavor the soup broth, and the rest during the last five minutes of cooking. This way, the herb flavor is more pronounced.

When replacing dried herbs with fresh you can increase quantity by three times. Likewise, if you are replacing fresh herbs with dried you should reduce it by one third. Spices can be added in the beginning of cooking as they hold up longer and don't lose their flavor over time.

Garnishes

Why garnish? It's the finishing touch of presentation. We "eat" with our eyes first. If a dish doesn't look appetizing, we don't expect it to taste appetizing. Garnishes are often fresh herbs such as scallions, parsley, dill, cilantro, basil, or earthier flavors such as oregano, thyme, or rosemary. Garnishes can also be a few pinches of dried spice such as cayenne or cumin, or sweet spices such as cinnamon or nutmeg. A little bit of garnish goes a long way in a bowl of soup. Garnish adds color and appeal and often a little *pizzazz*. For example, topping my *Creamed Winter Squash Soup* with chopped parsley adds a delightful contrast of flavor and color. Whatever your choice, garnishes can make an ordinary bowl of soup look extraordinary.

Fresh is Best

My experience is that my recipes taste best when the freshest and healthiest vegetables are chosen for the ingredients. To assure the best flavor and nutrition, organic vegetables are best. Please see the beginning of this book for more information about organic food and their nutritional importance.

Note: Most of my soups in this chapter make enough to serve six adults, so if you are feeding fewer people you will have extra for freezing. Most people will eat 1 to 1½ cups of soup per serving. Regardless of the serving amounts listed, I suggest you use a 4-quart size pot or larger.

Chicken Soup for the Soul

(Serves 6)

Ahh....yes, the soup that heals it all...

2   lbs organic skin-on and bone-in chicken (including breast, thigh, and leg with bone)
2   Tbs extra-virgin olive oil
1   small onion, chopped
1   cup sliced carrots (2 medium)
½   cup chopped celery (2 stalks)
1   small parsnip or white turnip, chopped
1   leek, white part sliced and chopped
6   cups organic chicken broth
2   bay leaves
½   tsp ground thyme
½   tsp ground sage
½   tsp dried rosemary
1   tsp sea salt
¼   tsp ground black pepper
¼   cup chopped fresh parsley (for garnish)

Optional: 1 cup precooked pasta or 1 cup leftover precooked brown rice

1. Preheat 2 tablespoons of olive oil in a large pot for 2–3 minutes on medium heat. Place chicken in pot, a few pieces at a time, cover and cook until skin browns, about 3–4 minutes each side. Turn chicken over and cook the other side. Repeat with all chicken parts. Remove and put in a bowl.

2. In the same pot, lower heat and sauté onion for 2 minutes or until it begins to soften. Add carrots, celery, parsnips, and leeks. Sauté 2–3 minutes more. Add chicken, chicken broth, bay leaves, herbs, salt, and pepper. Cover pot and bring to a boil. Reduce to medium heat and simmer until chicken is thoroughly cooked, about 30 minutes.

3. Check chicken by removing thigh and place in a bowl. With a fork and a knife try to pull the meat off the bone. If thigh meat removes easily from the bone, it is cooked thoroughly. If it does not pull away easily and the meat still looks a little pink, it is not completely cooked. Replace meat into the soup and continue cooking for another 10 minutes.

4. To remove meat from chicken once cooked, remove chicken parts to a bowl, cool, remove skin, and pull apart meat. Add meat into pot. Discard bones, skin, and cartilage. Discard bay leaves and adjust seasoning to taste. Add precooked pasta or rice if using. Garnish with parsley and serve.

Bites of Insight

Always use a fresh, bone-in chicken with the skin when making this soup. A skinless chicken breast will not be as tasty. You need the fat from the skin for flavor. After the chicken is cooked you can remove most of the fat by removing the skin.

Creamed Winter Squash Soup

(Serves 4–6)

This has always been my youngest son, Matt's favorite soup. I gave him "soup bottles" when he was a baby.

2   Tbs extra-virgin olive oil
1   cup chopped onion
4   cups cubed winter squash
    (either butternut, buttercup
    or Kobacha)
½   tsp sea salt
¼   cup chopped fresh parsley
    (for garnish)

Optional: 1 Tbs curry powder for a spicier variety, or add 1 tsp cinnamon, ¼ tsp ground cloves, ¼ tsp ground nutmeg for a pumpkin pie-flavored soup.

1. Peel, deseed, and cut squash into ½-inch cubes by cutting slabs of squash with a sharp knife. Place two slabs on top of each other, cut halves lengthwise into several pieces. Then cut cross cut into ½-inch pieces.

2. Preheat 2 tablespoons of olive oil in a large pot on medium heat and sauté onion for 2–3 minutes.

3. Add squash, salt, and 6 cups water. Cover and bring to a boil. Reduce heat to medium and continue to simmer for 20 minutes or until squash is very tender. Blend soup to desired consistency with a food processor or a handheld immersion blender. Add more water if necessary to reach desired creaminess. Serve garnished with parsley.

Note: Immersion blenders are wonderful and are inexpensive. You can leave the soup in the pot and blend!

Bites of Insight

Since the skin on most squash has been waxed and may contain pesticides, I highly recommend peeling them. If you get your squash in the Fall at a farm stand who grows their own, it won't be waxed. Acorn squash is too difficult to peel for a soup. I use acorn squash for baking wedges and for stuffing only.

Curried Split Pea Soup

(Serves 4)

Creamy with a hint of curry, which is optional. This is a great cold weather soup...

2   Tbs extra-virgin olive oil
½   cup chopped onion
1   cup chopped carrots
    (2 medium)
½   cup chopped parsnip
1   cup dried split green peas,
    rinsed and drained
3   bay leaves
½   tsp sea salt
1   tsp curry powder
2   scallions, chopped
    (for garnish)

1. Preheat 2 tablespoons of olive oil in a large pot and add onion. Sauté on medium heat for 2–3 minutes. Add carrots and parsnip to onions and sauté for 2 more minutes.

2. Rinse and drain split peas. Add split peas, bay leaves, and 6 cups water to pot. Cover and cook on medium heat for 30 minutes, stirring occasionally. Cooking time may be longer depending on your pot and stove. Do not add salt yet. If using smoked turkey, add it now to the soup. Add more water if necessary and continue to cook until peas have disintegrated and the soup has become creamy. Some people like thick pea soup, others prefer a lighter broth.

3. Next add salt and curry powder and continue to cook for 30 minutes longer. Adding salt too early to a pot of beans makes them tough and harder to cook; it is better to add salt about halfway through the cooking time. Garnish with scallions.

Note: You can cook this soup overnight in a slow cooker. Follow your slow cooker directions for bean soup. For added protein, you can add turkey hot dog pieces or smoked turkey leg to the soup for those who are missing the "ham hock" flavor.

Herbed Lentil Soup

(Serves 4)

If you've never tried lentils, this is a great introduction to their hearty flavor!

1   Tbs extra-virgin olive oil
1   cup chopped onion
½   cup chopped carrots
    (1 medium)
¼   cup chopped parsnips
1   cup dry brown lentils, rinsed,
    and drained
3   bay leaves
½   tsp dried sage
1   tsp dried thyme
2   Tbs soy sauce
½   tsp sea salt
2   scallions, chopped
    (for garnish)

Optional: Add a 15 oz can of diced tomatoes. For a heartier taste, add smoked turkey thigh or turkey bacon to soup in the beginning. Both can be purchased at a health food store.

1. Unlike most beans, lentils do not need to be presoaked. However, if you do it will cut down on cooking time. Presoak overnight or at least several hours. Rinse and drain lentils and set aside.

2. Preheat oil in large pot and sauté onions on medium heat for 2–3 minutes. Add carrots, parsnips, lentils, and bay leaves. Add 6 cups of water and cover. Bring to a boil and then reduce heat to medium and simmer for 30 minutes.

3. Add sage, thyme, soy sauce, and sea salt. Add salt to beans only when they are at least 60% tender, otherwise they will toughen. If you are using

the optional diced tomatoes, add them now. Continue simmering on medium heat for 15 minutes or more or until lentils have softened. Check soup and add more water if necessary.

4. Adjust seasoning to your own individual taste. Remove and discard bay leaves. Garnish with scallions and serve.

Bites of Insight

If you presoak an onion for 10 minutes in either warm or cold water before you peel or chop, you will avoid irritated eyes and the onion will peel much easier.

Hot and Sour Miso Soup

(Serves 4)

Exotic Japanese soup but easy enough for the everyday American table.

2 tsp sesame oil or toasted sesame oil

½ cup minced onion (1 small)

2 cloves garlic, minced

1 cup finely chopped or julienned carrots

4 dried shiitake mushrooms, presoaked in 1 cup boiled water

4 cups water or chicken broth

½ tsp sea salt

1 Tbs arrowroot or cornstarch

1 Tbs soy sauce

1 cup water or broth

2–3 Tbs apple cider vinegar

1 Tbs honey or natural sugar

¼ tsp hot chili oil for the "heat" (or to taste)

½ cup cubed firm tofu

1 Tbs dark miso

2 scallions, chopped (for garnish)

Optional: Mung bean sprouts, shredded green cabbage, napa cabbage, or bok choy cabbage

1. Presoak shiitake mushrooms for 20 minutes in 1 cup boiled water, set aside. Meanwhile, in a medium size pot, add oil and sauté onion and garlic on medium heat for 2–3 minutes. Add carrots and sauté another 2 minutes. Remove shiitake mushrooms, squeeze and remove stems, discard. Slice caps thinly and add to soup with the water used for soaking.

2. Add any optional cabbages at this time (except mung bean sprouts). Add 4 cups water or chicken broth and salt and bring to a boil. Reduce to medium heat and simmer for 5 minutes.

3. In a separate bowl, dissolve arrowroot or cornstarch and soy sauce in 1 cup cool water or broth. Add vinegar, honey or sugar, and chili oil to this mixture, stir again. Add this to the soup, cover and simmer for 2 minutes longer. Add tofu and reduce soup to low heat.

4. Remove 1 cup of soup broth into a bowl. Add miso and stir to dissolve the miso and remove lumps, pour back into soup. Do not boil soup after miso is added. Miso has important enzymes that are destroyed with high heat. If you are adding mung bean sprouts, add them now. Simmer on low for 3–4 minutes. Garnish with scallions and serve.

Note: If you make a big pot of this and want to reheat leftovers the next day, only reheat as much soup as you will eat. Constant reheating will destroy the enzymes in miso. Arrowroot is a starch that is a good substitute for cornstarch and is found in health food stores.

Jeweled Yam and Red Lentil Soup

(Serves 4–6)

This soup is warming, thick, and creamy with a hint of curry. This recipe makes a large amount so you can have leftovers to freeze.

1   Tbs extra-virgin olive oil
½   cup chopped onion
2   cloves garlic, minced
2   cups cubed yams or sweet potatoes (1 large)
1   cup uncooked red lentils, rinsed and drained (do not substitute with green lentils)
2   bay leaves
1–2 Tbs curry powder (or to taste)
1   Tbs minced fresh ginger
1   tsp sea salt
2   scallions, chopped (for garnish)

1. In large soup pot, add oil and sauté onion and garlic on medium heat for 2–3 minutes.

2. Peel yams and cut into ½-inch cubes, add to pot and continue cooking.

3. Add lentils, bay leaves, 6 cups water, curry powder, and minced ginger to pot. Cover, bring to a boil, and then reduce heat to medium. Simmer for 40 minutes, stirring occasionally. Add salt and continue to cook for 10 minutes longer.

4. Red lentils will be softened and dissolved by this time, and the yam will have broken down into a puree. If not, continue to simmer until it reaches a smooth consistency. Adjust flavors to your preference.

5. Remove bay leaves and garnish with scallions.

Bites of Insight

What we call yams are actually just a different variety of sweet potatoes. True yams are native to Africa and vary in size from a few ounces to over 100 lbs with over 600 varieties. Compared to sweet potatoes, yams are starchier and drier with flesh colored in white, pink, or brown, with a rough and scaly texture. Yams can be found in international markets sold in precut pieces. Sweet potatoes are relatively low in calories and have no fat. They are rich in vitamin A, having five times the RDA in one sweet potato, and potassium. The yam, a tuber, is a member of the lily family, and the sweet potato is a member of the morning glory family.

Marvelous Minestrone

(Serves 4)

The title says it all! A big hit with family, friends, clients, and students.

2   Tbs extra-virgin olive oil
1   cup chopped onion
    (1 medium)
2–3 cloves fresh garlic, chopped
1   small jalapeño pepper,
    minced (for a spicy soup)
½   cup chopped green bell
    pepper
½   cup chopped red bell pepper
3   carrots, chopped
½   cup chopped celery (2 stalks)
2   bay leaves
1   tsp each of dried basil and
    dried oregano
1   tsp sea salt
¼   tsp black pepper (or to taste)
1   cup precooked navy beans,
    rinsed and drained
½   cup chopped fresh string
    beans
1   small zucchini, chopped
1½ cups tomato sauce or
    15 oz can tomato sauce
1   cup precooked elbow
    macaroni
½   cup chopped fresh Italian
    parsley (for garnish)

Optional: ½ tsp wakame flakes
(a sea vegetable found in Asian
markets or health food stores)

1. In large pot, add oil and sauté onion and garlic for 2–3 minutes on medium heat.

2. Add jalapeño, peppers, carrots, celery, bay leaves, basil, oregano, sea salt, and pepper. Add enough water to the pot to cover the vegetables by 2 inches. You may add more water later (see Soup Tips in the beginning of this chapter). Cover, bring to a boil and then reduce heat to medium. Simmer for 5–8 minutes.

3. Add navy beans, chopped string beans, zucchini, tomato sauce, and wakame flakes if using. Check for desired thickness of soup before adding more water. Simmer string beans until tender, about 5 minutes. Adjust the seasoning. Remove bay leaves and discard.

4. Place the cooked macaroni in individual bowls. Ladle soup into bowls. When storing leftovers, it is a good idea to keep the noodles separate from any soup broth. This prevents the noodles from becoming too soft from absorbing too much liquid. Garnish with chopped parsley and serve.

Note: Use approximately 6 cups water total in this recipe, but add it in stages so you can control the thickness of the soup as you go. You can always add more water to a soup, but you can't take it out if you added too much in the beginning.

Mushroom Barley Soup with Dill

(Serves 6)

This is one of my most popular soups—it is being sold in supermarkets on the East Coast and most people who try it love it. Even my middle son, David, who dislikes mushrooms, loves this soup.

3–4 shiitake mushrooms, presoaked in 1 cup boiled water
2 Tbs extra-virgin olive oil
½ cup chopped onion
1 cup chopped carrots (2 medium)
½ cup chopped celery (2 stalks)
4 oz fresh mushrooms, sliced
1 cup precooked barley, rinsed (see *Whole Grain Cooking Chart*)
2 bay leaves
2 tsp sea salt
¼ tsp ground black pepper
¼ cup soy sauce
½ cup minced fresh dill, divided

1. Presoak shiitake mushrooms in 1 cup boiled water for 20 minutes. Mushrooms will be soft and easy to cut if soaked long enough.

2. Meanwhile, in large pot, add oil and onion and sauté on medium heat for 2–3 minutes. Add carrots, celery, and fresh mushrooms. Sauté for another 2–3 minutes. Add precooked barley, bay leaves, salt, pepper, and 5 cups water.

3. Remove shiitake mushrooms; squeeze out liquid, remove stems and discard. Slice mushroom caps and add to soup with the soaking water. Cover and bring to a boil, reduce heat, and simmer for 15 minutes.

4. Add soy sauce and ¼ cup fresh dill. Cook for an additional 10 minutes. You may add additional water until soup becomes the desired thickness. Adjust seasoning to taste. Garnish with remaining dill and serve.

Bites of Insight

If you like a clear soup like I do, place cooked barley in a colander and rinse under running water for a few minutes while turning the barley with a spoon to remove the starch. However, if you like a creamy, thick soup, don't rinse the barley. Just add cooked barley directly to the soup.

Parisian White Bean Soup

(Serves 4–6)

1 Tbs extra-virgin olive oil
½ cup chopped onion
2 cloves garlic, minced
½ cup chopped leek bottoms
½ cup sliced carrots
½ tsp sea salt
1 cup precooked white beans
   (cannellini), rinsed and
   drained
1 cup chopped spinach,
   prewashed
1 cup cleaned and thinly sliced
   leek tops
1 small roasted red pepper or
   ⅓ cup chopped fresh red
   pepper
½ cup chopped fresh basil
¼ tsp ground black pepper
2 scallions, chopped
   (for garnish)

Optional: 1 Tbs light miso

1. Preheat oil in large pot and sauté onion and garlic in olive oil for 2–3 minutes. Add leek bottoms and carrots. Add 2 cups water and sea salt, cover and bring to boil; reduce heat and simmer for 5 minutes.

2. Add beans, spinach, and leek tops, red pepper, basil, and black pepper with 2 ½ cups water, cover and simmer again for 10 minutes.

3. If using miso, remove a ladle of soup into a small bowl, add miso, and stir until miso is dissolved. Return to pot, but do not boil at this point, otherwise, you will destroy the important enzymes in miso. If not using miso, increase salt by ½ tsp. Garnish with chopped scallions and serve.

Bites of Insight

To roast peppers, place red pepper directly on open flame and char the skin on all sides. Or, lightly oil skin of pepper and place in a pan directly under broiler and broil until skin blackens. Continue turning until the entire pepper is black, remove and place in a covered bowl for 3–5 minutes. To remove skin, rub off with your fingers, remove seeds and white core, and chop into ½-inch pieces.

Potato Leek Soup

(Serves 4–6)

Potato soup lovers... you are going to love this one!

2 Tbs extra-virgin olive oil
2 cloves garlic, minced
1 small onion, minced
2 cups chopped leek bottoms
4 cups cubed new potatoes
1 cup chopped carrots
   (2 medium)
½ cup chopped celery (2 stalks)
5 cups vegetable or chicken
   broth
2 bay leaves
2 tsp dried thyme
1 tsp dried rosemary
2 tsp sea salt
¼ tsp ground black pepper
   (or to taste)
15 oz can light coconut milk

1. In a large pot, add oil and sauté garlic and onions on medium heat for 2–3 minutes.

2. Clean leeks by first cutting off green tops. Save tops for a soup broth or discard. Slice white bottoms down the center, then slice each piece again to get four long pieces. Cut crosswise into ¼-inch pieces. Soak chopped leeks in water for a few minutes while agitating the water occasionally with your fingers to dislodge any dirt. Drain and rinse, add to pot.

3. Add potatoes, carrots, celery, broth, bay leaves, thyme, rosemary, sea salt, and pepper. Cover and bring to boil. Reduce heat and simmer for 20 minutes or until potatoes are tender.

4. Remove bay leaves and discard. Using an immersion blender placed in the soup pot, blend soup until it is creamy. Add coconut milk and check for desired consistency. If you wish you can add more broth at this time. Adjust seasoning to taste and reheat for 2–3 minutes.

Bites of Insight

Light coconut milk has a mild flavor and can replace heavy cream or half and half in many recipes. Regular coconut milk will have more coconut fat and more coconut flavor and would work better in dishes when you want that strong Asian flavor.

Thanksgiving Soup

(Serves 4–6)

*I created this recipe to use up leftover wild rice stuffing (see **Stuffed Acorn Squash** recipe in **Amber Waves of Grain** chapter). A great autumn or winter soup.*

1   Tbs extra-virgin olive oil
1½ cups chopped onions
1   cup sliced fresh mushrooms
1   cup sliced carrots (2 medium)
½   cup chopped celery (2 stalks)
1   cup precooked brown rice
½   cup precooked wild rice
2   cups vegetable or chicken
    broth
2   Tbs soy sauce
2   bay leaves
2   tsp dried thyme
1   tsp dried sage
1   tsp sea salt
¼   tsp ground black pepper
¼   cup chopped fresh parsley

1. In large pot, add oil and sauté onions on medium heat for 2–3 minutes. Add mushrooms and sauté an additional 3 minutes.

2. Add carrots, celery, rices, 4 cups water, broth, and remaining ingredients except for parsley. Cover, bring to a boil and reduce heat to simmer. Cook for 15 minutes or until carrots are tender. Adjust the seasonings to your taste, add parsley and serve.

Serving Suggestion: For a light vegetarian meal, add beans to your soup. Or, have a bean side dish such as hummus with crackers, or add beans to a salad, giving you plenty of protein for this meal.

Note: This is a great way to use leftover cooked rice. You could also add some dried cranberries (¼ cup) at the beginning of the soup preparation. For cooking times for rice and other grains, see the *Whole Grain Cooking Chart* in the *Amber Waves of Grain* chapter.

Yam and Pinto Bean Soup

(Serves 4–6)

Yummy, sweet, spicy, creamy, and very filling!

2 Tbs extra-virgin olive oil
1 cup minced onion
2 cloves garlic, minced
2 Tbs minced fresh ginger or
   2 tsp dried ginger
3 cups peeled and diced yams
6 cups vegetable broth
2 tsp red pepper flakes
1 tsp ground cumin
2 tsp sea salt
1½ cups precooked pinto beans
   or 15 oz can organic pinto
   beans, rinsed and drained
6 oz can tomato paste
2 scallions, chopped or a few
   sprigs of parsley (for garnish)

1. In large soup pot, sauté onion and garlic in olive oil over medium heat for 2–3 minutes.

2. Peel a 2-inch piece of ginger with a potato peeler. Slice ginger thinly, then place on cutting board and slice into thin sticks. Slice across these sticks creating very small pieces. Add this to onion and garlic.

3. Add yams, broth, red pepper flakes, cumin, and sea salt. Cover and bring to a boil, then reduce heat to medium, and simmer for 20 minutes or until yams are tender. The longer the yams cook, the creamier your soup will be.

4. Add pinto beans and tomato paste and adjust seasonings to your taste. Serve garnished with scallions or parsley.

Bites of Insight

Almost any soup can be made creamier by adding blended beans. Other than canned refried beans, bean paste is not something you can buy. However, if you want to have a thick white cream base for a soup, for instance, blend a cup of cooked white kidney beans (cannellini beans) and add to the soup during the last few minutes of cooking.

Yellow Velvet Corn Soup

(Serves 4–6)

This is sooo delicious—creamy and sweet…but only use fresh, seasonal corn. Frozen on the cob or canned corn just will not give the same results.

6	ears of fresh, seasonal yellow corn
1	Tbs extra-virgin olive oil
1	cup chopped onion
½	cup oat bran or 15 oz can light coconut milk
1	Tbs light miso (found in health food or Asian markets) or 1 tsp sea salt
2	Tbs chopped fresh parsley (for garnish)

1. To build a sweet soup broth, remove corn from cobs and set aside. In a large pot, bring 6 cups water to boil. Cover and boil cobs in this water for 10 minutes. Remove cobs and cool on a plate. Reserve this broth and when cobs have cooled, wrap your hand around the cob over the pot and squeeze the rest of this sweet water off the cob. Discard cobs.

2. In a separate large pot, add oil and sauté onions for 2–3 minutes. Add cut corn kernels and enough corn broth to cover the corn and onions by 2 inches. If you start with too much water, you will lose the sweetness of the corn. Bring to boil, reduce heat, and simmer for 5 minutes.

3. Stir in oat bran or coconut milk. If using salt instead of miso, add it now. Cover and simmer for 3–5 minutes. Soup will be creamy and thick. You can add more broth if you wish to give it a thicker consistency. Freeze remaining leftover cob broth for future soup broths or use it to cook your next pot of rice.

4. If using miso, remove 1 cup of soup broth into a bowl. Add miso and stir to dissolve the miso to remove lumps, pour back into soup. Do not boil soup after miso is added. Miso has important enzymes that are destroyed with high heat. Simmer on low for 3–4 minutes. Garnish with chopped parsley and serve.

Variations: To make Mexican corn chowder, add the following to this basic recipe: 1 small chopped zucchini, ½ red bell pepper, chopped, sliced black olives, 1 Tbs ground cumin, 1 tsp chili powder, 15 oz can diced tomatoes, and ¼ cup minced fresh cilantro.

Amber Waves of Grain

• • •

Opposite: Chinese Fried Brown Rice and Stir Fry see page 146

Amber Waves of Grain

Whole grains are high-energy foods that contain the basic nutrients essential for life: water, complex carbohydrates, fats, protein, vitamins, minerals, and fiber. Whole grains are starch carbohydrates. If your body is craving starch for more energy, whole grains are the best source of energy you can eat. The American Cancer Society and the Nutrition Council recommend we increase our carbohydrate consumption to 60% of our overall diet. Vegetables, fruits, whole grains, pastas, and breads are all carbohydrates.

Grains are either whole (unrefined) or milled (refined). Whole grains are comprised of fiber or bran, germ (80% of the nutritional value) and endosperm (starchy part). The milling process removes the germ and bran layers and up to 80% of the nutritional value. Flours that have been milled and bleached will result in a product nearly devoid of important nutrients. Most commercially produced grain products that we eat today are made from this highly refined white flour. Breads, pastas, cereals, crackers, cookies, and degermed cornmeal (made into cereal, chips and tortillas) are some examples of these products. These flour products are simple carbohydrates (starches) that convert quickly causing a sudden rise in blood sugar. Called a high glycemic response, a drop in energy might soon follow. When our energy drops, we crave more starch to raise our blood sugar again. The cycle continues, causing us to overindulge in starch or sweets.

In stark contrast, whole grains are complex carbohydrates with the nutritious germ and fiber/bran left intact. They nourish us with protein, energy-giving complex starch, dietary fiber, vitamin B complex, vitamin E, iron, zinc, and magnesium. Eating cooked whole grains will give you long-lasting energy. Whole grains digest and release their natural sugars much slower because of the fiber. This helps stabilize our blood sugar levels and stops the cravings for refined starches and sweets.

A Look at Grain

Whole grains are seeds made up of three parts:

Germ - The nutritional powerhouse of the seed is high in essential minerals, protein, vitamin E, B-complex vitamins, and essential fatty acids. Vitamin E can help to reduce cancer-causing nitrosamines and inhibit oxidization in body tissues.

Endosperm (or starch) - This is the starchy bulk or center of the grain and is important as a basic fuel. It is not inherently fattening, only containing half the amount of calories as fat. This starch, when separated from the bran/fiber and germ, however, can cause a sudden rise in blood sugar.

Bran (or fiber) - Although it contains only 10% of the overall nutrients of the whole grain, it is high in dietary fiber. Whole grains contain several tough outer layers that are made of soluble and insoluble fibers that are called bran. Dietary fiber from bran comes in two forms and is found only in plant foods such as vegetables, fruit, nuts, beans, and whole grains:

Insoluble fibers act as sponges—drawing water into the intestinal tract to make waste matter soft and easy to pass. They are found in whole grains, vegetables, fruit, bran, and psyllium husk.

Soluble fibers remove toxins from the intestines and reduce levels of cholesterol and fats in the blood. Soluble fiber can be found in oats, corn, barley, brown rice, some fruits, beans, vegetables, and psyllium husks.

Americans average 12 to 15 grams of dietary fiber per day. Most researchers believe that figure should be doubled or even tripled.

Without adequate fiber in the diet, the process of eliminating wastes out of the body is slow, fostering the growth of bacteria that releases toxic waste, which can be potentially harmful and possibly carcinogenic. Research has shown that cultures around the world where people eat a diet high in fiber and low in fat have a low frequency of degenerative diseases and colorectal cancers. The best sources of dietary fiber are whole grains and whole grain products, fresh vegetables, and fruits.

Studies show that a high-fiber diet has a greater impact on lowering cholesterol and fat levels than simply a low-cholesterol diet.

Additionally, over-consumption of refined starchy foods also means consumption of high amounts of fats and sugars, bringing the overall calorie intake total much higher. Better known as empty calorie foods, these refined starchy foods don't fill us up or satisfy us. Whole grains, however, are high in fiber and low in fat with no added sugar and leave us with a satisfied, nourished feeling and can help to prevent overeating.

Whole Grains in your Meal Planning

To incorporate more whole grains in your diet, replace white rice with brown rice, white bread with whole grain bread, and white pasta with whole grain pasta. Whole grains are high in protein by themselves, but the protein is incomplete. For more information on vegetarian protein sources please refer to the beginning of this book. However, serving whole grains with beans, nuts, dairy, or seeds will increase the protein. A high protein vegetarian dinner can be *Easy Vegetable Stir-Fry with Teriyaki Sauce* (see *Vegetables* chapter) and *Chinese Fried Brown Rice* made with brown rice (see this chapter) or *Vegetarian Chili* over brown rice (see *Bean Cuisine* chapter). A summer meal could be a cold salad made from brown rice as in my *Dilled Rice and Green Pea Salad* or leftover quinoa can be made into a delicious salad such as my *California Fiesta Quinoa Salad* (both in the *Salads that Satisfy* chapter). These grain and bean combinations have as much protein and more fiber as most traditional meat and potato meals, but with less fat and cholesterol. Please refer to *Getting the Nutrition You Need* in the beginning of this book for more information on vegetarian meal planning. Experiment with your own combinations of flavors.

Cooking Tips

First, place the grain in the cooking pot and run water over it to allow debris to float to the surface for removal. Repeat this until the water is clear, usually once or twice, and drain. Measure the correct amount of clean water and pour into pot with the grain; bring to a boil. Add a pinch of sea salt for every cup of grain; cover pot and reduce to simmer, and cook according to instructions. Do not stir grain while cooking; it will make it sticky. After grain is cooked, shut off heat and let the covered pot sit for 10 minutes. Then, turn grain with a large spoon bringing the grain from the bottom to the top to allow for an even final steaming.

When cooking whole grains, if the heat is too high or your pot has a thin bottom, the water will boil away before the grain is cooked, possibly burning the grain on bottom. Be sure the heat is turned down to medium-low and your pot is a sturdy one with a tight fitting lid.

For added flavor, substitute chicken or vegetable stock for the water. Leftover grains do not freeze well, but they can be kept refrigerated for several days and reused in a variety of dishes. Adding different herbs, spices, vegetables, beans, or tofu can turn three-day-old rice into global cuisine possibilities. Alternatively, use leftover whole grains in soups, stews, stuffing, casseroles, or salads.

Use your imagination for limitless possibilities!

Whole Grain Cooking Chart

One cup of dry grain yields approximately 2 ½ cups of cooked grain. Most grains will double or triple their volume when cooked. If you have made more than you need for dinner, refrigerate and use it to make a completely new dish for another meal. Cooked grain can be refrigerated up to 4 days. Cook all grains in a covered pot. Cover pot, bring to a boil, then lower to a simmer and begin to time from when it started boiling. Avoid stirring grains while cooking—it will result in a sticky, gummy grain.

Whole Grain	Cooking Instructions	Serving Ideas
Amaranth	Cook ½ cup grain with 1 cup water. Simmer, covered, for 30 minutes.	Good in breakfast porridge.
Barley	Cook ½ cup grain with 3 cups water. Simmer, covered, for 60 minutes.	Wonderful in stews and soups. Good as cold grain salad.
Brown Rice - Jasmine or Basmati	Cook 1 cup grain with 1 ½ cups water. Simmer, covered, for 35–40 minutes.	Similar to long grain in texture. Has a delicate aromatic odor and taste. Great with seafood and poultry.
Brown Rice - Long Grain	Cook 1 cup grain with 1 ½ cups water. Simmer, covered, for 35–40 minutes.	Long grain rice remains separated and is good for cold salads, stir-frys, and pilafs.
Brown Rice - Short Grain	Cook 1 cup grain with 2 cups water. Simmer, covered, for 45 minutes.	Short grain is stickier and sweeter than long grain and good for burgers, sushi, puddings, and stuffing.
Buckwheat	Cook 1 cup grain with 2 cups water. Simmer, covered, for 15 minutes.	Good for wheat-free diets and is gluten-free. Good with pasta and in casseroles, soups, and porridge.
Bulgur Wheat	Cook 1 cup grain to 2 cups water. Boil water first, add grain, cover and let sit for 30 minutes until water is absorbed.	Great for cold salads such as tabbouleh. Nice as a hot pilaf (see *Bulgur Pilaf with Mushrooms*) or breakfast porridge.
Cornmeal - Yellow	Cook 1 cup grain with 4 cups water for polenta or corn grits porridge. Simmer on low heat for 20 minutes while stirring.	Makes a wonderful polenta to serve with sauces or vegetable dishes. Leftovers can be pan-fried and served with jam or apple butter for breakfast.

Continued on next page...

Continued from previous page...

Whole Grain	Cooking Instructions	Serving Ideas
Couscous	Cook 1 cup grain with 1 ½ cups water. Bring water to boil, add couscous, shut off flame and let sit, covered, for 5 minutes to reconstitute. Fluff with fork.	Not a whole grain but made from whole wheat flour. A light side dish to heavier meals especially with poultry or seafood.
Kamut	Cook 1 cup grain with 3 cups water. Simmer, covered, for 45 minutes.	Heirloom variety of wheat. Good in cold salads, stuffing.
Millet	Cook 1 cup grain with 3 cups of water. Place in boiling water first then simmer, covered, for 30 minutes. Fluff with fork.	Good in grain casseroles, soups, stuffing or added to beans. Also can be shaped into patties.
Quinoa	Cook 1 cup grain with 2 cups of water. Add to boiling water, simmer, covered, for 20 minutes. Fluff with fork.	Great as cold grain salad or in endless hot dishes, soups, and porridge. Gluten-free.
Rolled Oats	Cook ½ cup grain with 1 ½ cup water. Simmer, covered, for 10–15 minutes for porridge.	Add almond or rice milk instead of water for a creamier texture. Top with nuts, roasted seeds, maple syrup, and cinnamon. The bran in oats is the best source of cholesterol-reducing fiber.
Rye	Cook 1 cup grain with 2 ½ cups water. Simmer, covered, for 60 minutes.	Combine cooked grain with brown rice and add to soups.
Spelt	Cook 1 cup grain with 3 cups water. Simmer, covered, for 45 minutes.	Spelt flour can be used in breads and for baking. Or combine cooked grain with rice.
Teff	Cook 1 cup grain with 2 cups water. Simmer, covered, for 30 minutes.	Highest in Iron. Good in breakfast porridge.
Whole Oats (Oat Groats)	Cook ½ cup grain with 2 ½ cups water. Simmer, covered, for 50 minutes until creamy. Slow cookers work well. Make ahead for 2–3 days at a time.	Same as Rolled Oats. Whole oats are more nutritious and make a delicious creamy sweet porridge.
Whole Wheat (Wheat Berries)	Cook ½ cup grain with 2 ½ cups water. Simmer, covered, for 45–60 minutes until grains burst open and are tender.	Nutty flavored and a little crunchy, nice as a cold grain salad.
Wild Rice	Cook ½ cup grain with 2 cups of water. Simmer, covered, for 60 minutes.	Great stuffing for poultry, squash or as a cold grain salad.

Bulgur Pilaf with Mushrooms

(Serves 4)

Bulgur is a cracked precooked whole grain belonging to the wheat family. It is quick to prepare, nutritious, and high in fiber.

⅓ cup raw pumpkin seeds (pepitas)
2 Tbs extra-virgin olive oil
1 onion, chopped
1 cup sliced fresh mushrooms
¼ cup currants or raisins
2 tsp soy sauce
½ tsp dried rosemary
1 cup bulgur wheat
½ tsp sea salt

Optional: You can substitute sunflower seeds for pumpkin seeds.

1. Preheat oven to 325°F. Toast pumpkin seeds on a cookie sheet for 5 minutes. Alternately you can toast seeds in a dry frying pan on medium heat while stirring for 5 minutes. They will begin to pop and smell toasted, usually after 5–7 minutes. Remove from pan and set aside. If you are using pre-toasted and salted pumpkin seeds eliminate the salt in this recipe.

2. In a large frying pan, add oil and sauté onion and mushrooms for 2–3 minutes. Add pumpkin seeds, currants or raisins, soy sauce, rosemary, bulgur wheat, and sea salt. Stir for a few more minutes.

3. Add 3 ½ cups water, cover and bring to boil. Reduce heat to medium-low and simmer for 25 minutes or until all the liquid is absorbed. When done, toss thoroughly and serve immediately.

Bites of Insight

Bulgur is a parboiled, dried and partially de-branned (bran is removed) whole grain. Bulgur is sometimes confused with cracked wheat, which is crushed wheat grain that has not been parboiled. Currants are a small tart fruit grown in the Northeast that are high in antioxidants, potassium, and vitamin C. One cup of currants gives you as much vitamin C as three large oranges. Dried currants are very similar to raisins, and are a great substitute in many recipes calling for raisins.

Chinese Fried Brown Rice

(Serves 4–6)

Use refrigerated leftover long grain rice that has gotten a bit dry for best results!

2   Tbs sesame or dark toasted sesame oil
1   cup diced carrot (1 large)
¼   cup chopped string beans
2   cups precooked long grain brown rice
¼   cup frozen peas
2   large eggs, scrambled and chopped
¼   cup chopped scallions (2 scallions)
1   Tbs fresh ginger juice (from 3-inch piece)
2   Tbs soy sauce
½   cup peanuts, roasted and chopped or almond slivers

1. Preheat oil in pan. Add carrots and string beans, cover, and sauté for 2 minutes on medium heat.

2. Layer remaining ingredients by adding rice, frozen peas, scrambled eggs, and chopped scallions. Cover without stirring and simmer for 3–4 minutes. If rice is hard and dry, add 1–2 Tbs of water at a time to rehydrate.

3. Without peeling the ginger, grate it on a fine metal grater such as a handheld cheese grater. Squeeze this ball of ginger over rice mixture to distribute juice evenly. Discard remains. Drizzle in soy sauce and add nuts. Now stir rice thoroughly, making sure all ingredients are distributed evenly. Adjust seasoning with additional soy sauce and ginger according to your preference.

Bites of Insight

Toasted sesame oil has a delicious unique flavor and is best in Asian dishes. It has a shorter shelf life because it is toasted so keep it refrigerated and it will last three to six months.

Caribbean Black Beans and Rice

(Serves 4)

Using precooked rice and beans, this takes just 15 minutes for a complete entrée that is very flavorful and colorful!

2 Tbs extra-virgin olive oil
½ cup chopped onions
2 cloves garlic, minced
½ cup chopped red bell pepper
½ cup chopped celery (2 stalks)
½ cup diced tomatoes (fresh or canned)
¼ tsp chili powder
½ tsp dried thyme
½ tsp dried oregano
¼ tsp ground allspice
½ tsp sea salt
½ cup precooked black beans, rinsed and drained
2 cups precooked long grain brown rice
¼ cup chopped scallions (2 scallions)
¼ cup chopped fresh cilantro

1. In a large frying pan, add oil and sauté onions and garlic on medium heat for 3 minutes until onions are tender. Add red bell pepper and celery and simmer for another 3 minutes.

2. Stir in tomatoes with juice, spices, herbs, and salt. Simmer covered for another 2–3 minutes.

3. Add beans, rice, and scallions. Reduce heat, cover, and simmer for 5–8 minutes or until liquid is absorbed. Sprinkle with chopped cilantro.

Serving Suggestion: Sprinkle the top with shredded cheddar cheese right before serving. There are many dairy-free cheeses on the market including those made from almonds and rice. This can also be a stuffing inside a roasted pepper for an entrée.

Greek Couscous with Feta

(Serves 4)

Couscous originates from Morocco. These tiny balls of semolina flour need only hot water to turn them into delightful fluffy pasta. This light and colorful salad will be a welcomed light dinner on a warm summer night.

1 ½ cups couscous
½ cup halved sun-ripened cherry tomatoes
1 cup shredded zucchini
2 Tbs chopped roasted red pepper
½ cup black olives, pitted and chopped (Kalamata are my favorite)
⅓ cup chopped fresh parsley
⅓ cup chopped fresh mint

Dressing:
½ cup extra-virgin olive oil
4 Tbs lemon juice
1 tsp lemon zest
½ tsp sea salt
¼ tsp ground black pepper or red pepper flakes (your favorite)
1 clove garlic, minced
½ cup crumbled feta cheese

1. Bring 2 ¼ cups water to a boil in a covered medium size pot. Add couscous and turn off heat and remove from hot burner. Allow couscous to sit covered for 5 minutes. If you wait too much longer, the couscous will become hard and it will be difficult to separate the grains. Using a fork (not a spoon), lightly scrape top layer of couscous into bowl and continue scraping layer by layer until all couscous has separated into the bowl. Fluff grains and allow to cool in the refrigerator.

2. Prepare dressing by drizzling in olive oil as you whip lemon juice. Add lemon zest, salt, pepper, and minced garlic.

3. Toss all vegetables, olives, fresh herbs, and couscous together. Add dressing, toss, and serve.

Serving Suggestion: If you add cooked beans, like garbanzo or kidney, you boost the protein considerably. Serve with a green salad for a light lunch or dinner.

Bites of Insight

Zest is the minced thin outer layer of citrus fruits. Using a vegetable peeler, gently peel off a thin layer of a lemon. Be careful not to get the much of the white pithy part as it is very bitter. Mince small with a knife. You can also use a kitchen tool, called a zester, specifically for this purpose.

Japanese Soba Noodles with Sesame Sauce

(Serves 4–6)

Soba noodles made from buckwheat flour have a unique flavor—serve hot or cold!

½ lb soba noodles (1 package)
4 dried shiitake mushrooms, presoaked for 30 mins in 1 cup boiled water
2 Tbs toasted sesame oil or light sesame oil
3 cloves garlic, finely minced
½ cup sliced red bell pepper
½ cup sliced snow peas
½ cup sliced scallions (4 scallions)
¼ cup chopped fresh cilantro

Sesame Sauce:
3 Tbs sesame tahini
1 Tbs soy sauce
¼ cup brown rice vinegar
¼ tsp hot pepper oil
2 Tbs toasted sesame oil
1 Tbs peeled and minced fresh ginger
1 cup mushroom soaking liquid

1. Precook soba noodles by shocking method (see *Bites of Insight*) or according to package directions. Drain, rinse, and cool. This can be done a few days ahead.

2. Remove mushrooms from water and squeeze out excess liquid, reserving liquid for sesame sauce. Remove and discard mushroom stems and slice caps thinly.

3. In a large frying pan, preheat oil and sauté garlic on medium heat for 1 minute. Add red peppers and shiitake mushrooms, cover, and sauté for 3 minutes. Add snow peas and scallions. Cover and sauté 2 minutes or until peas are bright green but tender. Toss vegetables with noodles.

4. Add sesame sauce ingredients into a blender and process until smooth. Mixture should be thick but able to pour (if not add 1 Tbs water). Add noodles to vegetables and cilantro and toss. Serve at room temperature.

Bites of Insight

Soba means "buckwheat" in Japanese. Made with wheat flour, these noodles have a unique flavor. They are found in most grocery stores, Asian markets, and health food stores. Tahini is a paste made from ground sesame seeds and is found in most grocery or health food stores.

Long Grain Brown Rice

(Serves 4–6)

This is a basic rice recipe that you can make once and turn into three makeover meals during the week. Cooked brown rice is a staple in our house.

2 cups long grain brown rice
¼ tsp sea salt

Optional: For additional protein, add cooked beans, tofu, or nuts.

1. Rinse rice thoroughly to remove any hulls or dust. Drain and add to pot with 3 cups water and add salt. Cover, bring to a boil, then reduce heat to medium-low and simmer for 35–40 minutes. Do not stir rice as it will make it mushy. When all water is absorbed and the rice is tender, it's ready.

Serving Suggestion: Long grain rice is good for cold rice salads, rice molds, and fried rice. It is not the best rice for burgers that require sticky rice like short grain brown rice. See *Salads that Satisfy* chapter for ideas on using fresh cooked brown rice.

Variations: You can add other grains to the rice in the beginning of cooking for variety. I recommend a 3 to 1 ratio of brown rice to another grain.

Example: Long grain brown rice and bulgur wheat
Long grain brown rice and quinoa
Long grain brown rice and millet
Long grain brown rice and whole wheat berries

Whole wheat takes longer to cook and is best when presoaked or pressure cooked with medium rice. In some cases, you need to adjust the amount of water to accommodate the additional grain. The combinations above need 1 to 2 ratio of grain to water. Refer to cooking chart in the beginning of this chapter for more clarification on times and amounts of water.

SWEET BROWN RICE WITH CORN *(variation of Long Grain Brown Rice)*

(Serves 4)

My youngest son's favorite rice dish and it's made from leftovers!

1 cup uncooked long grain brown rice or 2 cups precooked rice
½ tsp sea salt, divided
1 Tbs extra-virgin olive oil or butter
1 small onion, chopped
1 ear fresh corn, kernels removed or 1 cup frozen corn

Optional: Replace rice with precooked quinoa

1. If you are using precooked rice, skip to step 2. To cook fresh rice, thoroughly rinse rice several times and drain. Place in large pot with 1 ½ cups water and ¼ tsp salt. Cover and bring to boil, reduce heat to medium-low, and simmer for 45–50 minutes. Do not stir as it makes the rice gummy.

2. Preheat oil or butter in frying pan and sauté onion for 2–3 minutes until translucent. Add corn, ¼ tsp salt, and 1–2 Tbs water to prevent onions from sticking. Cover and simmer 2–3 minutes.

3. Add rice to the pan, cover, and allow rice to soften for 3–5 minutes.

Bites of Insight

If you presoak an onion for 10 minutes before you peel and chop, you will avoid irritated eyes, and the onion will peel much easier. Sorry, should have told you earlier.

Moroccan Couscous

(Serves 4–6)

Beautiful colors, East Indian flavors and a great party salad.

2   Tbs extra-virgin olive oil,
    divided
4   cloves garlic, minced
1–2 Tbs curry powder
½   cup chopped carrots
½   tsp sea salt
1   cup couscous
½   cup frozen or fresh green
    peas
⅓   cup chopped red bell pepper
⅓   cup chopped green bell
    pepper
¼   cup chopped black olives
½   cup yellow raisins
½   cup chopped roasted peanuts
¼   cup chopped scallions
    (2 scallions)

Optional: Substitute couscous
with long grain brown rice or
quinoa.

1. In a medium sized pot, sauté garlic in 1 Tbs oil for 10 seconds on low heat. Add curry powder and sauté for an additional 10 seconds. Add carrots, salt, and 1 ½ cups water. Cover, bring to boil; add couscous, stir, turn off heat, and remove from hot burner and let sit for 5 minutes with lid on.

2. Add green peas to top of couscous, return lid and allow to steam 3 more minutes. Using a fork (not a spoon), lightly scrape top layer of couscous into bowl and continue scraping top layer until all couscous has separated into the bowl. Fluff grains and allow to cool.

3. In small frying pan, sauté red and green bell pepper in 1 Tbs oil on medium heat for 2–3 minutes. Add to couscous. Add olives, raisins, peanuts, and scallions. Toss gently and adjust seasoning to your preference.

Bites of Insight

Curry is not a single spice but a combination of as many as twelve spices. All curry is balanced for a unique flavor; some curry is spicier than others. Be careful when selecting curry in Asian markets as they tend to be a hotter blend than American varieties.

Quinoa Yam Burgers

(Makes 8 burgers)

Yummy! Quinoa is versatile, quick-cooking, and high in protein.

1   cup precooked quinoa
1   peeled and chopped yam
2   Tbs extra-virgin olive oil
1   Tbs minced garlic
2   Tbs minced fresh ginger
1   Tbs curry powder or 1 Tbs
    dried green curry paste
¼   cup minced fresh parsley
½   cup blanched almonds,
    toasted and ground to
    a powder
½   tsp sea salt

Optional: ⅓ cup bread crumbs
or one large egg if needed for
binding

1. Cook quinoa ahead of time (even several days ahead) to save time or use any leftover grain. To make fresh quinoa, boil 2 cups water, add 1 cup quinoa, cover, and simmer on medium low until light and fluffy, about 18–20 minutes. Remove to large bowl, cool, and set aside.

2. Steam yam in steamer basket for 15 minutes or for a better flavor use leftover baked yam. I usually bake more yams than I need for dinner just to have them on hand. I like adding them to stews, soups, and burgers. Measure one cup of mashed yam.

3. In medium frying pan, sauté garlic and ginger in 2 Tbs oil on low for about 2–3 minutes. Stir in mashed yam and curry. Adjust flavors for your taste, keeping in mind that flavors will mellow when added to the quinoa. Cool and add this mixture to quinoa and parsley and blend until thoroughly mixed.

4. Add ground almonds and blend again. Form into ½-inch thick and 3-inch wide patties. If batter is too soft or it doesn't hold together when pressed into a patty, add bread crumbs until it begins to hold together.

5. Preheat oil in frying pan on medium-high heat. The oil is ready when a few drops of mixture immediately begins to sizzle. When the oil is hot, fry burgers on one side for approximately 3 minutes, gently turn over and repeat on the other side. Don't overcrowd the pan with burgers or they will not brown.

Bites of Insight

What we call yams are actually a different variety of the sweet potato. True yams are native to Africa and vary in size from a small potato to over 100 lbs with over 600 varieties. Compared to sweet potatoes, yams are starchier and drier with flesh colored in white, pink or brownish-black with a rough and scaly texture. Yams can be found in international markets sold in precut pieces. Sweet potatoes are relatively low in calories and have no fat. They are rich in vitamin A, having five times the RDA in one sweet potato, as well as potassium. The yam, a tuber, is a member of the lily family, while the sweet potato is a member of the morning glory family.

Red Rice with Mango Chicken Salad

(Serves 4)

Wehani rice is nutty and a great complement to sweet mango.

1   cup red rice (wehani)
¼   tsp sea salt
1   chicken breast
2   Tbs extra-virgin olive oil
½   cup chopped scallions
    (4 scallions)
½   mango, peeled and chopped

Dressing:
⅓   cup extra-virgin olive oil
2   Tbs lemon juice
1   Tbs soy sauce
½   tsp lemon zest
1   clove garlic, minced
1   Tbs grated ginger juice

Optional: Substitute wild rice for the wehani

1. Rinse rice and drain. Place the rice and 2 cups of water in a medium size pot. Add salt, cover, and bring to a boil. Reduce heat to simmer and continue to cook for 40–45 minutes. Remove rice to a bowl and allow to cool.

2. Meanwhile, in a small frying pan, cook chicken in 2 Tbs of oil for 3 minutes, turn over and cook approximately 3 minutes on other side. Chicken should not be pink in the center but still tender. When cool, cut into bite-size pieces.

3. Toss scallions with cooled rice. To chop mango, hold fruit straight up so you see the stem end on top. Placing your knife a half inch away from this stem end, slice down along the large flat seed in the center of the fruit. Turn mango around and repeat on the other side. You will have two halves. Make criss-cross marks across the flesh on each half, being careful not cut through skin. Invert skin inside out. The fruit will "pop" up away from the skin; slice fruit off skin into cubes. Add mango to rice.

4. To grate ginger, use a handheld cheese grater with small holes. Leaving the skin on, grate the ginger until you get a tablespoon of pulp. Squeeze this pulp in the palm of your hand into a bowl. Discard the pulp.

5. Combine olive oil, lemon juice, soy sauce, lemon zest, garlic, and ginger juice. Mix thoroughly. Add to rice salad along with chicken and toss.

Rocky Road Rice

(Serves 4–6)

A party pleaser....if you love nuts and garlic you will love this dish!

½ cup chopped nuts, any variety or combination
2 Tbs extra-virgin olive oil, divided
3 cloves garlic, minced
1 cup coarsely chopped mushrooms
2 cups precooked brown rice (any variety)
1 Tbs soy sauce
½ cup chopped scallions (4 scallions)

Optional: Use shiitake mushrooms instead of button mushrooms or combine both to total 1 cup.

1. To roast nuts, place on cookie sheet in toaster oven or conventional oven at 350°F for 5 minutes. My favorite variations include walnuts, almonds, sunflower seeds, and pumpkin seeds.

2. In a deep frying pan, sauté garlic for 1 minute in 1 Tbs oil on low heat. Don't let the garlic brown or it will be bitter. Add another 1 Tbs of oil and add mushrooms. Cook for 2 minutes or until softened. If using dried shiitake mushrooms, presoak in boiled water for 20 minutes. Squeeze out excess liquid. Remove stem and slice very thin and add to frying pan.

3. Add rice, nuts, soy sauce, and 1 Tbs water; mix to coat evenly. Cover and steam for 2–3 minutes.

4. Add scallions and heat for another few minutes. Serve immediately.

Serving Suggestion: Because this rice is combined with nuts, it is high in protein. Serve with a salad or a broccoli side dish. Simple, quick, and easy if you have leftover rice in the refrigerator begging for creativity.

Bites of Insight

Almonds are more alkalizing than other nuts and higher in calcium. Almonds are a "tree" nut as opposed to peanuts which are in the legume family and have a higher amount of fat than almonds. I love almonds and almond butter.

Spicy Thai Noodles

(Serves 4)

I love this noodle salad with lots of flavor and texture, and it's great as a leftover.

8   oz Thai rice noodles
2   Tbs light sesame oil
⅓   cup dried shiitake mushrooms,
      soaked in boiled water for
      20 minutes
3   cloves garlic, minced
1   cup shredded green cabbage
1   small jalapeño pepper, minced
      or ½ tsp hot red pepper
1   red bell pepper, sliced thin
1   cup broccoli florets
¼   tsp sea salt
½   cup snow peas, sliced
      diagonally
½   cup chopped scallions
      (4 scallions)

Sauce:
2   Tbs light sesame oil
2   Tbs dark toasted sesame oil
2   Tbs soy sauce
1   tsp honey
1   Tbs lime juice
½   tsp crushed red pepper flakes
      (or to taste)
½   cup chopped fresh cilantro
      (for garnish)

Optional: Near the end of cooking,
you can add cubed firm tofu to
add more protein to this dish.

1. Boil at least 2 quarts of water. Add noodles, shut off heat and let them stand for 10 minutes or follow package directions. Remove and drain.

2. Presoak shiitake mushrooms in boiled water for 20 minutes or until soft, remove, and squeeze. Remove stem and discard. Slice thinly and set aside for now.

3. Preheat 2 Tbs of sesame oil in wok or large frying pan and sauté garlic for 1 minute. Add cabbage, jalapeño pepper, red bell pepper, mushrooms, broccoli, and salt; stir for another 3–4 minutes.

4. Add drained noodles and mix with vegetables. Add snow peas and scallions and mix again.

5. Mix together light and dark toasted sesame oil, soy sauce, honey, lime juice, and red pepper flakes. Add to rice mixture and toss thoroughly. Adjust to your taste. Garnish with cilantro.

Spring Vegetable Bulgur Pilaf

(Serves 4)

Great way to get more veggies in your diet!

1 Tbs extra-virgin olive oil
⅓ cup chopped onions
⅓ cup chopped carrots
   (1 medium)
⅓ cup chopped string beans
¼ cup corn
¼ cup green peas
½ cup chopped scallions
   (4 scallions)
½ cup roasted sunflower seeds
¾ cup bulgur wheat
2 tsp soy sauce
¼ cup chopped fresh parsley

1. In a large frying pan, sauté onion for 2 minutes in olive oil on medium heat. Add carrots and string beans, cover, and sauté for an additional 2 minutes.

2. Bring 1 ¼ cups water to boil. Add corn, sunflower seeds, bulgur wheat, and soy sauce. Cover and reduce heat to medium-low and simmer for 15 minutes or until all water is absorbed. Bulgur will be tender and fluffed. Add peas and scallions and toss all ingredients together.

Serving Suggestion: You can prepare this dish with any leftover grain by cooking all the vegetables and herbs in a skillet, adding leftover grain, cover, and simmer for 5–10 minutes.

Bites of Insight

Bulgur is parboiled, dried, and partially de-branned whole wheat. Bulgur is sometimes confused with cracked wheat, which is crushed wheat grain that has not been parboiled.
P.S. Soy sauce, shoyu, and tamari are the same.

Summer Quinoa

(Serves 4–6)

A light and refreshing grain that is perfect for (but not limited to) spring and summer meals.

1   cup quinoa
¼   tsp sea salt
1   Tbs extra-virgin olive oil
1   small onion, finely chopped
1   ear of fresh corn or 1 cup
     frozen corn

Optional: You may add chopped
winter squash to make a sweet
and delicious dish.

1. Bring 2 cups of water to boil. Rinse quinoa in a fine mesh strainer and then add quinoa and salt to boiling water. Cover, reduce heat to medium-low, and simmer for 20 minutes.

2. Remove corn from cob by slicing kernels off as close to cob as you can.

3. In a medium sized frying pan, sauté onion in 1 Tbs of oil on medium heat for 2–3 minutes. Add corn and ¼ cup water, cover, and simmer on medium-low for 4–5 minutes. Add to cooked quinoa and stir.

Serving Suggestion: Leftover quinoa can be tossed with vegetables and vinaigrette for a delightful beach or picnic salad. Look in my *Salads that Satisfy* chapter for recipe ideas using cooked quinoa. To use quinoa for breakfast porridge, use 3 times the amount of water to quinoa.

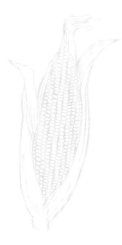

Bites of Insight

Quinoa is the only whole grain that is a complete protein and gluten free! The quinoa germ separates after cooking and looks like a white piece of string attached to the grain.

Sushi - Made Easy

SUSHI - THE BASICS

Basic Ingredients:
Sushi rice (cooked white or brown rice)
Nori (seaweed)
Pickled ginger (shoga or gari)
Wasabi (Japanese horseradish)
Rice vinegar (seasoned)

Optional:
Raw seafood (tuna, roe, salmon, etc., your choice)
Cooked seafood (shrimp, smoked salmon, eel,
    crabmeat, or tuna)
Dried fish flakes called bonito flakes (denbu) usually
    colored and sweetened
Marinated and baked tofu (Asian markets or health
    food stores)
Marinated tempeh (soybean cake from health food
    stores)
Raw veggies (cucumber match sticks, red bell pepper,
    water cress, scallions, daikon radish sprouts,
    avocado)
Blanched veggies (asparagus, carrot sticks, spinach,
    shiitake mushrooms, broccoli, string beans)
Pickles (dill, ginger, kimchi, takuan pickled daikon,
    turnip, sauerkraut, dried gourd strips, Kampyo)
Toasted sesame seeds both black and brown
    (roasted goma)
Omelet sliced (tamago-yaki)

1. Lay out all the ingredients out on a large platter or cooking sheet so when you are ready to assemble you will have everything prepared.

2. Blanch and cool veggies you will be using; cut seafood into small pieces; drain and cut pickles.

3. Cook rice one or more hours ahead of time so it can cool. Hot rice will wilt the nori so it must be room temperature. Remove rice from pot, place in a large bowl (preferably a wooden rice mixing tub or "hangiri"). Mix in seasoned vinegar as you turn the rice to cool it. Traditionally, the sushi helper would fan the rice while the chef turned it to help cool and glaze the rice with the vinegar.

4. Have ready a water dipping bowl for your hands, a very sharp knife, a bamboo mat, plastic wrap (for California Roll) and a serving platter.

SUSHI - COOKING THE RICE

2 cups sushi white rice
   (prewashed and drained)
¼ cup seasoned rice vinegar

1. Rinse rice 2–3 times in a strainer until the water is clear. In heavy pot add rice and 2 ¼ cups water, cover with a tight lid and let it soak without heating for 10 minutes. Bring to a boil and cook for 3 minutes then immediately reduce heat to simmer on medium-low for 15 minutes. Turn off heat and let it sit for another 10 minutes to allow rice to continue steaming. Do not stir rice while it is cooking. Fluff the rice with a wooden spoon from the bottom of the pot. Turn out into a larger bowl to begin cooling.

2. Sprinkle ¼ cup seasoned vinegar while you turn over the rice and cool with a fan (if you have a helper). Rice should not be too hot when you begin to make sushi otherwise nori will curl and wilt and become chewy—yuck!!

3. Once rice has cooled, keep a damp clean dish towel over bowl while working so rice does not dry out on the top layer.

Optional: For brown rice sushi, use 2 cups short grain brown rice in 4 cups water and a pinch of sea salt. Bring to boil and lower to simmer for 45 minutes or until all water is absorbed. Toss with seasoned rice vinegar (¼ cup) and cool before using.

STYLES OF SUSHI

Maki - means wrap, so:
Maki-zushi (rolled sushi)
Futo-maki (thick roll)
Hoso-maki (thin roll)
Tekka-maki (tuna roll)
Kappa-maki (cucumber roll)
Te-maki-zushi (te means rolled sushi in smaller pieces)
Nigiri - means grip, so Nigiri-zushi is hand pressed sushi. This is usually served with raw fish on top of rice, without nori seaweed.
Oshi-zushi or Hako-zushi is mold pressed sushi. You can buy molds at Asian markets.
Hana-zushi is flower-shaped sushi with fermented fish and is a regional favorite in Japan. There are many other variations depending on the region.
Chirashi-zushi means scattered sushi. This is served without fish, but usually with vegetables and pickles scattered on rice.
Inari-zushi is a fried and flavored tofu pouch. It is usually filled with simple rice or flavored with veggies. Tofu pouches can be purchased frozen or fresh in Asian markets. Their texture is better if they are fresh.

SUSHI - FILLINGS

Condiments:
Umeboshi plums, ginger pickles, sauerkraut, kimchi, dill pickles, wasabi, hot radish pickles. There are many varieties of hot and spicy pickles at Asian markets.

Vegetables:
Cucumber, carrots, scallions, watercress, spinach, asparagus, zucchini, avocado, shiitake mushrooms, string beans and snow beans.

Protein:
Scrambled egg, baked tofu, fried tempeh, seitan (wheatmeat). Cooked fish could include crabmeat, smoked eel, blanched shrimp, seared ahi tuna, smoked trout, smoked salmon, etc.

Noodles:
Udon (wheat) noodles, soba (buckwheat) noodles; green tea noodles or mugwort noodles will give you a green noodle color. To prepare them, take a small bunch of noodles (they will double in size) and using a clean rubber band placed about one inch from edge, wrap noodles tightly. You will cut this section off when you lay it on the nori after it has dried. Cook several bundles in a large pot of water until done. Drain and rinse noodles. When they cool, squeeze out excess water and lay the bundles on a cookie sheet to dry. If you put noodles in a nori when they are wet, they will soften the nori and it will fall apart.

To Serve:
Arrange cut sushi pieces, flat side up on the plate. Garnish with fresh flowers, ferns, or parsley. On a dipping plate or on the sushi plate, form a wasabi pyramid shape. Place gingered pickles on the plate. In a small bowl, serve soy sauce. As an alternative for dipping, blend equal amounts of soy sauce and water with a little fresh grated ginger.

Storage:
Nori-makis can be refrigerated up to 3 days if wrapped well. Do not cut nori-maki rolls if you are planning to refrigerate them. They are best eaten the same day they are made.

Sushi Etiquette:
Mix a small amount of wasabi paste and soy sauce into the dish. Dip nori-maki pieces into this mixture. You can also spread a little wasabi paste directly on the nori-maki.

Sushi Party:
Once you get a hang of this, invite some friends over for a sushi rolling party! Purchase bamboo mats, sake, and prepare the rice, seafood, pickles, and vegetables ahead of time. Pour the sake and provide instructions and watch the fun!

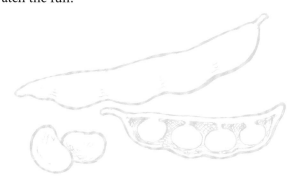

Brown Rice Nori-Maki

In Japanese Cuisines, Nori (Lava) is the seaweed used to wrap the rice, and Maki means wrap in Japanese. Sushi actually means vinegar rice, not raw fish. These basic instructions just get you started. Let your imagination fly with different combinations of vegetables, pickles, protein, rice, noodles, and seasonings.

2 cups of short grain brown rice
½ tsp sea salt
¼ cup brown rice vinegar or
   sushi vinegar (to taste)
1 pkg of sushi nori (10 sheets)
   Bamboo sushi mat

Optional: Replace ½ cup of the short grain brown rice with ½ cup sweet brown rice

Fillings:
See ingredient suggestions in *Sushi - The Basics* and *Sushi - Fillings*.

1. Rinse rice and put in pot. Add 3 3/4 cups water and salt, cover and bring to boil; reduce heat and simmer for 45 minutes. Turn off heat and remove pot from hot burner. Let rice sit in pot without stirring for 15 minutes. Remove to a bowl, sprinkle in vinegar and mix thoroughly. Allow to cool. I cook my rice at least an hour before I will use it. Hot rice will "melt" the nori when you wrap it. Leftover rice that has been refrigerated more than a day will not stick together, so cooled fresh rice is best.

2. Blanch and cool vegetables that you will be using. Don't overcook; you want them to be crisp and brightly colored.

3. On the sushi mat, place one sheet of nori with the shiny side down. If it is positioned correctly the edges of the nori will come to the first line of stitches in the mat. Wet your hands and grab about a softball size (about 1 cup) of rice and spread it out on the nori without packing it down. Spread rice to the left and right edges but leave a half inch clearance at the edge close to you and an inch clearance at the end away from you.

4. Along the edge closer to you, spread condiments across the bottom of the rice. Arrange fillings in a lengthwise row on top of the condiment. Add protein if you are using it.

5. Start to roll the sushi by picking up the bottom of the mat. Tuck under and roll tightly with uniform pressure to form a cylinder. To seal the roll, flip the roll over and roll the nori-maki back up into the sushi mat and gently press along the edge. Remove mat and let the roll rest on the seam. Continue rolling until you have finished all nori-makis. Wet a sharp knife and in quick back and forth motion; slice the roll into eight pieces, occasionally cleaning the knife to assure neat slices.

Bean Cuisine

• • •

Opposite: Hot Tamale Pie with Red Beans, see page 176

Bean Cuisine

Beans are in the legume family. Along with whole grains, they have been a major source of sustenance throughout the world for more than ten thousand years. Farmers discovered that planting grain crops year after year without rotating them would eventually deplete the nutrients in the soil. Eventually they learned to rotate grain crops with bean crops which produce nitrogen as they grow. They found this improved the soil from year to year and produced better crops for both grain and beans.

Nutritional Value of Beans
Beans contain vitamins and minerals, helping to make them an excellent source of nutrition for the whole family. Beans are high in protein, complex carbohydrates, dietary fiber, and low in unsaturated fat (no cholesterol) and calories. Beans are an excellent low-cost protein, well-stocked with B vitamins, zinc, potassium, magnesium, calcium, and iron. Despite their long cooking time, beans retain 70–90% of most vitamins and minerals after cooking. The B vitamins and folacin, however, are most affected by cooking, dropping 35–50% of their nutrient value.

Beans are a Great Source of Iron
A cup of most cooked beans offers 25% of the RDA of iron for women and 40% for men. The iron in beans and other plants is non-heme iron, which the body does not absorb as well as heme iron, which is supplied by animal protein. However, combining vegetables that are high in vitamin C with your beans (such as tomatoes or peppers) will increase absorbability of this iron.

Got Protein?
Beans contain more protein (22% per dry weight) than any other plant protein. Like most vegetable products, bean protein is incomplete. Protein consists of a chain of amino acids in varying ratios. If a food is incomplete it means that either some of these amino acids are missing or they are not in the right ratio for us to derive the most benefit. Animal food and animal food by-products (dairy and eggs) have all the essential amino acids to make them a complete protein. All beans, except for soybeans, are incomplete proteins. Combining them with any whole grain, dairy, egg, whole grain breads and pasta, nut or seed helps to make a complete protein.

Soybeans, although a complete protein, take several hours to cook and may be difficult to digest. You can eat soybean by-products and obtain the same or similar protein benefits. Fermented soy products are recommended instead of the overly processed and manufactured soy derivative products on the market today. Soy products such as tempeh, tofu, soy sauce, and miso are easiest to digest. Find out more about soybeans in the *To Meat or Not To Meat* chapter.

Beans against Beef
Compare 3 ½ ounces of cooked kidney beans with 3 ½ ounces of a choice grade broiled sirloin. The beans offer 9 grams of protein, 1 gram unsaturated fat, no cholesterol and lots of fiber! The sirloin

supplies 30 grams of protein and 9 grams of fat (one-third saturated) and about 90 milligrams of cholesterol and no fiber!

Cooking Beans:

Always rinse beans first. Place in a big pot and cover with cold water. Broken, cracked, or damaged beans will float to the top. Discard them and drain the water.

Presoak beans for 3–6 hours or overnight. Now pour fresh water in the pot three times the volume measurement of the beans you are cooking. Presoak beans for at least 3–6 hours. To prevent fermentation, soak in the refrigerator. Soaking is essential to soften the bean, help reduce cooking time, and make them more digestible. After soaking, drain the beans, rinse and discard this soaking water. Use fresh water to cook the beans by following the cooking chart in this chapter. Split peas and lentils do not need to be presoaked, but soaking will reduce their cooking time and help the lentils hold their shape after cooking. Presoak lentils for 30 minutes if you wish.

Begin cooking by covering the beans with at least 2 inches of water above the beans. The heavier and deeper the pot, the better it is for cooking beans. Cover lightly and bring to a boil, then reduce heat to medium. Cooking time varies greatly between beans—refer to the chart for detailed information. Periodically check the water level and add more if necessary.

Add kombu to the beans instead of salt to increase minerals, alkalize and soften the beans, and to improve digestion. Kombu, the Japanese word for

kelp, is a sea vegetable available in health food stores and Asian markets.

Add salt when the beans become tender. *Knowing when to add salt is crucial to a great tasting, well-cooked bean.* Use ¼ to ½ tsp of salt per cup of dried beans. Do not add salt in the beginning or it will toughen the bean. If added too late, the bean will not absorb the salt. Salt helps to sweeten and soften the beans and make them more digestible. An unsalted bean will taste flat and starchy no matter how long it is cooked. If you have to restrict salt in your diet, reduce the amounts in other areas of preparation but do not cut out salt when cooking beans.

Continue cooking until beans are tender. After salt is added, replace lid and continue cooking until beans pass the "squish test" (see below). At this point, vegetables, herbs, and spices can be added to create a simple bean stew. You may also use these as a base for endless recipe possibilities that include soups, loaves, burgers, croquettes, salads, and spreads.

Squish Test: A properly cooked bean will squish easily against the roof of your mouth using only your tongue. If you have to chew it, keep cooking it.

Alternative Cooking Methods:

Quick-soaking method. Boil the beans in a pot without a lid for 5 minutes, shut off the heat and let them soak in this water for one hour. Drain, add fresh water, and cook according to the chart.

Pressure cooking reduces cooking time by half. Always use a stainless steel pressure cooker and follow the instructions provided. Don't fill pressure cooker more than half full as beans expand and will often foam. Never cook lentils, split peas, black-eyed peas or soybeans in a pressure cooker as their skin and foam can clog the pressure cooker vents.

Slow cookers are especially good for cooking beans. I recommend that you boil beans for 20 minutes in a pot before adding to slow cooker. The slower and longer that beans are cooked, the sweeter and more concentrated their flavors will be.

Musical Beans?

If you are having trouble digesting beans, this is why: Beans contain two starches, stachyose and raffinose. In the intestine, special bacteria work on the ironclad bonds that link the elements in these starch chains together. As the bacteria work, carbon dioxide and hydrogen are given off, thus resulting in gas. When beans are soaked and cooked correctly, these starches are broken down during cooking, making the bean more digestible and less "gassy."

Even when well cooked, some beans are harder to digest than others. Lentil, kidney, soybeans, and broad beans are the toughest to digest. If you are having a gas problem, try one of the popular bean enzymes on the market or just abstain from these beans for a while. As specific intestinal bacteria that break down starch are encouraged to grow over time, it becomes easier to digest beans.

The recipes in the following chapter are some of my family's favorites. I include beans when I make soups, casseroles, burgers, stews, and salads. There are more than two dozen varieties of beans available and many can be substituted in recipes.

Save Time in the Kitchen

With both whole grains and beans, I always cook more than I need for the evening meal. Although whole grains can be frozen, it does change the texture. Beans freeze very well and can be measured and placed in ziplock bags for future dinners. There is now a great variety of organic cooked beans on the market.

I recommend cooking large quantities of beans which can then be frozen in small containers for later use in quick dinners. For more bean recipes look in my For the Love of Soups *or* Salads that Satisfy *chapters!*

Salvaging Burned Beans

Burned your beans? Sometimes they are salvageable. Start by removing the pot from the stove and keep the lid on until they cool. Then turn the pot over into another pot or bowl and allow the beans to fall out. DO NOT scrape the bottom of the pot. The beans that are stuck to the bottom are beyond repair. Add water to the new pot so the beans are covered by several inches. Swish your hands in the water a few times and you will see some beans start floating to the top. These beans will likely have a black spot on them, which is carbon from the burn. These beans float because carbon is lighter than water. Carefully, remove and discard these burned beans. Repeat this a second time with fresh water. The beans that remain on the bottom will have little or no burned flavor and you can proceed to cook them for the remaining time with fresh water. Ta-da!! Saving burned dishes is a chef's specialty!

Guide to Dried Beans

Dried Bean Iron Content

Legumes, Beans or Seeds	Serving Size	Iron Content
Black Beans	1 cup	3.6 mg
Black-eyed Peas	1 cup	1.8 mg
Cashews	½ cup	2.65 mg
Chickpeas	½ cup	3.0 mg
Kidney Beans	½ cup	2.2 mg
Lentils	1 cup	6.6 mg
Lima Beans	½ cup	2.3 mg
Navy Beans	1 cup	4.5 mg
Peanuts	½ cup	1.5 mg
Pinto Beans	1 cup	3.6 mg
Soybeans	1 cup	8.8 mg
Soy Milk	1 cup	1.4 mg
Sunflower Seeds	1 ounce	1.4 mg
Tofu, firm	½ cup	3.4 mg
Walnuts	½ cup	3.75 mg

Dried Bean Cooking Times

Dried Beans (1 cup)	Cooking Time
Needs Presoaking:	
Adzuki Beans	45–60 minutes
Black (Turtle) Beans	45–60 minutes
Garbanzo (Chickpeas)	1 ½–2 hours
Great Northern	1 hour
Kidney Beans	1–1 ½ hours
Lima, Large	1–1 ½ hours
Lima, Baby	45–50 minutes
Navy Beans	1 hour
Pinto or Pink Beans	1 ½ hours
Red Chili Beans	1 hour
Soybeans	3 hours
Non-soaking:	
Black-eyed Peas	30 minutes
Lentils, Green	45–60 minutes
Lentils, Red	30 minutes
Peas, Split (green or yellow)	45–60 minutes

⅓ cup dry beans = 1 cup cooked beans
½ cup dry beans = 1 ½ cups cooked beans
⅓ cup dry beans = 2 cups cooked beans
1 cup dry beans = 3 cups booked beans
2 cups (1 pound) dry beans = 6 cups cooked beans

Black Bean & Garden Vegetable Enchiladas

(Serves 4–6)

Very filling and tasty vegetarian enchiladas....

2   Tbs extra-virgin olive oil
2   tsp minced garlic
⅓   cup diced onions
¼   cup each of diced green and red bell pepper
½   jalapeño pepper, minced (or ½ tsp chili powder)
1   carrot, diced
⅓   cup diced zucchini
1   tsp ground cumin
1   tsp dried oregano
½   tsp sea salt
⅓   lb firm tofu, cut into tiny cubes
½   cup diced tomatoes
1 ½ cups precooked black beans, rinsed and drained
½   cup chopped cilantro
4   cups enchilada sauce
6   flour or corn tortillas
1   cup shredded cheddar cheese (cow's, rice, or almond cheese)

1. Preheat oven to 350°F. In a large frying pan, sauté garlic and onions in oil on medium heat for 2–3 minutes. Add green and red peppers, jalapeño, carrot, and zucchini, cover and simmer for 5 minutes or until vegetables are tender. Add cumin, oregano, and salt.

2. Add tofu and diced tomatoes, stir, and cover for 1–2 more minutes. Add black beans, cilantro, and ½ cup enchilada sauce to bind it, cover again.

3. Spray oil in a small frying pan, place tortilla in it and cover. Heat on low for 1–2 minutes, just long enough to soften the tortilla. This will prevent the tortilla from breaking when rolling it. Place on cutting board, fill with bean mixture and add some shredded cheese if you wish. Wrap enchilada style (cigar shape). Repeat for remaining tortillas.

4. In an 8 x 8-inch oven-safe dish, layer 2 cups of the enchilada sauce on the bottom of the pan. Place tortillas close together on top of sauce with seams placed down into the sauce. Pour the remaining sauce between and on top of each tortilla. Sprinkle with remaining cheese.

5. Bake uncovered 20–30 minutes. Cheese will melt as it is heated through.

Bites of Insight

Tofu is very high in protein. An 8 oz serving has the same amount of protein as a 5 oz hamburger, without the cholesterol. The fat in tofu is unsaturated and contains about 85% water. If calcium sulfate is added (not all tofu contains this), the tofu is a good source of calcium. Tofu also contains a fair amount of iron, phosphorus, and B-complex vitamins.

Chickpea Fritters

(Serves 4–6)

This was a favorite dish of my sons…children love the sweet flavor of chickpeas (garbanzo beans)!

3 cups precooked chickpeas (garbanzo beans), rinsed and drained
1 small onion, finely minced
¼ cup grated carrots
¼ cup minced fresh parsley
3 Tbs arrowroot, organic cornstarch, or unbleached wheat flour
½ tsp ground cumin
½ tsp sea salt
2 Tbs expeller pressed sesame oil

1. Strain chickpeas of any residual cooking juice. Drier beans will hold together better. Mash with a pastry cutter, potato masher, or in the food processor (pulse long enough to create a course mash). The bean shape should still be obvious. Be careful not to over mash into a paste. The bean mixture should be coarse and thick like cookie dough.

2. In a medium bowl, combine chickpeas, onions, carrots, parsley, arrowroot or organic cornstarch, cumin, and salt. Mix together until smooth. Mixture should hold together when pressed into a patty. Add more flour if needed.

3. Form the mixture into patties about 3 inches across, otherwise they will not hold together well.

4. Preheat oil in a frying pan on medium-high heat. To test if the oil is ready, place a little of the batter in the oil. If it begins to sizzle right away it is ready for frying. If it isn't, wait another minute and try again. Place patties in the pan leaving plenty of space. If you overcrowd the pan the patties will not brown and might fall apart before they cook. Fry patties on one side until browned. Turnover and repeat. If you need more oil, add after you remove the patties. Never add new oil in the middle of cooking a batch of patties or it will make them soft. Reheat oil again and start a new batch.

Serving Suggestion: Serve with a whole grain, salad, or fresh-steamed greens for a tasty vegetarian meal. To increase the protein content, add some leftover millet or rice to the bean mixture.

Bites of Insight

If you presoak an onion for 10 minutes before you peel and chop, you will avoid irritated eyes, and the onion will peel much easier. Sorry, should have told you earlier.

Cannellini Bean and Tomato Basil Salad

(Serves 4–6)

This is a summertime favorite salad for one of my clients. Fresh from the garden flavors yet hearty enough for a meal.

1 ½ cups precooked cannellini beans (white kidney beans), rinsed and drained
1 ½ cups chopped heirloom tomatoes or red tomatoes
²/₃ cup seeded and chopped cucumbers
⅓ cup chopped red bell pepper
⅓ cup chopped green bell pepper
¼ cup chopped fresh basil
¼ cup chopped fresh cilantro
2 cloves garlic, minced

Dressing:
1 lemon, juiced
2 Tbs white or red wine vinegar or white balsamic vinegar
⅓ cup extra-virgin olive oil
¼ tsp sea salt
⅛ tsp ground black pepper

1. Stand tomatoes stem side up. Slice tomatoes straight across into ½-inch slabs. Lay flat on board and make 3 long cuts and then several cross cuts. This is the easiest way to cut cube pieces of tomatoes for salads. Remove any seeds or juice that falls onto your cutting board.

2. If using large cucumbers, cut cucumbers in long slabs and then into long pieces. The center piece will contain most of the seeds, discard the seeds. Then cross cut into ½-inch cubes. Toss with tomatoes.

3. Add beans, red and green bell peppers, basil, cilantro, and garlic. Toss again.

4. Make dressing by combining all the ingredients. Mix well and toss with bean salad. Serve immediately. This will keep up to 5 days refrigerated.

Bites of Insight

Cannellini beans a very popular in Italy, especially Tuscany. They are mild flavored and related to the kidney bean. Navy beans or great northern beans can be substituted. The many health benefits of cannellini include: low in fat, high in protein, high in fiber, minerals, and B vitamins. This bean is a staple of minestrone and other soups, salads, and stews.

Hot Tamale Pie with Red Beans

(Serves 6–8)

I have taken this to parties and potlucks and it's everyone's favorite – very visually attractive and is a sure hit! Don't let the ingredient list stop you; this is well worth the effort and it freezes well.

1   Tbs extra-virgin olive oil
1   small onion, chopped
3   cloves garlic, minced
⅓   cup chopped green bell pepper
⅓   cup chopped red bell pepper
½   cup chopped fresh tomato or 15 oz can diced tomatoes
½   tsp ground cumin
1   tsp dried oregano
¼   tsp chili powder
¼   tsp sea salt
2   cups precooked red chili beans (or pinto or kidney), rinsed and drained
½   cup fresh or frozen corn, blanched
¼   cup tomato sauce

1. Preheat oven to 400°F.

2. In a large frying pan, sauté onion and garlic for 3 minutes on medium heat. Add green and red bell pepper and sauté for 3 minutes. Add tomato, cumin, oregano, chili powder, and salt. Sauté, covered, another 2 minutes.

3. Add precooked red beans, corn, tomato sauce, and ½ cup water. Cover and cook on medium heat for 5 minutes or until flavors have blended. Test for flavor and add more chili, cumin, or tomato sauce if you prefer.

4. Spread mixture evenly in a 13 x 9-inch ungreased baking dish. Continue to *Hot Tamale Pie Crust Topping* on following page.

Bites of Insight

In a bean and cornbread casserole such as this, it is important that the bean mixture not be too "soupy" or too dry. If it is too "soupy" it will prevent the cornbread from drying out as it bakes. It if is too dry, the sauce will evaporate into the cornbread and you will have beans stuck up into the cornbread, which is still delicious but too dry. Making it a few times will guide you to the right consistency for the best results.

Hot Tamale Pie Crust Topping

Dry Ingredients:
½ cup corn flour
½ cup unbleached white flour or whole wheat pastry flour
1 tsp baking powder
¼ tsp sea salt

Wet Ingredients:
½ cup yellow coarse cornmeal
⅓ cup extra-virgin olive oil
¼ cup honey or agave syrup
1 large egg

Optional Garnish:
1 cup sour cream
1 small tomato, sliced into half moons
½ ripe avocado, sliced
6 black olives, sliced

1. Bring 1 cup of water to boil. Pour water over coarse cornmeal. Let sit for 10 minutes to soften the grits.

2. In a separate bowl, combine dry ingredients: corn flour, unbleached white flour, baking powder, and salt.

3. In another bowl, mix remaining wet ingredients: oil, honey or agave syrup, and egg, blending well. Then add softened cornmeal with water.

4. Combine both dry and wet ingredients. Mix well and spread evenly over the bean mixture by drizzling batter slowly over the top of beans as you move the bowl up and own in rows over the casserole. You will not be able to spread mixture with a spoon.

5. Bake at 400°F for 15 minutes. Reduce heat to 350°F and bake another 15 minutes or until cornbread topping looks dry. Place a knife in the center of the cornbread 1 inch deep; if it comes out dry then it is done. Remove and cool for 10–15 minutes before garnishing.

6. If you want to create single serving portions (optional), top the cornbread with evenly spaced garnishes starting with a tablespoon of sour cream, topped with a slice of tomato and avocado, and a few black olives. This will define the portions to cut into if you are bringing this dish to a party or a potluck. For dinner with family and friends, serve with a green salad for a complete and delicious vegetarian meal.

Lentil Provençal with Orzo

(Serves 2–4)

You can substitute quinoa for orzo or bulgur if you wish to avoid wheat.

⅓ cup uncooked orzo or bulgur
2 Tbs extra-virgin olive oil
⅓ cup chopped onion
2 cloves garlic, minced
½ cup green beans
½ cup chopped zucchini
¼ cup chopped celery
1 cup chopped tomatoes
½ tsp sea salt
1 cup precooked lentils (start with ¼ cup raw lentils cooked in 1 cup water for 15 mins)
½ cup tomato sauce
2 tsp red wine vinegar
¼ tsp ground cayenne (for spicy, or less to taste)
1 tsp dried basil or 2 Tbs minced fresh basil

1. If using orzo, cook according to package directions. If using bulgur, boil 1 cup water, turn off heat, add bulgur and cover. Let sit to reconstitute the grain, approx. 15–20 minutes, or until all the water is absorbed. This can be done ahead or the day before.

2. In medium sized frying pan, sauté onion and garlic in oil for 2–3 minutes on medium heat. Add green beans, zucchini, celery, chopped tomatoes, and salt. Cover and simmer for 5 minutes or until green beans are tender.

3. Add lentils, tomato sauce, red wine vinegar, cayenne, and basil. Stir and adjust for taste and simmer another few minutes. Serve over orzo or bulgur.

Serving Suggestion: Lentils served with orzo pasta, brown rice, or bulgur grain increases the protein in this dish. For a vegetarian dinner, no other protein is necessary. Serve with a fresh salad.

Bites of Insight

Orzo is simply rice-shaped pasta. Orzo is Italian for barley which describes the shape and size of the pasta. Orzo is popular in the Mediterranean nations and the Middle East. The best orzo comes from durum semolina wheat, a hard wheat variety that will retain its shape during cooking.

Stuffed Poblano Peppers

(Serves 4)

If you love Mexican food, you will love this dish…..

4 fresh poblano peppers
2 Tbs extra-virgin olive oil
½ cup minced onion
2 cloves garlic, minced
½ cup corn
½ cup precooked black beans or pinto beans, rinsed and drained
1 ½ cups precooked brown rice
¼ tsp sea salt
½ tsp ground black pepper
¾ cup shredded cheddar cheese (cow's, rice, or almond)

Salsa Verde:
6 tomatillos (husks removed)
1 clove garlic, minced
¼ cup chopped fresh cilantro
2 Tbs fresh lime juice (1 lime)
¼ tsp sea salt

1. Preheat broiler to 450°F. With a paring knife, cut a vertical slit into one side of the pepper from ½ inch right under the cap to 1 inch from the bottom. Carefully remove seeds with your fingers and the thin layer of membrane running down the inside of the pepper and discard.

2. Roast poblano peppers under broiler, rotating peppers as soon as each side blackens until charred black on all sides. Don't roast too long as you want them still a little firm. Place in a bag or in a covered bowl for 3 minutes. When cooled you can remove the skin easily by rubbing it off with your fingers.

3. Turn oven to bake and preheat to 375°F.

4. For salsa verde, place tomatillos and 1 clove garlic in small pot with enough water to cover and bring to a boil. Reduce heat, cover and simmer for 5 minutes. Drain and puree in blender. Add cilantro, lime juice, and sea salt and puree again. If you wish, substitute this sauce for bottled salsa verde found in most food stores. Spread enough sauce to cover the bottom of an 8 x 8-inch baking pan, reserving 2 Tbs for stuffing the peppers.

5. In a small frying pan, sauté onion and 2 cloves garlic in olive oil until tender. In a bowl, toss this with corn, beans, rice, salt, pepper, 2 Tbs remaining salsa verde sauce, and 2 Tbs cheddar cheese. Mix well. Stuff about ¼ cup mixture in each poblano pepper and place in baking dish. Sprinkle with remaining cheddar cheese. Cover and bake in preheated oven for 25 minutes.

Note: Poblano chilies are commonly available in the southern and western states. If you cannot find them, substituting green Italian frying peppers or ordinary green peppers will do quite nicely. The poblano chilies are mildly hot. Tomatillos are small, tangy green tomatoes found in many grocery stores. If you cannot find them, substitute bottled salsa verde.

Stuffed Peppers with Beans & Rice

(Serves 4–6)

Great way to use up leftover rice and beans!

4   bell peppers (in a variety of colors if you wish)
1   Tbs extra-virgin olive oil
¾   cup finely chopped onion
2   cloves garlic, minced
½   cup chopped green bell pepper
½   cup corn
1 ½ tsp chili powder
1   tsp oregano
1   tsp sea salt
1 ½ cups chopped tomatoes or 15 oz can diced tomatoes
½   cup precooked red chili beans or pinto beans, rinsed and drained
2   cups precooked brown rice (long or short variety)

Optional: 6 slices of your favorite cheese

1. Preheat oven to 375°F.

2. Trim ½ inch off tops of peppers and clean out seeds and white membranes. Trim bottoms if necessary so peppers can stand upright, being careful not to cut a hole through the bottom. Place in baking pan cut side down, spray or brush with olive oil and bake for 15 minutes. Allow peppers to cool before stuffing.

3. In a medium sized frying pan, sauté onion and garlic in olive oil for 2–3 minutes on medium heat. Add chopped green bell pepper, corn, chili powder, oregano, and salt. Sauté for an additional 2–3 minutes.

4. Add tomatoes and beans and simmer for a few minutes until flavors blend. Add precooked rice and mix well.

5. Stuff each pepper to the top and, if you wish, add a slice of cheese on top. Bake uncovered for 15 minutes. If you have more stuffing than you need you can just heat and serve this mixture without peppers!

Bites of Insight

Short grain brown rice will make sweeter and stickier rice. Long grain rice is better for pilafs. Either one is good in this recipe. Most whole grains double in volume when they are cooked. If you want 2 cups of cooked rice start with 1 cup of rice and 2 cups of water. See Amber Waves of Grain *for more information on cooking whole grains.*

Thai Coconut Chickpeas

(Serves 4)

Sweet, creamy and so delicious—one serving will not be enough!

2 cloves garlic, minced
1 tsp extra-virgin olive oil
1 medium sweet potato or yam, peeled and cut into ½-inch pieces
1 cup bean juice from cooking, or vegetable broth or water
1 Tbs curry powder
2 cups precooked chickpeas (garbanzo beans), rinsed and drained
15 oz can light coconut milk
½ tsp sea salt
½ cup chopped fresh cilantro
½ cup chopped fresh basil

1. In a medium sized frying pan, sauté garlic in oil for 2–3 minutes on medium heat. Add sweet potato, juice or broth, and curry powder. Cover and simmer for 5–8 minutes or until potato is almost tender.

2. Add chickpeas, coconut milk, and salt. Cover and simmer on medium-low for 5 minutes. Add cilantro and basil and simmer for another 2 minutes, just long enough to wilt herbs.

Serving Suggestion: Serve with a whole grain such as brown basmati rice or Naan bread—an Indian flatbread that is similar to a pita. Always serve a green vegetable with a wholesome meal. There is plenty of protein, carbohydrates, vitamins, minerals, and some good quality fat in this dish. Serving a light salad or steamed broccoli will finish it off nicely.

Makeover: Leftovers can be made into a quick soup by blending some of the beans to a paste and then adding additional broth and curry. Actually, any leftover bean dish is a great beginning for a soup.

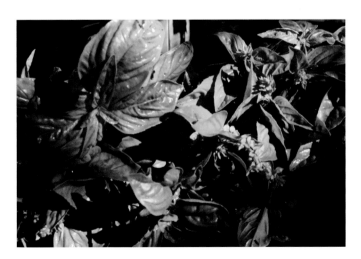

Three Sisters Stew

(Serves 4–6)

Native Americans referred to squash, beans, and corn as the three sisters, which were a major part of their diet.

2　Tbs extra-virgin olive oil
1　small onion, chopped
2　garlic cloves, minced
½　cup chopped red or green bell pepper
½　jalapeño pepper, minced or ½ tsp hot red pepper flakes
1　cup peeled and chopped butternut squash
½　cup chopped celery (2 stalks)
1　tsp ground cumin
1　tsp dried oregano
1　tsp sea salt
1　quart vegetable broth
15 oz can pinto beans or 2 cups precooked beans, rinsed and drained
15 oz can tomato sauce
½　cup fresh corn, blanched
15 oz can refried pinto beans
⅓　cup chopped parsley (for garnish)

1. In a medium sized soup pot, sauté onion and garlic in olive oil for 2–3 minutes on medium heat. Add red or green bell pepper and jalapeño pepper and sauté another 2 minutes.

2. Add squash, celery, cumin, oregano, salt, and vegetable broth. Cover and bring to a boil. Continue to simmer until squash is tender, about 8 minutes.

3. Add beans, tomato sauce, and corn. Return to medium heat. Simmer for 5 more minutes.

4. Add refried beans and stir until all ingredients are well mixed and heated. Add more vegetable broth or water until mixture reaches desired consistency. Garnish with chopped parsley and serve.

Serving Suggestion: Serve with a salad and whole grain bread for a hearty vegetarian stew.

Tuscan White Beans

(Serves 4)

More like a bean and vegetable stew....colorful and hearty!

2 Tbs extra-virgin olive oil
⅓ cup chopped onion
1 tsp minced garlic
⅓ cup green string beans
⅓ cup chopped red bell pepper
½ cup coarsely chopped zucchini
1 cup chopped fresh tomatoes
¼ cup chopped celery
½ tsp dried basil or 1 Tbs fresh basil
½ tsp dried oregano or 2 tsp fresh basil
1 tsp sea salt
¼ tsp ground black pepper
1 ½ cups precooked white beans (great northern or navy), rinsed and drained
1 cup tomato sauce
2 Tbs minced fresh parsley, minced or ½ tsp dried parsley

1. In a medium sized frying pan, sauté onion and garlic in oil for 2–3 minutes on medium heat.

2. Slice celery by cutting once or twice vertically along the rib. Depending on the size of the celery you might need to cut it in thirds. Then cut again crosswise into ½-inch pieces. Add string beans, red bell pepper, zucchini, tomatoes, celery, basil, oregano, ¼ cup water, salt, and pepper. Cover and simmer for 3–5 minutes or until string beans are tender but still bright green.

3. Add white beans, tomato sauce, and parsley. Cover and cook for another 3–4 minutes.

Serving Suggestion: Serve with brown rice, couscous, or quinoa for a great vegetarian meal or serve as a side to any poultry dish.

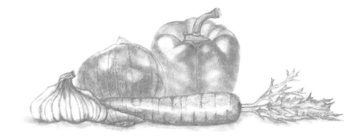

Bites of Insight

The easiest way to peel a clove of garlic is to place it on your cutting board and lay your knife blade flat side down on top of the clove. With your other hand, make a fist and hit the blade with one hard smack. It will crack the clove and split the skin, making it easier to peel.

Vegetarian Chili

(Serves 4–6)

My family's favorite chili! Even meat-eaters love it. This freezes well for future quick meals.

2   cups precooked red beans (kidney, chili, or pinto), rinsed and drained
1   Tbs extra-virgin olive oil
½   cup chopped onion
3   cloves garlic, minced
½   cup chopped green bell pepper
1   medium carrot, chopped
1   stalk celery, chopped
28 oz can crushed tomatoes
¼   cup bulgur wheat
2   bay leaves
1   tsp chili powder
1   tsp ground cumin
1   tsp dried oregano
1   Tbs soy sauce
½   tsp sea salt

Optional: ½ cup corn

Garnish with ¼ cup diced red onion, ½ cup chopped fresh cilantro, and ½ cup shredded cheddar cheese

1. In a medium sized soup pot, sauté garlic and onion in oil for 2–3 minutes on medium heat.

2. Add beans, peppers, carrots, celery, 1 cup water, and all remaining ingredients. Cover and bring to a boil. Reduce heat and simmer 15 minutes. Adjust seasoning for your taste, adding more chili powder, cumin, or soy sauce to your liking.

3. You can serve in individual bowls garnished with chopped raw onion, cilantro, and shredded cheese (cow's, rice, or almond).

Serving Suggestion: When a whole grain (bulgur wheat) and bean are combined they offer a complete protein, so no additional protein is needed. Serve with a fresh green salad or fresh steamed broccoli. Cornbread would be a wonderful addition to this hearty chili. For a meatier chili see *Bison Chili Con Carne* in the *Meat or Not to Meat* chapter.

White Bean and Cauliflower Madras

(Serves 4–6)

Golden curried yellow vegetables are eye appealing as well as delicious! Even better the next day!

1   Tbs extra-virgin olive oil
1   cup chopped onion
1   inch piece of ginger, peeled and minced
2   cloves garlic, minced
1   cup chopped green cabbage
1   cup sliced carrots
1 ½ Tbs curry powder
¼   tsp ground cardamom (optional)
1   tsp sea salt
1 ½ cups precooked white beans or garbanzo beans, rinsed and drained
1 ½ cups chopped cauliflower
½   cup vegetable broth or water
15 oz can light coconut milk
1   cup green peas, frozen or fresh
⅓   cup chopped fresh cilantro

Optional: Use ½ lb cubed firm tofu instead of beans

1. In a medium sized frying pan, sauté onion, ginger, and garlic in oil for 2–3 minutes on medium heat. Add cabbage and carrots, cover and cook about 3–4 minutes. Stir in curry powder, cardamom, and salt.

2. Add beans, cauliflower, and vegetable stock or water. Simmer covered, for 5 minutes.

3. Add coconut milk, peas, and cilantro. Cover again and simmer long enough for peas to soften, about 2 minutes. Serve immediately.

Serving Suggestion: If you wish, serve a dollop of yogurt on top as a garnish for each serving. Serving this with long grain brown rice would also increase the protein.

Bites of Insight

Light coconut milk can be substituted for cream, half and half, or yogurt in many recipes if you need to avoid dairy. Light coconut milk has fewer calories and less of a coconut flavor. You can freeze unused coconut milk. If you wish to have a stronger coconut flavor, use regular coconut milk.

Vegetables–Nature's Bounty

. . .

Opposite: Easy Stir Fry with Teryaki Sauce, see page 202

Vegetables—Nature's Bounty

Color is your first and best clue to nutrient-rich vegetables. Most yellow and orange vegetables, including carrots, winter squash, or sweet potatoes get their color from beta-carotene and other carotenoids (antioxidants), which are precursors to vitamin A. Dark green leafy vegetables also contain carotenoids, and chlorophyll, which gives them their green color. The more intense the vegetable's color (especially green or orange), the more beta-carotene it contains. Generally higher in calories than salad leaf vegetables, intensely colored vegetables are good sources of vitamin C, a great antioxidant. These vegetables offer a myriad of flavors and textures that makes them useful for seasonings and accents as well as a staple food.

The recipes in this chapter will contain some unfamiliar but extremely nutritious vegetables.

Bites of Insight: Did you know that some vegetables are really botanically defined as fruits:

- eggplant
- pumpkin
- zucchini
- peppers
- cucumbers
- avocados
- tomatoes

These are technically fruits rather than vegetables because they have a fleshy pulp and seed-bearing body. In the culinary world, though, we use them like vegetables and refer to them as such.

Vegetables = Vitamins & Minerals
Fruits and vegetables are the nutritional powerhouses of your diet. They brim with vitamins, minerals, fiber, and phytochemicals. These may protect against cancer, heart disease, strokes, and other health problems. Vegetables are low in calories and fat and provide almost every important vitamin and mineral your body needs. The exception is vitamin D and for that you will need sunshine. Most cooked vegetables contain 50 calories per ½ cup serving. Starchy vegetables, including beans, potatoes, peas, winter squash, beets, and corn will be twice that. To stay healthy, the recommendation is to eat seven to nine servings of fruits and vegetables a day. Yet the most recent survey states that less than 10% of Americans achieve that goal.

Our house motto is "greens-a-day-keep-the-doctor-away." Green leafy vegetables like kale, collards, Swiss chard, broccoli, mustard greens, and turnip greens are high in calcium, iron, vitamins E and C and beta-carotene (which converts into vitamin A in the body). My children and I had a side dish of one of these vegetables with every dinner. You can also add these leafy greens to soups and casseroles. Many delicious salads can be made with finely chopped kale tossed with other crunchy vegetables and a dressing.

Of course, leafy salad greens can be eaten raw, but do not rely on them for a source of calcium or iron. Spinach, although it contains both, also has oxalic acid, which binds up the calcium and iron, and prevents much of it from being absorbed. Additionally, iron is best absorbed when vitamin C-rich foods such as tomatoes and peppers are included in the meal.

Folic acid (B complex vitamin) deficiencies are common in the U.S. Research shows diets deficient in folic acid are linked to an increase risk of lung and cervical cancer. As this vitamin is essential to build red blood cells, a deficiency can also lead to certain types of anemia. Vegetables like Brussels sprouts, asparagus, broccoli, cabbage, corn, peas, raw spinach, romaine lettuce, and dried beans are good sources of folic acid.

It is essential that we get vitamin C from our food. Humans, guinea pigs, some bats, and some birds cannot synthesize vitamin C like the rest of the animal kingdom (we're in great company). It is speculated that a possible mutation happened in humans that prevented us from manufacturing our own vitamin C. Fortunately, vitamin C is plentiful in fruits and vegetables. However, cooking these foods at high temperature or for longer than 10 minutes destroys most of this vitamin.

In general, fruits and vegetables contain a more diverse group of minerals and vitamins than any other food group. The health protection that these nutrients can give us is widely documented. I encourage you to research on your own (internet is easy) to get a list of nutrients contained in these food groups.

Frozen vs Fresh vs Canned

I am a big believer in eating in-season, locally grown, organic fresh fruits and vegetables, but I do believe there are instances where substitutes are helpful. For many in colder climates, the availability of fresh local fruits and vegetables is limited or non-existent.

Out of season fruits and vegetables can travel from 1500–3000 miles before they reach your grocers' shelves. To withstand long transport times these crops will be picked before their peak of ripeness when the food contains the maximum level of nutrients. To consumers, most of these foods will look ripe but they are anything but. Many nutrients are lost (or were never there in the first place) with some of this "fresh" produce.

Frozen vegetables are generally picked at their peak of ripeness and processed quickly. The first step of freezing is blanching them in steam or hot water to kill bacteria. This causes some water-soluble nutrients like vitamin C and the B vitamins to be lost. The next step however, of flash-freezing, locks the vegetables in a relatively nutrient-rich state. The problem then arises when you, the consumer, might take these frozen vegetables, put them in water and boil them for another 10 minutes to defrost them. Water logged again, not many water-soluble nutrients will survive. So, when cooking frozen vegetables boil your water first and add vegetables for one minute. The best method is to put vegetables above boiling water in a covered steamer basket.

The only frozen vegetables I keep on hand are organic green peas and corn. Frozen peas are high in iron and well, corn, I just love it and would prefer organic. I do not recommend canned vegetables, other than tomatoes and cooked beans, except in an emergency.

Eat a Rainbow of Vegetables

It is essential to eat a variety of vegetables as they differ in the nutrients they offer. So keep a variety of root vegetables, round vegetables, and leafy vegetables on hand. Root vegetables, such as onions and carrots, are grown underground, and tend to have more minerals and fat-soluble vitamins but less chlorophyll than other vegetables. Round vegetables that grow on the ground like broccoli, cabbage, cauliflower, and squash contain a good amount of beta-carotene and vitamins. Leafy vegetables like salad lettuces and hardy winter greens (kale, spinach, Swiss chard, etc.) offer the greatest amount of chlorophyll (rich in nutrients). If you are relying on salad bars to offer you a variety of nutrient rich vegetables, then I guarantee that you are not getting enough variety of minerals and vitamins. Some of the best nutrient-rich vegetables are the varieties that need to be cooked. So think outside the salad bowl and start experimenting with a variety of vegetables.

Cooked vs. Raw vs. Juiced

Eating only cooked vegetables means you will not be getting the necessary enzymes available in raw vegetables. Additionally, there is vitamin loss when vegetables are cooked. When cooking vegetables rich in vitamin C, as much as 45–90% of this vitamin can be lost, depending on the length of time it is cooked and the style of cooking. Boiling in a large amount of water for a long period of time will result in the greatest nutrient loss. So eat some of your vegetables raw in salad, some cooked as side dishes, and some juiced. You want to have a greater proportion of your vegetables raw, steamed, blanched, or juiced in the warmer months. Whereas, in the colder months you might be drawn to more stew recipes containing longer-cooked and heartier vegetables. This is seasonal cooking and helps your body adjust to the climate.

Juicing vegetables is a great way to increase your vitamin and mineral intake without overdoing the bulk. Fresh made vegetable juice bars are popping up all over the country so it's easier to find fresh squeezed juices. Be cautious, however, on the amount of fruit juices you consume. Often containing frozen yogurt they are very high in calories and sugar. Once you become a juice enthusiast, I recommend that you purchase your own electric juicer. It need not be expensive or fancy. I recommend the juicers that have a gear mechanism to crush the vegetables instead of the spinning basket types.

If you are in an area that offers wild food foraging classes, it is a great way to get to know the wonderful plant foods easily available to you. Wild onions, garlic, parsnips, carrots, dandelion, watercress, fiddlehead ferns, and spearmint are some common greens in the Northeast where I grew up. You might be surprised how many of the "wild weeds" are edible. Never eat wild vegetables taken from grounds that have been sprayed with weed killers or pesticides. Even if you don't spray, educate yourself first before you forage in your own backyard.

Bites of Insight

Celtic literature refers to carrots as "honey underground." Becoming popular only in England during the time of Elizabeth I, they were already being eaten daily in Ireland, Scotland, and Wales. Carrots were originally red or yellow until an orange hybrid cross was developed. The Queen of Holland declared that this would be henceforth referred to as a carrot as it matched the colors of her Coat of Arms. Red and yellow carrots are now called "heirloom carrots" and are coming back at some farmers markets. Heirloom carrots are a delicious and colorful alternative. See my *Honeyed Carrots with Black Sesame Seeds* recipe in this chapter.

Know Your Vegetables

Select vegetables in their proper season to ensure freshness and maximum nutritional value. When selecting any fresh produce, look for brightly colored, firm vegetables. Limp, wrinkled, discolored, or bruised vegetables and fruits are best avoided. Look for mushrooms with closed, firm caps that are sweet smelling. Avoid root vegetables that have already sprouted. For most vegetables, look for a deep color as it will contain more vitamins, minerals and a greater chance that it was "sun-ripened." Most fresh veggies will have a bright and shiny complexion.

Baby carrots are not babies at all. They are cut, reshaped carrots and they have 1/10th the nutritional value of a whole carrot!

As I have mentioned before, buying organic produce is very important. When possible, buy fresh, seasonal food that is grown locally. Less fungicide and pesticide chemicals are used when long-distance shipping and prolonged storage are not required. America imports produce from China, Mexico, New Zealand, and Costa Rica to name just a few countries. There is a greater possibility for a higher pesticide and fungicide residue with imported produce than homegrown, so buy American! Many vegetables (cucumbers and rutabagas for example) are sprayed with wax coating. That wax often contains small amounts of fungicide. I always peel vegetables that are waxed and never peel those that are not. In my kitchen, most vegetables get a good scrub under running water and that is it!

All refrigerators today are frost-free and automatically remove the air moisture and consequently make vegetables limp faster. So it is important to keep them wrapped in the vegetable crisper.

Preparing Vegetables—Big Bites of Insight!
To remove the skin from garlic, place the clove on your cutting board and lay the flat side of your knife on the garlic. With your right hand, make a fist shape and whack the center of the knife with your hand. It will crush the clove and the skin will slip off easily. Then you can then either chop, mince, or use in a garlic press.

Peel onions without shedding a tear by soaking them in water (any temperature) for 10 minutes before peeling. The peel softens and is easier to remove.

Leeks are wonderful, versatile, sweet vegetables but need thorough cleaning. To do this, remove any bruised or tough outer leaves. Cut off the first few inches of the top green stem and the root end. Discard or save for a later soup stock. Slice the leeks lengthwise once and then crosscut into ½-inch pieces. Place in a bowl of water and clean as you would greens. The upper green leaves of a leek are the dirtiest. I use both the tender green tops and bottoms in most recipes. I put the lower white root in my recipe early in the preparation and the upper green tops get added later so they don't get overcooked and lose their bright green color.

Green leafy vegetables - kale, collards, spinach, Swiss chard, and mustard greens can be cleaned by first chopping them. Place a few leaves on top of each other on your cutting board, and then cut out the hard stem (also called the rib). Slice the leaves down the center. Place one half on top of the other and slice

Storing Vegetables
To keep vegetables fresh at home, wash them thoroughly and wrap individually in damp paper towels or return them to their original plastic bags in the crisper. Some stores shrink wrap fruits and vegetables but it is best not to leave them in this packaging as they might deteriorate faster if there are any soft spots on them. Vegetable crispers (drawers) protect the vegetables and fruit from dehydration but they still need to be protected.

again lengthwise. Turn them to face you horizontally and chop into ½-inch pieces all the way up the leaves. Now place them in a large bowl in the sink and fill the bowl with water. Wash thoroughly by dunking the leaves in the water. Debris will settle to the bottom; pour off water and repeat. Lift vegetables out of water and place in a colander to drain. They are now ready to cook or be stored. To save time I will prepare two heads of kale or collard greens at a time. After they are drained (even if they are still a little damp) I place them in a plastic bag and tie the end. Poke a hole in one of the lower corners to let excess water drain, then place in another bag for storage in the refrigerator crisper drawer for up to 3 days.

Fresh herbs - Curly leaf parsley and Italian parsley, dill, and cilantro can be washed and easily chopped. Without removing the rubber band or twist tie, take the bunch of herbs and repeatedly dunk in a large bowl of water several times. You will see dirt start to collect at the bottom of the bowl. Pour off and repeat with fresh water, separating some of the leaves with your fingers so the water can get deep into the head. Shake out the head thoroughly and place on your chopping board. Gather the leaves in a tight bunch and mince from the top down to the band. Discard the stem that is below the band.

If you have not used the entire bunch of herbs, keep them fresh by standing them in a jar of water. Place a produce bag over the top covering the herbs. This can be refrigerated up to 7–10 days. Change the water at least every 5 days.

Dried mushrooms need to be presoaked in boiled water for at least 20 minutes before preparing them. Discard the stem as it is usually too dry to use even after soaking. After presoaking, remove mushrooms and squeeze out excess water and slice thinly. Add to your recipe according to the directions. Dried mushrooms are worth the extra step. They add a wonderful earthy flavor to soups and stews.

Preserving nutrients in the vegetables. Cut vegetables so they will cook quickly. You can steam, broil, sauté, grill, blanch, bake, or roast them. Whatever preparation you choose, be sure not to overcook your vegetables. When ready to eat, they should still be a little firm and brightly colored.

Some people see vegetables as a side dish, but most of them are hearty enough to stand alone as a main entree. With the addition of some protein (tofu, beans, tempeh, or nuts), vegetables can serve as a meal in itself. For a light and nutritious dinner or lunch, serve vegetables over pasta or with your favorite whole grain.

On the following pages are some of my favorite vegetable dishes. When you find you do not have the exact vegetable the recipe calls for, try substituting. Experimenting with substitutes is how new recipes are developed! Choose a similar vegetable in flavor, texture, or color. For instance, if a recipe calls for carrots, substitute sweet potatoes, or if it calls for string beans, substitute any green vegetable from the pod family (snow peas, snap peas, lima beans, etc.). Do not be daunted by lack of ingredients; play, experiment and come up with your own version.

Bites of Insight
After ten minutes of cooking most vegetables have lost 60% of their vitamin C! Cut your vegetables instead so they will cook in under 5–8 minutes.

Acorn Squash Stuffed with Rice Pilaf

(Serves 4)

This will stuff 3 squash, or 2 with leftover rice to serve as a side dish for another meal.

¼ cup wild rice
¾ cup brown rice
⅛ tsp sea salt
3 large acorn squash
2 Tbs natural vegetable oil
½ cup minced onion
1 stalk celery, chopped
4 oz fresh shiitake or regular mushrooms, chopped
2 Tbs soy sauce
¼ tsp dried thyme
¼ tsp dried sage
½ cup sunflower seeds, roasted
¼ cup chopped fresh parsley

Optional: Muenster or soy cheese, sliced in strips, 2 for each squash half

1. Preheat oven to 350°F.

2. Measure wild rice, rinse thoroughly, and drain. Cook wild rice in small pot with 2 cups water for 55 minutes or until the rice "splits" and opens. In another pot, place brown rice, 1 ½ cups water, and salt (can eliminate if desired). Cover, bring to boil, reduce heat to low and cook for 40 minutes.

3. Meanwhile, cut acorn squash in half lengthwise, and scoop out seeds and stringy pulp. Place squash face down in baking pan. Add ¼-inch of water to prevent it from sticking. Cover with foil. Bake 30 minutes or until squash is a little tender. DO NOT OVERCOOK or squash will not hold the stuffing.

4. When squash comes out of oven, place sunflower seeds on cookie sheet and roast 3–5 minutes or until they start to turn a golden brown.

5. Preheat oil in large fry pan and add onion, sauté for 3 minutes. Add celery and mushrooms to onions and continue to sauté for 3 more minutes.

6. Add both cooked rices, soy sauce, thyme, sage, sunflower seeds, and parsley. Toss well. Cover and simmer for 5 more minutes. Fill each squash half with rice mixture, mounding on top. Crisscross 2 pieces of cheese on top of the rice. Bake for 20 minutes.

Serving Suggestion: This recipe can be made up to 2 days ahead. Bring squash to room temperature, put in oven for 30 minutes at 350°F to reheat thoroughly.

Chinatown Sweet and Sour Bok Choy

(Serves 4–6)

1 head bok choy
2 Tbs light sesame oil
1 Tbs fresh ginger root, peeled and minced
½ cup shredded red cabbage
½ cup julienned carrots
1 tsp sea salt

Sauce:
1 Tbs arrowroot or organic cornstarch
1 Tbs soy sauce
½ cup honey
3 Tbs raw apple cider vinegar

1. Separate leaves of bok choy and discard outer leaves that might be bruised or pithy. Rinse bok choy thoroughly. Cut away bottom white section of bok choy from the green leafy tops. Place 2 stems of the white bottoms on top of each other and slice down the middle lengthwise. Cut into ½-inch diagonal slices. Place the leafy green tops on top of each other and cut in half. Fold over and cut again in half lengthwise, then cut crosswise into ½-inch pieces. Keep separate for now.

2. Preheat sesame oil in frying pan and sauté ginger root for 30 seconds. Add red cabbage and carrots and sauté for another 2 minutes. Add bottoms of bok choy and salt. Cover and simmer on low heat for 3 minutes.

3. Prepare sauce by dissolving arrowroot or cornstarch in 1 cup cold water. Add soy sauce, honey, and vinegar, and mix. Place in pan with the red cabbage and stir until sauce begins to thicken. Now place the greens on top of vegetables in pan. Do not stir them in. Cover and steam for 2 minutes. Serve immediately.

Cranberry Glazed Yam Casserole

(Serves 6)

This is a favorite holiday side dish for our family. Better and healthier than the marshmallow and sweet potato or pineapple version.

Yam Casserole:
3–4 yams or sweet potatoes
¼ cup butter (½ stick)
¼ cup pure maple syrup
1 tsp ground cinnamon
½ tsp sea salt

Cranberry Glaze:
8 oz bag whole fresh cranberries, rinsed
⅓ cup golden or dark raisins or dark raisins
¼ tsp ground cloves
½ tsp ground cinnamon
⅓ cup organic cane sugar
⅛ cup maple syrup
1 Tbs arrowroot or organic cornstarch
½ cup fresh squeezed orange juice

Topping:
1 cup chopped pecans, toasted
¼ cup organic cane sugar

1. Bake 3–4 yams in a 400°F oven for 45 minutes or until tender. Cool, split open, and scrape pulp into a large bowl, discard skins. This can be done days in advance if you need to save time. Add remaining ingredients: butter, maple syrup, cinnamon, and salt. Blend for 2–3 minutes with an electric blender. Spoon mixture into a baking pan and use a spatula to spread evenly.

2. Place cranberries, raisins, cloves, cinnamon, sugar, and syrup in a medium sized pot. Cover and simmer on low for 5 minutes, stirring occasionally. Check frequently to be sure cranberries do not stick and burn. After a few minutes they will begin to break down and their juices will be released.

3. Add 1 Tbs arrowroot or organic cornstarch to orange juice and stir to dissolve. Add to cranberry mixture and stir. Continue to simmer and stir for a few more minutes until the glaze thickens. Remove from heat.

4. Smooth the cooled cranberry glaze over the top of the yam casserole. Mix together the chopped pecans and sugar. Spread on top of the glaze.

Easy Vegetable Stir-Fry with Teriyaki Sauce

(Serves 4–6)

This is an easy stir-fry that doesn't get stirred! Layering vegetables is the key to this quick, delicious dish. Don't be discouraged at the length of the recipe…these are mostly suggestions.

Choose 4 cups mixed fresh vegetables, cut into bite-size pieces. I suggest picking 4–6 vegetables of a variety of colors largely depending on what veggies you have on hand. Be sure to pick contrasting colors and textures.

Vegetable Suggestions:

Longest cooking vegetables:
Carrots - cut diagonally or into matchsticks
String beans - cut in half
Red, green, or yellow bell peppers - ½ cup sliced
Red or green cabbage - ½ cup sliced

Longer cooking vegetables:
Broccoli - cut into bite-size pieces
Cauliflower - cut into bite-size pieces

Quicker cooking vegetables:
Bok choy or Napa cabbage bottoms - sliced
Green zucchini squash - sliced diagonally or into matchsticks
Yellow summer squash - sliced diagonally or into matchsticks

Quickest cooking vegetables:
Snow peas or snap peas - ½ cup sliced in half
Mung Bean sprouts - ½ cup
Bok choy green tops

(continued on the following spread)

Teriyaki sauce:
½ cup soy sauce
½ cup water
2 tsp arrowroot or organic cornstarch
1 tsp grated ginger
½ tsp minced garlic
1 Tbs white vinegar
1 Tbs organic cane sugar

Stir-Fry:
2 Tbs light sesame oil
1 Tbs dark toasted sesame oil
½ tsp sea salt

Note: If you like it hot and spicy, add a dash of hot sesame oil. If you like a sweet and sour sauce, add 1 tsp of apple cider vinegar and 2 tsp of honey or other natural sweetener.

(continued from the previous spread)

1. For teriyaki sauce, combine soy sauce, ½ cup water, and arrowroot or cornstarch in a small pot. Stir to dissolve. Add ginger juice (see *Bite of Insight* below), garlic, vinegar, and sugar. Simmer on low while stirring for 1–2 minutes or until sauce thickens. Remove from stove and set aside. Add this sauce to the stir-fry after it comes off the stove. Adding this to the vegetables while cooking will result in unappetizing brown colored vegetables.

2. For stir-fry, preheat oils on medium-high heat in frying pan. Add longest cooking vegetables first: carrots, cabbage, and bell peppers; cover and cook for 1–2 minutes. Vegetables will cook longer as more layers are added.

3. Increase heat to high and wait a minute until the pan gets hot. Now add broccoli and cauliflower without stirring. Quickly add ¼ cup of cold water and salt to the pan, and replace lid immediately. Cook at high heat for another 3 minutes. Longest cooking vegetables mentioned above will brighten in color but still feel firm when poked with a fork.

4. Reduce heat to medium-high and add other vegetables, such as summer squash or bok choy bottoms, and cook for an additional minute. Now add bok choy leaves and snap peas, cover and simmer another minute without stirring. Check vegetables, they should not be overcooked.

Serving Suggestion: Serve over brown rice or prepare my *Chinese Fried Brown Rice* found in the *Amber Waves of Grain* chapter. If you choose, you can add precooked chicken, shrimp, or beef during the last few minutes of cooking. This is an excellent way to get your family to eat more vegetables and less meat.

Bites of Insight

You don't need to peel ginger. The skin is quite clean, similar to a carrot peel and is edible; it is just a tougher fiber. With a handheld ginger grater or small handheld cheese grater, grate ginger into a small ball of pulp. Squeeze this pulp in the palm of your hand into the sauce, and discard pulp.

Golden Squash Casserole

(Serves 6)

So simple, easy, sweet, and delicious, plan to make extra!

1 medium winter squash
   (butternut, buttercup,
   delicata, Hokkaido, or
   kabocha)
1 medium onion, chopped
2 Tbs extra-virgin olive oil
⅛ tsp sea salt

1. Preheat oven to 375°F. Peel squash, cut in half, remove seeds and loose fiber. Chop into ½-inch pieces. Place chopped onion in 9 x 14-inch baking dish. Spread squash on top of onions. Drizzle with oil and sprinkle with salt.

2. Cover baking dish with lid or aluminum foil. Bake 35–40 minutes or until squash is very tender.

Serving Suggestion: Leftovers can be blended and creamed to make soup by adding a little water and a few spices. See *Creamed Winter Squash Soup* in *For the Love of Soups* chapter.

Honeyed Carrots with Black Sesame Seeds

(Serves 4)

Heirloom carrots are available at some grocery stores and at the farmer's market, and come in an array of colors from purple to yellow. If heirloom carrots are not available, substitute with traditional orange carrots.

1 orange carrot, cut into matchsticks
1 red carrot, cut into matchsticks
1 white carrot, cut into matchsticks
1 Tbs butter
¼ tsp sea salt
1 Tbs honey
1 tsp black sesame seeds (found at Asian markets) or white sesame seeds

Optional: Add ½ cup chopped walnuts

1. Remove stems and leaves from carrots and scrub well to remove any dirt. Do not peel carrots. To make matchsticks, cut carrots in long thin diagonal slices. Then take 2–3 slices at a time stacked on top of each other and cut into long thin straight sticks. Continue cutting the rest of the carrots.

2. In a large skillet, melt butter, add carrots and salt, cover, and simmer on medium-low for 3 minutes.

3. Remove lid, add honey, and toss carrots for a few minutes until the honey begins to thicken and the carrots become glazed. If using walnuts, add at this time. Keep lid off while the honey thickens. Sprinkle with black sesame seeds and serve immediately.

Bites of Insight

Celtic literature refers to carrots as "honey underground." Carrots became popular only in England during the time of Elizabeth I. Carrots were eaten daily in Ireland, Scotland, and Wales in soups, puddings, and stews. Carrots were originally red or yellow, until a hybrid variety was developed that was orange. The Queen of Holland liked it and as it matched the color of her Coat of Arms, she declared that the orange variety would henceforth be referred to as the carrot. Red and yellow carrots are now called heirloom carrots.

Hurry Curry Vegetables

(Serves 6)

Creamy, hot, and sweet…all at the same time! Great served over brown rice, couscous, or quinoa.

1   Tbs extra-virgin olive oil
1   small onion, chopped
3   red potatoes, cut into ½-inch chunks
2   carrots, chopped into ½-inch rounds
½   green or red bell pepper, chopped
3 ½ Tbs curry powder
¼   tsp sea salt
1   cup bite-size cauliflower pieces
1   cup fresh or frozen peas
¼   cup chopped fresh cilantro
1   Tbs arrowroot or organic cornstarch
15 oz can light coconut milk

1. Sauté onion in oil over medium heat, about 2–3 minutes. Add potatoes, carrots, peppers, curry powder, salt, and ½ cup water. Cover and cook until potatoes are tender, about 10 minutes.

2. Increase heat to medium and add cauliflower, cover and cook 5 minutes until tender. Add peas and cilantro and warm through for another 1–2 minutes.

3. Add arrowroot to ¼ cup of water and stir to dilute until it appears milky. Add coconut milk and stir again. Add to vegetables and simmer for an additional 2-3 minutes or until liquid has thickened.

Serving Suggestion: For a lower calorie dish, omit the coconut milk. You can use unsweetened almond milk instead. Use the same ratio of arrowroot and proceed as above. It will be less creamy but still intensely curry flavored.

Bites of Insight

Curry is a combination of 11–16 different herbs and spices. It is not necessarily hot as it depends largely on who has mixed the curry. Everywhere you travel in India you will taste different curries mixed in their own unique ways. Some very hot curries will usually state the "BTU" on the label. BTU stands for British Thermal Units and it measures the heat output, so you know it's super spicy. I recommend getting a standard store bought curry and adding your own unique twist to it. I love ginger for instance, so I add more ginger to my curry dishes but if you like it spicier, add cayenne pepper.

Polenta with Wild Mushrooms

(Serves 6– 8)

Fresh and dried wild mushrooms will make this dish extra special. Do not use only fresh as the dried mushrooms are what give this dish its "meaty" flavor. Serve over polenta (see following recipe) or spaghetti squash.

1   oz dried wild mushrooms, such as porcini, oysters, or chanterelles
3–4 garlic cloves, minced
2   Tbs extra-virgin olive oil
2   shallots or 1 small onion, minced
½   lb fresh wild mushrooms, porcini and/or chanterelles
½   lb fresh mushrooms, button, cremini, or baby bellas
1   tsp dried thyme (or to taste)
½   tsp chopped fresh rosemary or crumbled dried rosemary

Sauce:
2   tsp arrowroot or organic cornstarch
1–2 Tbs soy sauce
½   cup dry red wine
1   cup soaking water from the dried mushrooms
¼   tsp sea salt
¼   tsp ground black pepper (or to taste)

1. Pour 2 cups boiled water over dried mushrooms in a small bowl and cover for 30 minutes.

2. Heat 2 Tbs oil in large frying pan and add garlic and shallots or onions. Sauté 2–3 minutes until tender. Add fresh wild and regular mushrooms, cover, and sauté 4 more minutes until they begin to release their juices.

3. Drain, squeeze, and slice dried wild mushrooms, remove stems, and discard. Reserve 1 cup soaking liquid for sauce. Add mushrooms to the frying pan of fresh mushrooms. Add thyme and rosemary.

4. Combine soy sauce, wine, and 1 cup of the reserved mushroom soaking water; dissolve arrowroot in this liquid. Add this to mushrooms along with salt and pepper. Cover and simmer for 5 minutes. If sauce is too thin, remove lid and simmer until liquid thickens.

Serving Suggestion: Add some cubed firm or extra firm tofu, or a cooked chicken breast. Serve as an entrée over polenta (see *Good Ole' Polenta* on following page), making an indentation in polenta and pouring wild mushrooms in the center.

Good Ole' Polenta

(Serves 4–6)

1   tsp sea salt
½   lb coarse stone-ground
    cornmeal
2   Tbs chopped fresh parsley
    (for garnish)

Optional: Add 3-4 Tbs fresh grated Parmesan cheese or rice Parmesan cheese, found in health food stores.

1. Bring 5 cups water to boil and add salt. Add ½ cup of cornmeal at a time, stirring constantly. Continue doing this until all cornmeal is added. Simmer on low heat, stirring often. This will take 10–15 minutes. Be careful—as the polenta thickens it can burn very easily.

2. Polenta is ready when it's thick and creamy. Stir in Parmesan cheese. Spread polenta on large serving platter and garnish with parsley.

Note: You can buy premade polenta in most grocery and health food stores. Just slice and pan fry or heat in a toaster oven.

Bites of Insight

Polenta is made from course ground cornmeal and was commonly eaten as porridge or gruel in the early 1900s. Polenta is still considered a peasant food in some parts of the world. Polenta was also eaten with buckwheat, farro, and chestnut flours. Cooked polenta can be shaped into balls, patties, or sticks and fried to a golden brown. Fried polenta is popular in Southern Brazil.

Kale with Garlic

(Serves 3–4)

A powerhouse of nutrition, this vegetable is one of my kids' favorites! Only wheatgrass has more nutrients.

1 bunch fresh kale
2 Tbs extra-virgin olive oil
2 cloves garlic, minced

Optional: Add a thinly sliced carrot and/or ½ tsp fresh ginger

Serving Suggestion: Kale and collard greens are very similar and are interchangeable in this recipe. You may also wish to try winter squash or yellow summer squash. Thinly slice and sauté, covered, for 3–4 minutes before you add kale.

1. To remove stems from kale, hold leaf up by its stem. Wrap your fingers around the stem and pull down toward the top of the leaf, tearing if off. Or, hold leaf up by its stem and with a knife shave off leaves from the rib. Once you have the leaves removed, take several of them at a time, and slice across into ½-inch pieces. Place cut kale in large bowl, pot, or sink and fill with water. With your hands push the kale in and out of the water as if you were washing clothes by hand. Kale is very curly and easily holds dirt in its leaves.

2. Lift kale out of the water with your hands and drain in colander. Since the kale is lighter than dirt, the kale will float while the dirt and sand settles to the bottom of the bowl. That's why lifting it out of the water helps leave the dirt behind.

3. In a large frying pan, preheat oil; add garlic and sauté for 30 seconds. If using other vegetables add them now and sauté for another minute.

4. Add kale to frying pan. With a pair of kitchen tongs, turn kale over occasionally, allowing it to cook evenly. If all the water has evaporated and the kale is still tough, increase heat and add ¼ cup water. Cover and simmer for another 2–3 minutes.

5. Remove lid and serve immediately. Kale will be bright green and shiny and the leaves a little tender. Kale is in the cabbage family so it will always remain somewhat chewy.

Bites of Insight

When purchasing kale, look for dark, even green color with firm, fresh leaves. Wilted kale is a sign of water loss. Varieties of kale include very curly leaf, red leaf, and a flat leaf variety commonly referred to as Tuscan kale or dinosaur kale. Kale is available year-round but for the best flavor, buy it in the fall and winter when it is the sweetest. Like the cabbage family, kale gets sweeter with cold nights.

Roasted Asparagus with Prosciutto

(Serves 4)

The saltiness of the cured ham with asparagus is wonderful!

½ package of prosciutto ham
1   bunch of fresh asparagus
1   Tbs extra-virgin olive oil

1. Preheat oven to 350°F. Rinse asparagus and snap off or cut lower white bottoms. If the asparagus is very large, steam first for 2–3 minutes in water, drain, and then continue with recipe.

2. Slice prosciutto in half so you have long strips of cured ham. Starting down at the bottom of the asparagus hold ham on an angle and begin wrapping around the asparagus as you come up to the tip. Place asparagus spears side by side on an oiled cookie sheet with seams down.

3. Place in oven and roast for 5–8 minutes or until ham begins to sweat and the asparagus is a little tender.

Serving Suggestion: If you avoid animal protein you can skip the prosciutto and just roast asparagus without it. However, spray with olive oil and dust with a little bit of salt and garlic powder before putting it in the oven.

Bites of Insight

Asparagus has no fat or cholesterol, is low in sodium, and has less than 4 calories per spear! Asparagus is a nutrient-dense food high in folic acid and is a good source of potassium, fiber, vitamin B6, vitamins A and C, and thiamin. A 5 oz serving provides 60% of the recommended daily allowance for folacin which is necessary for blood cell formation, growth, and prevention of liver disease. Asparagus is a member of the lily family. Under ideal conditions, an asparagus spear can grow 10 inches in a 24-hour period—now that's fast!

Ratatouille over Spaghetti Squash

(Serves 4–6)

I love the colors and flavors of this vegetable stew. Vary the ingredients depending on what you have on hand.

1   spaghetti squash, medium
2   Tbs extra-virgin olive oil
1   small onion, cut into ½-inch pieces
3   cloves garlic, chopped
½   green or red bell pepper, chopped
2   medium zucchini, cubed
1   small eggplant, cubed
1   tsp dried basil or ¼ cup chopped fresh basil
1   tsp dried oregano or 1 Tbs chopped fresh oregano
½   tsp dried thyme or 1 Tbs chopped fresh thyme
½   tsp sea salt
⅛   tsp ground black pepper
2   large tomatoes, peeled and chopped
2   cups tomato sauce

Optional: Vegetarian—Add 1 cup precooked white beans
Meat Lovers—Add 2 precooked chicken breasts and the beans—everyone needs fiber!

1. Slice squash in half crosswise with heavy knife. Scoop out seeds. Place cut side down in a wide baking pan filled with 2 inches of water. Cover and place in oven at 350°F for 30 minutes. You can also cook squash on top of the stove in a covered large pot in 2 inches of water for 25–30 minutes. Squash is ready when a knife is easily inserted but squash still feels a little firm.

2. In a large frying pan, sauté garlic and onion in oil for 2–3 minutes. Add bell pepper. Cut zucchini and eggplant into 1-inch cubes, and add to frying pan along with herbs, sea salt, and pepper. Cover and sauté for 5 minutes or until the onion is translucent.

3. To peel tomatoes, drop in boiling water for 1 minute, remove, and cool. Peel should slip off easily. Cut into 2-inch pieces and add to frying pan. Cover and simmer for 3–4 minutes more.

4. Add 2 cups tomato sauce, cover, and cook over medium heat for 5 minutes or until vegetables are tender.

5. When ready to serve, run a fork gently along the inside of the squash to pull out spaghetti strands. Place on individual plates or on a large platter. Spoon ratatouille over squash and serve immediately.

Bites of Insight

Spaghetti squash is a wonderful low carb alternative to pasta. If the squash is cooked just right you will be able to pull strings out of the squash with a fork. Overcooking will result in a mushy but tasty vegetable.

Sweet Winter Collards

(Serves 2–4)

A favorite vegetable in Southern cooking, collards are one of the highest nutrient-dense green vegetables you can eat! Collards are a member of the cabbage family and they are the sweetest when harvested during the colder months.

1   bunch fresh collard greens
1   Tbs extra-virgin olive oil
1   large carrot, cut into
     matchsticks
     pinch of sea salt

1. Remove leaves by holding stem at the end and running your knife along each side of the rib to separate leaves from the rib. You can also place leaves on the cutting board, cut along both sides of the rib and remove the leaves. Discard stems or use in vegetable juice if you juice. Or if you are going to cook the ribs, slice ribs on a diagonal to ensure quick cooking. Place a few halves of the leaves on top of each other and slice vertically, then cut crosswise into ½-inch pieces.

2. Wash collards thoroughly in a large bowl in the sink. Swish leaves in water to remove dirt. Drain.

3. To create matchsticks, slice carrot into thin diagonal cuts. Then stack a few of these cuts on top of each other. Slice very thin long sticks vertically down the carrots. Preheat olive oil in large frying pan and add carrot matchsticks and sauté without a lid for 1–2 minutes before adding the collards.

4. Add chopped collard greens and sea salt, and sauté for 3–4 minutes on medium heat. Increase heat to high and add 2 Tbs water. Cover and steam for 3–4 minutes. Collard greens are done when they are bright, shiny green and the leaves are slightly tender. Collard greens never become extremely tender because they are part of the cabbage family.

Optional: Kale and collard greens are very similar and interchangeable in many recipes. You may also sauté very thin slices of winter or summer squash for 5 minutes with a covered lid, then add the collard greens and cover again and sauté until tender.

Bites of Insight

Kale, collard greens, mustard greens, turnip greens (tops), watercress, and parsley are just a few leafy greens that are high in calcium, beta-carotene, vitamin E, and iron. Beta-carotene can act like an antioxidant in the blood, destroying free radicals that cause aging and cell degeneration. A rich source of vitamins and minerals should be included in your diet every day.

Roasted Summer Vegetables

(Serves 4–6)

An abundance of fresh summer vegetables can be grilled or roasted to bring out their natural sweetness.

1   large onion, sliced into wedges
2   zucchini, sliced into 1-inch thick rounds
1   red bell pepper, sliced into 2-inch squares
1   green bell pepper, sliced into 2-inch squares
1   small eggplant, cubed into 2-inch pieces
1   yellow summer squash, sliced into 2-inch pieces
3   Tbs extra-virgin olive oil
3   cloves garlic, crushed
1   tsp dried oregano
2   tsp dried basil
¼   tsp sea salt

1. Preheat oven to 400°F. Cut vegetables and toss in bowl with oil. Then add garlic, herbs, and salt, and toss again.

2. Arrange in a baking dish large enough for the vegetables to be spread in a single layer. Bake for 30 minutes uncovered. Check if vegetables are tender by piercing them with a fork. If too firm, cook another 5–10 minutes.

Serving Suggestion: You can add other spring/summer vegetables such as asparagus, string beans, or baby artichokes when available. This is a great side dish with any entrée and wonderful over pasta with homemade sauce.

Bites of Insight

To cut onions into wedges, leave root end on when removing the skin. Stand the onion up with root end on top and slice through this root end in half. Take each half onion and repeat this step. You will have 6 wedges of onions held together by a piece of the root end still intact.

Roasted Winter Vegetables

(Serves 4–6)

I love this vegetable dish with my fall and winter dinners. Roasting vegetables is an easy, tasty, and healthy way to enjoy winter vegetables. They also smell wonderful while they roast!

1 cup peeled and cubed winter squash (butternut or buttercup)

1 large sweet potato, peeled and cut into 1-inch thick large matchsticks

1 medium parsnip, unpeeled, cut into ½-inch matchsticks

1 medium turnip, unpeeled, sliced and then cut into ½-inch matchsticks

1 large leek, green top removed, bottom sliced into 1-inch diagonals

1 small rutabaga, peeled and cut into ½-inch matchsticks

8 small white onions or 1 medium yellow onion, peeled and quartered

6 Brussels sprouts, halved

3 Tbs extra-virgin olive oil

1 tsp dried rosemary

2 tsp dried thyme

¼ cup minced fresh parsley

1 tsp sea salt

1. Preheat oven to 425°F. Clean and remove outer leaves of Brussels sprouts and cut in half. Put cut leek bottoms in a small bowl of water and let them soak for 5 minutes. This will help remove the dirt in between the leaves. Place all cut vegetables in a large mixing bowl.

2. Drizzle oil over the vegetables and toss thoroughly to coat. Add thyme, rosemary, parsley, and salt and toss again. Arrange vegetables in one single layer on a baking sheet. If the pan is too small to accommodate all these vegetables use a second pan. Bake uncovered for 40 minutes. Vegetables will be tender and slightly caramelized at their tips. Depending on the size of the cut you make, you will have to adjust cooking time a little less or more. The smaller the cut, the quicker the vegetables will cook. The quicker it cooks the less it will caramelize.

Serving Suggestion: This is a wonderful side dish to serve with a bean casserole, chicken, turkey, lamb, or seafood steak. It is very sweet and satisfying and you will want to have extras.

Bites of Insight

Dried herbs can be exchanged for fresh herbs in most recipes, but dried herbs do not have the same intensity and freshness. When a recipe calls for fresh herbs and you want to substitute dried, decrease quantity by one third. When the recipe calls for dried and you want to substitute with fresh herbs, increase quantity by three.

Sweet Potato Home Fries

(Serves 2–3)

Craving a bag of chips? Quick…make some home fries! Certainly these are a better choice of starch because of all the vitamins and minerals and fiber in these potatoes. Can you say "guilt-free binge?"

2   medium yams or sweet
    potatoes, peeled
1   Tbs extra-virgin olive oil
⅛   tsp cayenne pepper
¼   tsp ground paprika
¼   tsp ground cumin
½   tsp ground thyme
⅓   tsp sea salt

1. Preheat oven to 450°F. Grease a cookie sheet with oil or use parchment paper.

2. After peeling the potatoes, slice lengthwise into ½-inch long slabs. Then cut each slab into large matchsticks. You will get about 2 dozen matchsticks from two potatoes. Place in a large bowl.

3. Drizzle oil over potatoes and toss until thoroughly coated. Combine spices, herbs, and salt in a small dish. Sprinkle on the potatoes and toss again until the herbs are evenly distributed.

4. Place a single layer of potatoes on a cookie sheet and place on the middle rack of the oven for 5 minutes. Remove cookie sheet, and with a pair of tongs, flip the matchsticks onto opposite side. Place in oven for another 5 minutes. Potatoes should be a little browned on the outside and tender on the inside.

Serving Suggestion: Anytime or anywhere you crave starch, consider sweet potatoes and yams which are a lower glycemic starch than white potatoes. By the way, you can cook white potatoes the same way as above. Enjoy!

Bites of Insight

What we commonly refer to as yams are actually a different variety of the sweet potato. True yams are native to Africa and vary in size from a small potato to over 100 lbs with more than 600 varieties. Yams are starchier and drier than sweet potatoes. Yams will have flesh colored in white, pink, or brownish-black with a rough and scaly texture. In international markets yams are sold in precut pieces. Sweet potatoes are relatively low in calories and have no fat. They are rich in vitamin A, having five times the RDA in one sweet potato as a white potato, as well as potassium. The yam, a tuber, is a member of the lily family, while the sweet potato is a member of the morning glory family.

To Meat or Not to Meat

• • •

Opposite: Crunchy Corn Crusted Picnic Chicken, see page 240

To Meat or Not to Meat

Or do you want to "meat" in the middle? If this is a question you are pondering, please read on. Are you a vegetarian on the verge? Or maybe a "flexitarian" or "depends-on-what's-around" vegetarian? Do you love eating vegetables but just can't give up meat entirely? I strongly believe that people need to choose what type of diet is best for them. Most people think that following the latest diet craze will give them more energy, vitality, and health. What I know is that the vitality we desire results from sensible, balanced, and consistently healthy lifestyle choices that include diet. So wisely consider your dietary choices and their implications for your health.

If you choose to include animal protein in your diet, it is very important that you choose fresh, unprocessed natural proteins. Today, most poultry, meats and even fish are "factory farmed." These animals are fed a steady diet of antibiotics and growth hormones designed to enhance production for the meat industry. It is widely known that these pharmaceuticals are easily absorbed into our bodies along with the meat. Using more antibiotics increases bacteria resistance leading to the need for more antibiotics.

It is important to read and understand labels to avoid these chemically/ pharmaceutically altered foods. The following are definitions of the terms you will likely find:

Organic applies to poultry, meat, dairy, and eggs. An organic label stipulates that animals must be raised on organically-grown feed, be free range, and grass-fed with no antibiotics or growth hormones added.

Wild Caught refers only to seafood which includes fish and shellfish. It defines fish that were harvested in the open ocean vs farm-raised. At present, organic regulations do not apply to seafood as the ocean environment cannot be controlled. As of this publication there is a growing industry that is "farm-raised organic" which includes sustainable methods of feeding and harvesting.

Farm-raised refers to seafood which might include shellfish. Farm-raised seafood is raised in man-made ponds often along coastal waters, in foreign countries, or facilities in the desert where land is cheap. The ponds are potentially subjected to contamination and severe pollution problems. Fish may come from "beds" or "net-pens" that are located in controlled ocean or river waters but have fresh seawater. Even so, these beds can be as contaminated as man-made ponds.

Natural or All Natural does not mean organic. Surprisingly, as of now, there are no regulated standard for these terms. The USDA defines "natural" as not containing any artificial flavoring, colors, chemical preservatives, or synthetic ingredients added to the processing of the food after slaughter. This, however, does not eliminate antibiotics, growth hormones, or the pesticides and herbicides used on the feed given to the animals before slaughter.

Free Range applies to chickens and eggs. This term is misleading, simply meaning the animals have space to roam freely inside the barn and outside for an "undetermined period each day." USDA standards are weak in this area.

Antibiotic-Free is free of antibiotics but not necessarily free of growth hormones.

Grass-Fed or Free Roaming refers to cattle that are allowed to graze on open land for a period of time. They will be barn fed for part of the time to help "finish" them or fatten them up. Completely grass-fed, free range meats tend to be very lean and somewhat tough unless they are "finished" with grain. These cattle differ from factory farmed feedlot cattle, which may never see, let alone eat, a blade of grass for most of their life.

No Hormones or Hormone Free can refer to poultry, meat, dairy, and eggs. These animals were not given growth hormones. However, most likely they were given antibiotics and non-organic feed.

Numerous studies have shown that the residual antibiotics in our food encourage the development of disease-causing micro-organisms that are immune to antibiotics. Data was so overwhelming that some of the larger chicken producers voluntarily cut back on the quantity of antibiotics in their animal feed. Growth hormones, referred to as rBGH (or Recumbent Growth Hormone), are fed to 17% of US dairy cattle. It causes a 20–40% increase in milk production and necessitates longer milking time. This leads to a dramatic increase in mastitis, a painful bacterial infection of the udder causing inflammation, swelling, pus and blood secretions into the milk. The dairy industry relies on antibiotics and pasteurization to destroy this bacterium. However, bacteria produce a lot of toxic waste which is not destroyed by pasteurization or antibiotics. This is yet another way we Americans are being affected by the overuse of antibiotics.

Feedlot raised cattle are fed growth hormones to increase their body weight twice as fast (one year instead of two) as a typical grass-fed animal. Growth hormones allow ranchers to bring animals to auction sooner, which turns their investment into profit more quickly. Growth hormones increase the potential for infections, then requiring the use of more antibiotics. Research studies show a link between growth hormones in our food supply and early onset menses for adolescent girls.

Got E. coli?

Feedlot raised cattle have four times the amount of E. coli in their gut as grass-fed cattle! Their diet consists mainly of genetically modified corn and soybean meal, liquid vitamins, and minerals. Grass-fed? There is not a blade of grass to be found in these mud holes of stench.

Organic is always my first preference when purchasing meats, poultry, and dairy. If organic is not available in your area, try to find labels that read "growth hormone and antibiotic free" or "no rBGH," or "free range" chicken or "grass-fed" beef. Look for "growth hormone free" on the label of milk by-products such as butter, cream, yogurt, cheese, kefir, and ice cream.

Seafood is a great choice of animal protein. The best choice is wild caught fish or fish freshly caught by you or a family member. Wild caught fish are more expensive than farm-raised fish, which are more widely available. Each year, we feed 14 million tons of wild caught fish (including anchovies, sardines, mackerel, and herring) to pigs and chickens around the world. That amounts to 17 percent of all the wild

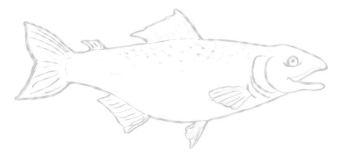

fish caught. Pigs and chickens eat double the amount of fish that the people of Japan consume annually, and six times more seafood than the entire U.S. population eats each year. Additionally, these fish tend to be higher in Omega-3 EFA, an essential fatty acid lacking in the standard American diet, so why are we feeding them to livestock?

Processed meats such as sausage, hot dogs, jerky, bacon, lunchmeat, and even meats in canned soup products are made with sodium nitrites or sodium nitrates. These ingredients convert into highly carcinogenic nitrosamines, potent cancer-causing chemicals that accelerate the formation and growth of cancer cells (especially pancreatic and colorectal cancer) throughout the body. Nitrite and nitrate free products are available in health food stores and will be marked on the label as such.

Proportions

Animal protein is a heavier protein to digest than the protein in beans, nuts, or whole grains. Additionally, the by-products of digestion from animal proteins are potentially more toxic. Therefore, it is necessary to balance meals that contain animal protein with at least three times more vegetables. Vegetable side dishes can include soup, vegetable juices, salads, and cooked vegetables. The majority of vegetables have an alkalizing effect and all animal protein has an acidifying effect. By balancing your meals with more vegetables than protein, you help keep your pH (acid/alkaline ratio) balanced. Additionally, the water and

fiber in vegetables helps keep waste matter moving through your system. Carnivores (meat eaters) have the shortest elimination tract which moves toxic waste matter through their elimination system quickly. Herbivores (plant eaters) have a longer tract, allowing for a very slow digestion of fibrous plant protein that makes up their diet. Humans are omnivores (meat and plant eaters) having a longer elimination tract than carnivores and shorter than herbivores. Fibrous vegetables and whole grain products help assist us in keeping things "moving along."

Shop Wisely

When purchasing fish, avoid pre-wrapped fish. If I cannot smell the fish first, I don't buy it. I will at times purchase frozen fish, as long as it is vacuum packed to prevent the fish from drying out. Frozen fish loose in a bag, no matter how cheap, will always be dry and tasteless.

Little or no odor indicates the first sign of freshness in meat or fish. I always purchase my meat from a butcher where I can view, smell, and choose cuts of meat before I buy. That is why I prefer to shop in smaller stores or health food stores that carry fresh cut meats rather than larger grocery chains where I am forced to choose from pre-packaged meats and seafood. Yes, I do believe in spending more to get better quality because my health and my family's health is worth it.

Storing

Use meats and poultry within three days of purchase, or freeze for later use. Most meats will have a "fresh by" date that will help determine how long you can keep it in your refrigerator. Cooked leftovers of poultry and beef can be "made over" into another meal up to 3–4 days later. My *Chicken Garden Enchiladas* is an example of how to use leftover cooked chicken. The protein in animal food is not lost after cooking or storage. Animal protein and fat does not contain large quantities of water-soluble vitamins, making it stable in most types of cooking, except high heat frying.

Should you use previously cooked vegetables? NO! Many vitamins and minerals are lost when vegetables are cooked, especially the water-soluble vitamins B and C. More than 60% of the vitamin C is lost after the first ten minutes of cooking. That is why having a variety of raw vegetables in salads, freshly squeezed vegetable juices, and freshly prepared are the best ways to get a wide range of vitamins. Reheating vegetables further depletes what is left. Cooked vegetable side dishes should be prepared and eaten fresh every day or at the latest, as part of the following day's meal.

Preparing Chicken

The juiciest chicken that you can make is easier than you may think. Keep boneless, skinless chicken breasts whole while cooking. Whether you are frying or simmering in a sauce, don't cut the chicken until it is cooked. Chicken has very little juice and if you cut it before it is cooked you will lose the juice and the chicken will become tough.

To cook chicken evenly, trim the breasts first. Take the breast and place on the cutting board with the thin side closest to you. With your knife held horizontally, slice off the thicker part of the chicken. Smaller sliced-off pieces can be cooked for sandwich ingredients or are a perfect kid-size portion. This will give you a breast filet that is evenly thick. Some would

recommend using a meat tenderizer to pound the filet but I think this causes too much juice loss. After it is cooked (usually 5–8 minutes), place on your board and cut into cubes or slices. If you prefer slicing, notice the direction of the "grain" or the muscle. Slice across the grain to get thin filet slices that will hold together.

Searing Meats

When you are searing or pan frying meats and poultry, it is best to use expeller pressed oils instead of extra virgin olive oil. Although I use extra virgin olive oil 90% of the time, I have other healthy oils in my pantry for higher heat cooking. Extra virgin olive oil has a low heat point and will foam when brought to higher temperatures. The foam contains air bubbles that will prevent the oil from getting hot enough. This is fine if you are sautéing, but if you want to sear or panfry you'll need oil that will not foam at higher temperatures. I use expeller pressed sesame oil (untoasted) for most of those needs. Organic canola oil or organic grape-seed oil are also good choices. You can find these oils at health food stores.

What, no meat?

Many people I meet today abstain from eating red meat with little understanding or knowledge of its dietary contribution of iron. Iron is an essential nutrient involved in oxygen transport. Two thirds of iron is found in hemoglobin, the protein in the red blood cells that carries oxygen to tissues. This oxygen is used for the energy required for proper cell growth and development, and provides fuel for other life-sustaining metabolic processes. A deficiency of iron limits oxygen delivery to cells, resulting in fatigue, poor work performance, decreased immunity, and anemia. On the other hand, excess amounts of iron can result in toxicity and even death. So, be sure if you are taking iron supplements, take the recommended daily allowance or consult your health practitioner.

Iron deficiency anemia is a worldwide health problem that is especially common in young women and children. Our bodies are not capable of absorbing all types of iron with equal efficiency. In other words, not all iron we consume is available to our bodies for use. Heme iron, found in red meat, seafood, and poultry, has the most bioavailability (most readily absorbed). Non-heme iron, which is less readily available, is found in whole grains, green leafy vegetables, beans, and sea vegetables. Consuming foods with both types of iron boosts the bioavailability. Additionally, the presence of vitamin C in a meal can increase the non-heme iron absorption up to six-fold. Eat vegetables containing vitamin C, such as broccoli, cauliflower, peppers, and tomatoes. Remember, cooking these vegetables more than 10 minutes can destroy much of the vitamin C. Caffeinated teas and coffee consumed with meals can block iron absorption.

Non-Heme (non-meat) Iron Rich Foods

RDA (recommended daily allowance) for iron is 18 mg for adult menstruating women and 8 mg for men.

Legumes, Beans or Seeds	Serving Size	Iron Content
Black Beans	1 cup	3.6 mg
Black-eyed Peas	1 cup	1.8 mg
Cashews	½ cup	2.65 mg
Chickpeas	½ cup	3.0 mg
Kidney Beans	½ cup	2.2 mg
Lentils	1 cup	6.6 mg
Lima Beans	½ cup	2.3 mg
Navy Beans	1 cup	4.5 mg
Peanuts	½ cup	1.5 mg
Pinto Beans	1 cup	3.6 mg
Soybeans	1 cup	8.8 mg
Soy Milk	1 cup	1.4 mg
Sunflower Seeds	1 ounce	1.4 mg
Tofu, firm	½ cup	3.4 mg
Walnuts	½ cup	3.75 mg

Whole Grains	Serving Size	Iron Content
Brown Rice	1 cup (cooked)	.8 mg
Whole Wheat Bread	1 slice	.9 mg
Whole Wheat Germ	2 Tbs	1.1 mg
Oatmeal	1 cup	1.6 mg
Total Cereal, fortified	1 ounce	18 mg
Cream of Wheat	1 cup	10 mg
Raisin Bran Cereal	1 cup	6.3 mg
Grits, enriched	1 cup	1.5 mg

Vegetables	Serving Size	Iron Content
Artichoke	whole	3.9 mg
Beets	1 cup	1.8 mg
Beet Greens	1 cup	1.0 mg
Broccoli, cooked	½ cup	.7 mg
Collard Greens	1 cup	2.0 mg
Green Beans	½ cup	.8 mg
Grean Peas	½ cup	1.8 mg
Jicama	⅓ cup	.8 mg
Kale	1 cup	1.1 mg
Mustard Greens	1 cup	.8 mg
Parsley	½ cup	1.8 mg
Potato with skin, baked	1	4.0 mg
Spinach, fresh	½ cup	3.2 mg
Swiss Chard	½ cup	2.0 mg
Turnip Greens	1 cup	.6 mg
Wheat Grass	1 ounce	1.8 mg

Miscellaneous	Serving Size	Iron Content
Apricots, dried	1 cup	7.2 mg
Egg	1	1.0 mg
Molasses, blackstrap	1 Tbs	3.5 mg
Peaches, dried	1 cup	9.3 mg
Prunes	½ cup	1.9 mg
Prune Juice	½ cup	5.2 mg
Raisins	½ cup	2.55 mg

Best Fish Tacos!

(Serves 4)

This is everyone's favorite! Do not be turned off by the ingredient list....it's simpler than it looks and to save time, you can purchase salsa instead of making it from scratch.

4-6 fillets orange or white roughy
3-4 Tbs extra-virgin olive oil or enough to cover the pan ¼" deep

Salsa:
2 cups chopped tomatoes
½ cup finely chopped green bell pepper
½ jalapeño pepper, minced
¼ tsp sea salt
⅓ cup minced red onion
⅓ cup chopped cilantro
2 Tbs lemon juice

Taco Sauce:
1 ripe avocado
1 cup salsa verde
1 clove garlic, minced
1 Tbs mayonnaise
¼ cup chopped fresh cilantro

1. Prepare salsa by combining ingredients in a medium bowl. Set aside.

2. Prepare taco sauce by placing ingredients in blender or food processor and blending until smooth and creamy. Set aside.

3. Prepare taco topping by slicing cabbage, romaine, and cilantro very thin. Chop enough to garnish the fish tacos.

4. Prepare fish topping by combining all ingredients except eggs in a shallow bowl. In a separate shallow bowl beat eggs. Cut fillets in half lengthwise. Dip fish in egg and then in topping on both sides, pressing down on each side. Place on a plate or paper towel as you continue to coat all the fillets.

5. Preheat oil in large frying pan on medium heat. Test oil by dropping a little of the breading into the oil. If it begins to sizzle immediately it is ready for the fish. If oil is hot enough, place as many fillets as you can fit in the pan without overcrowding. The key to crispy fried fish is to keep the oil hot by not overcrowding the pan and keeping the flame on medium-high. Continue to panfry all the fillets until golden brown on both sides. Remove fish and drain on paper towels.

6. To assemble a taco, place a corn tortilla in a dry small frying pan on low heat and sprinkle some cheddar cheese down the middle. Cover and allow cheese to melt while tortilla warms, about 1–2 minutes. Remove tortilla, pile a piece of fish, then sauce, cabbage topping, and salsa on top, fold, and enjoy! These are easy to overeat as they taste so good.

Serving Suggestion: If you have leftover sauce or salsa you can freeze it up to two months. Fish, unfortunately, never tastes the same the next day so make only as much as you need for one meal.

Fish Topping:
2   large eggs, beaten
1   cup Panko flakes (found in
    most grocery stores or Asian
    markets)
⅓   cup unbleached flour
½   tsp sea salt
½   tsp dried thyme leaves
½   tsp garlic powder
½   tsp ground cumin
½   tsp chili powder
1   tsp dried oregano leaves

Taco Topping:
1   cup shredded cheddar
    cheese (cow's, rice, or
    almond cheese)
8   corn tortillas
⅛   head green cabbage, thinly
    sliced
¼   cup chopped fresh cilantro
6   romaine leaves, thinly sliced

Bison Chili Con Carne

(Serves 4–6)

Yes, bison (or buffalo) is a flavorful alternative to beef that is low in fat, and free range without hormones or antibiotics. Found in larger health food stores or on the web shipped directly to you!

3 Tbs extra-virgin olive oil, divided
1 cup chopped onion
3 cloves garlic, minced
½ cup chopped green or red bell pepper
1 jalapeño, minced (less if you don't like spicy)
½ lb ground bison or bison stew cuts
2 bay leaves
3 cup precooked red beans (kidney, chili, or pinto), rinsed and drained
28 oz can crushed tomatoes
¼ tsp chili powder
2 tsp ground cumin
1 tsp dried oregano
1 Tbs soy sauce
½ tsp sea salt

Optional: ½ cup corn. Ground beef can be substituted for bison.

1. Preheat 2 Tbs oil in a large soup pot; add onion and garlic, and sauté for 2–3 minutes on medium heat. Add bell pepper and jalapeño and sauté for another 2 minutes. Remove from heat and set aside.

2. In a large frying pan over medium-high heat, add 1 Tbs oil and bison. If using ground meat, break up with a spoon in order for heat and oil to reach the meat. Continue stirring and breaking up meat until it is browned.

3. Add bison to pot with vegetables along with remaining ingredients: beans, tomatoes, 1 cup water and spices. Cover, heat on medium-high until it begins to boil, and then reduce heat to simmer on medium-low. Cook for another 15 minutes. Check for seasoning and adjust to your liking.

Serving Suggestion: Serve with a fresh green salad or steamed broccoli. My *Corn and Chili Bread* (following recipe) would be a wonderful addition to this hearty chili.

Comparison of Ground Meats (per 3.5 oz serving)

Animal	Calories	Protein	Total Fat	Saturated Fat	Cholesterol
Bison, grass-fed	146	20.23 g	7.21 g	2.917 g	55 mg
Beef, 90% lean	176	20.00 g	10.00 g	4.058 g	65 mg
Pork, 84% lean	218	17.99 g	16.00 g	5.362 g	68 mg
Turkey	149	17.46 g	8.26 g	2.250 g	79 mg
Chicken	143	17.44 g	8.10 g	2.301 g	86 mg

Corn and Chili Bread

(Serves 9)

Just a little sweet and spicy, this is a great cornbread to serve with my **Bison Chili Con Carne** *or* **Vegetarian Chili** *in the* **Bean Cuisine** *chapter.*

Dry ingredients:
1 ½ cups unbleached white flour
⅓ cup yellow cornmeal
¼ cup organic cane sugar
1 Tbs baking powder
1 tsp sea salt

Wet ingredients:
¾ cup buttermilk (or cow's, rice, or almond milk)
2 Tbs extra-virgin olive oil
2 large eggs, beaten

Veggies:
2 scallions, minced
⅓ cup finely chopped fresh cilantro
½ small jalapeno pepper, minced or 4 oz can pickled jalapeno
½ cup fresh corn, preferably roasted on the grill, or frozen

1. Preheat oven to 350°F. Lightly oil a 9 x 12-inch baking pan or 8-inch cast iron frying pan.

2. In a medium sized bowl, mix dry ingredients thoroughly. In a separate small bowl mix wet ingredients thoroughly. Now combine wet and dry ingredients together and mix well. Toss in vegetables and mix again.

3. Pour into baking pan. Bake for 35–40 minutes or until a toothpick inserted in the center of the pan comes out clean. Let cool for 5 minutes before cutting.

Serving Suggestion: You can eliminate the veggies and just have a simple and delicious cornbread. I love plain cornbread with organic butter and organic raspberry jam.

Bites of Insight

To roast corn on the cob, boil or steam shucked corn for 5 minutes. Remove from heat and drain. Have grill on high heat. Brush corn with olive oil and a little salt. Place on grill and turn every minute for even browning. To grill corn with husks, first remove outer tough green husk. Pull back but do not remove inner husk and remove silk. Brush corn with butter. Wrap corn with the husks and tie to secure. Place on grill for 20–30 minutes while turning frequently.

Black Bean and Sausage Stew

(Serves 4–6)

*Inspired by my husband as the "meat" version of my **Three Sisters Stew** in the **Bean Cuisine** chapter. Another one of our favorites.*

2   Tbs extra-virgin olive oil
1   small onion, chopped
2   cloves garlic, minced
½   cup chopped red or green bell pepper
½   jalapeño pepper, minced or ½ tsp hot red pepper flakes
1   cup chopped carrots
½   cup chopped celery
1   tsp ground cumin
1   tsp dried oregano
1   tsp sea salt
1   quart chicken broth
15 oz can black beans or 2 cups precooked black beans, rinsed and drained
15 oz can diced tomatoes
½   cup cooked corn
4   chicken sausages, precooked (mix with spicy varieties)
⅓   cup chopped scallions (for garnish)

1. In a medium sized soup pot, sauté onion and garlic in olive oil for 2–3 minutes on medium heat. Add bell pepper and jalapeño pepper and sauté another 2 minutes.

2. Add carrots, celery, cumin, oregano, salt, and chicken broth. Cover and bring to a boil. Continue simmering until carrots are tender, about 5 minutes.

3. Add beans, diced tomatoes, and corn. Return to medium-high heat. Simmer for 5 more minutes.

4. Cut sausage into 1-inch pieces. Add sausage and mix thoroughly and reheat. Add more vegetable broth or water to reach desired consistency. Garnish with chopped scallions and serve.

Serving Suggestion: Serve with a salad and whole grain bread.

Note: Prepared chicken sausages are widely available in a variety of

flavors. Almost any flavor will work in this recipe except a chicken apple variety. I like combining a spicy cajun or andouille sausage with a milder variety to add some kick.

Chicken Garden Enchiladas

(Serves 4–6)

A satisfying and filling meal for any occasion. Use your leftover cooked chicken for this quick dinner.

2   Tbs extra-virgin olive oil
¼   cup chopped onion
2   cloves garlic, minced
¼   cup each chopped green and
    red bell pepper
½   jalapeno pepper, minced
⅓   cup diced zucchini
¼   cup minced fresh cilantro
1   tsp ground cumin
1   tsp dried oregano leaves
½   tsp sea salt
1   chicken breast and 1 thigh,
    cooked and shredded or
    chopped
8   oz diced tomatoes (approx. ½
    15 oz can)
½   cup precooked black or pinto
    beans, rinsed and drained
2   4 oz cans enchilada sauce
⅓   cup shredded cheddar
    cheese
4   corn tortillas

Optional: Add ¼ tsp chili powder
if you like more spice.

1. Preheat oven to 375°F. Preheat oil in large frying pan and sauté onions and garlic for 2–3 minutes on medium heat. Add green and red peppers, jalapeño, zucchini, and cilantro. Simmer, covered, until vegetables are tender, about 4 minutes. Add cumin, oregano, and salt and stir.

2. Add chicken and canned tomatoes, stir, and cover for 2–3 more minutes. Add beans, a little enchilada sauce (to bind), and cover again. Mixture should be firm. Remove from heat.

3. Heat tortillas in small frying pan or in oven for 1 minute to soften. If desired you can add some shredded cheese to the inside of the tortilla before wrapping. Once soft, fill with chicken mixture and wrap enchilada style (rolled up). Spread a little of the enchilada sauce evenly on the bottom of a square 8 x 8-inch baking pan, Place enchiladas close together on top of sauce with seams facing down. Drizzle more sauce between each enchilada and cover with cheese.

4. Bake uncovered for 20–30 minutes, until cheese melts and enchilada is heated through. These can be prepared in advance and refrigerated prior to cooking. If they are coming out of the refrigerator, allow at least 30 minutes to heat through.

Serving Suggestion: Just add a salad and you have a complete dinner. An additional pan of enchiladas can be prepared, wrapped well with plastic wrap (yes, pan and all) and frozen for another dinner, but don't melt cheese before freezing.

Blackened Red Snapper with Corn Relish

(Serves 4)

This spicy snapper is balanced with a cool summer relish of corn, tomatoes, and avocados. Substitute other fillets such as catfish if you wish, as long as they are firm and thick.

4   red snapper fillets
2   Tbs extra-virgin olive oil

Seasoning mix:
½ tsp each of dried thyme, dried oregano, cayenne pepper, ground paprika, and ground black pepper
1   tsp onion powder
1   tsp arrowroot or organic cornstarch

Relish:
¼ cup fresh or frozen corn
1   cup coarsely chopped tomatoes
1   avocado, cubed
¼ cup minced red onion
¼ cup chopped fresh cilantro
2   cloves garlic, minced
2   limes (one for garnish, one for juicing)
½ tsp sea salt

1. To make relish, combine corn, tomatoes, avocado, onion, cilantro, garlic, lime juice, and salt and refrigerate until ready to serve.

2. To make seasoning, combine all the ingredients in a small bowl and transfer to plate. Press both sides of fillets in mixture and set aside.

3. Preheat oil in a medium sized frying pan on high heat. Test oil for readiness by dropping a little seasoning in the pan. If it begins to sizzle immediately, it is ready. Place a few fillets slowly into the oil and fry on both sides until fish is tender and flaky. Serve with relish and lime wedges.

Note: Arrowroot comes from the tuber root of an arrowroot plant and can be substituted for cornstarch in most dishes.

Bites of Insight

Do not overcrowd pan or the oil will cool and the fish will absorb too much oil. The trick to lightly frying is that the temperature of the oil must remain consistent, which is achieved by not overcrowding the pan.

Chicken Parmesan

(Serves 4)

So quick and easy, you will want to serve this many times! Make extra, and before melting cheese, freeze it for another dinner. A vegetarian version, **Tofu Parmesan,** *is found in the* **The Other White Meat—Soy** *section at the end of this chapter.*

4   chicken breasts
1 ½ cups Italian bread crumbs
2   Tbs extra-virgin olive oil
2–3 cups prepared tomato sauce
      or pasta sauce
½   lb mozzarella cheese,
      shredded or sliced
2   large eggs, beaten

1. Preheat oven to 375°F. In a shallow bowl large enough to accommodate a chicken breast, beat eggs with a fork and set aside. Place bread crumbs in another shallow bowl.

2. Rinse and pat dry chicken breasts. Trim off fat with kitchen shears or a knife. Use a knife to horizontally slice off the thickest side of the breast, so the chicken will cook evenly. Or, flatten with a meat mallet.

3. First dip both sides of chicken into egg mixture, then dip both sides into bread crumbs. Place on plate and repeat until all the chicken is breaded.

4. Preheat a medium sized frying pan with ¼-inch of oil. To test oil for readiness, drop some bread crumbs in the pan. If it begins to sizzle immediately, it is ready for the chicken. Place breaded chicken breasts in hot oil. Do not overcrowd pan or the oil will cool and the chicken will absorb too much oil. The trick to lightly frying is to keep the temperature of the oil consistent, which is achieved by not overcrowding the pan.

5. Fry chicken in oil on medium to high heat until lightly browned on both sides. Once browned, remove chicken and allow to drain on paper towels. Only add more oil if there is no oil remaining, and always add before the next new batch of chicken. Also remove any burned bread crumbs before each new batch of chicken.

6. Spread tomato sauce on the bottom of a 9 x 13-inch baking dish, about one inch deep. Place chicken breasts on top of sauce, side by side. Do not layer chicken, and do not add sauce over chicken.

7. Sprinkle with shredded mozzarella cheese, cover with foil, and bake for 15–20 minutes. Remove foil and bake an additional 10 minutes.

Coconut Shrimp with Mango Salsa

(Serves 4)

12 jumbo raw shrimp, peeled, with tails on
1 large egg, beaten
¼ cup unbleached white flour
⅓ cup finely shredded coconut
⅓ cup white sesame seeds
   natural vegetable oil (canola, peanut, safflower, etc.)

Salsa:
1 mango, peeled and diced
½ small red onion, finely diced
¼ cup chopped fresh cilantro
1 lime, juiced
⅛ tsp each sea salt and ground black pepper (or to taste)

1. To butterfly the shrimp, cut three-quarters into (but not through) the underside of the shrimp. Remove the vein and spread open each "wing" and press down to flatten.

2. Beat egg in a small bowl. Set aside 2 more bowls, one with the flour, and one with the coconut and sesame seed mixture.

3. Dip each shrimp first into the flour, then into the egg mixture, followed by the coconut mixture, making sure to press down so ingredients adhere to shrimp. Place shrimp fanned out on cookie sheet and refrigerate for 15 minutes to firm up again.

4. Cut mango into cubes by holding the mango on its edge with the stem end up. Take a sharp large knife and cut straight down about a half inch away from the stem end. The mango nut is a flat wide seed in the center so cut the mango in half on both sides of this wide seed. You will feel your knife along the side of the seed as you slice down. Turn mango around and repeat on the other side of the stem end. Now taking mango half in your hand and with a smaller knife, make scoring cuts about a half inch apart into but not through the mango. Now turn the mango and cut across these scoring cuts. You will have cut cubes of mango. Grabbing with both your hands, turn skin inside out. Mango cubes will pop up and you can easily slice them off into a bowl. Add the diced onion, cilantro, lime juice, salt, and pepper.

5. Preheat oil in frying pan. To test oil for readiness, drop a little coconut in oil. If it sizzles immediately the oil is ready. Place shrimp in oil and fry for 20–30 seconds or until the shrimp turns pink. Be sure not to crowd the frying pan or it will cool the oil while making the shrimp soggy. Remove and cool on paper towel. Serve on a bed of lettuce (3 shrimp per person) and garnish with salsa.

Chicken Stew with Garden Vegetables

(Serves 2–3)

2 boneless and skinless chicken breasts
3 Tbs extra-virgin olive oil, divided
3 cloves garlic, minced
¼ cup finely chopped onion
1 carrot, diced
1 celery stalk, diced
¼ cup corn, fresh or frozen
3 red potatoes, quartered
1 cup chicken broth
¼ cup chopped fresh parsley
¾ tsp dried thyme
¼ tsp dried sage
¼ tsp dried rosemary
1 tsp sea salt
¼ tsp white or black pepper
8 string beans, halved
½ cup green peas, fresh or frozen

Roux or White Sauce:
2 Tbs butter
1 Tbs unbleached white flour
1 cup milk or unsweetened almond milk

1. Rinse chicken breasts and pat dry. Place breast on a cutting board with the fattest side away from you. With a sharp knife held horizontally, slice off the top of the thicker part of the chicken. Preheat 2 Tbs oil in medium frying pan and cook chicken on medium for 4–5 minutes or until chicken is browned. Remove from pan and set aside.

2. Preheat 1 Tbs oil in medium frying pan and sauté garlic and onion in olive oil for 2–3 minutes. Add carrots, celery, corn, potatoes, and chicken broth. Cover pan and simmer for 5 minutes or until vegetables are tender.

3. Add string beans and peas. Cut cooked chicken into ½-inch cubes and add to frying pan. Add herbs. Simmer, covered, for 4–5 minutes or until string beans are tender but still bright green. Turn off heat and keep covered.

4. To make a roux (gravy base), melt butter in a small frying pan, add flour, and slowly stir for 2–3 minutes. Slowly add milk while stirring, breaking up any lumps that may form. Continue adding milk until a creamy consistency is achieved. Make gravy a little thicker than you ultimately want it.

5. Combine gravy with vegetables and chicken. Add dumplings (see following recipe). You can also serve this stew with homemade biscuits. Or you can pour stew into a round baking dish and cover with premade pie crust top, crimp edges, and bake for 30 minutes.

Dumplings for Chicken Stew

(Serves 2–3)

Dumplings go back to the colonial days when pioneers traveled by covered wagon without ovens, so cooking biscuits on top of the stews was common. Later, many folks took the same batter and made baked biscuits to serve on top of the chicken stews. I have asked several people about their childhood version of chicken and dumplings, and have received a variety of preparations. The more common one is a biscuit batter baked on top of the casserole in the oven instead of steamed dumplings in a pot. Both are good, but quite different.

2 ½ cups unbleached flour
3   tsp baking powder
1   tsp sea salt
3   Tbs shortening or butter
2   Tbs chopped fresh parsley
1 ¼ cups milk

1. Mix dry ingredients together. Using either two knives or a pastry blender, cut in shortening or butter until mixture is coarse and grainy. Add chopped parsley and slowly add milk. Do not overmix. It should only take a few turns to incorporate the milk.

2. Drop large spoonfuls on top of simmering stew. Simmer 5 minutes with the lid off the pot and then cover and simmer 15–20 minutes longer. Dumplings should be light and fluffy. Serve immediately.

Note: Spectrum Naturals has a vegetable shortening that does not contain hydrogenated fats or oils. It looks and works similarly to the shortening you might have used before, but is made from expeller pressed oils. It is available in health food stores only.

Crunchy Corn Crusted Picnic Chicken

(Serves 4)

I love the way this chicken comes out! This is a frequent picnic for the sailing days on our boat!

1 lb chicken tenders

Marinade:
2 cups buttermilk
½ tsp Tabasco sauce
½ tsp sea salt

Cornflake Batter:
2 cups ground cornflakes (find flakes that are organic and low in sugar)
1 tsp dried basil leaves
1 tsp dried oregano leaves
½ tsp dried thyme leaves
½ tsp ground cumin
½ tsp sea salt
⅛ tsp ground black pepper
½ tsp granulated garlic
   Canola or safflower spray cooking oil

1. Combine marinade ingredients, add chicken and refrigerate overnight or at least a few hours. Remove chicken, drain on paper towel leaving some marinade on the chicken. Cut into long bite-size pieces. Discard marinade. You can skip the marinade step if you are in a hurry. Preheat oven to 400°F.

2. Place cornflakes in ziplock bag and crush with rolling pin. If you don't have a rolling pin, any hard cylinder will do (side of a can) or even the back of your hand will work too. Do not over crush them or you'll end up with corn flour. Add remaining spices, close bag, and shake to blend.

3. Pour cornflake mixture onto a flat dish. Dip chicken, and roll on both sides into the corn flakes. Transfer to a wire cookie rack that is placed over a cookie sheet. Place chicken on rack and spray chicken with cooking oil on both sides. Bake for 5 minutes. Turn chicken over and bake again for 5 minutes. Serve with my dipping sauce (see following recipe) or your own favorite sauce.

Serving Suggestion: If making chicken ahead of time, allow it to cool completely and store it in an airtight container in the refrigerator. This recipe tastes best when made the same day.

Dipping Sauces for Crunchy Corn Crusted Picnic Chicken

(Serves 4)

Two dipping sauce possibilities…very different and both very good—if you have time, make both!

Spicy BBQ Sauce:
1 Tbs extra-virgin olive oil
1 small onion, minced
2 cloves garlic, minced
1 stalk celery, chopped
¾ cup ketchup
1 tsp ground paprika
½ tsp cayenne pepper
½ cup beer (dark ale is best)
¼ cup apple cider vinegar
1 Tbs Worcestershire sauce
¼ tsp hickory liquid smoke
1 tsp brown sugar
½ tsp sea salt

1. In a medium frying pan, sauté onion, garlic, and celery in oil for 2–3 minutes on medium heat.

2. Combine remaining ingredients in a small bowl. Now add cooked onion, garlic, and celery and mix thoroughly. Refrigerate for at least an hour. This spicy and sweet sauce really balances the Picnic Chicken.

Serving Suggestion: The spicy sauce will last for a month in the refrigerator (maybe longer, but ours never stays around that long). Add it to meat dishes or use as part of the sauce for the *Spicy Orange Beef* recipe in this chapter. Try this dipping sauce as a sandwich spread, with fried fish, or with my *Sweet Potato Home Fries* recipe in the *Vegetables— Nature's Bounty* chapter.

Dijon Dipping Sauce:
¼ cup Dijon mustard
1 Tbs mayonnaise
1 Tbs honey or agave syrup
1 tsp dried tarragon
¼ tsp sea salt

1. Combine all ingredients and chill for 1 hour before serving with chicken.

Crusted Ling Cod with Orange Ginger Sauce

(Serves 4)

This elegant and delicate fish entrée is great for company. I prepared this entrée for a private cooking class and it was a big hit!

4   6 oz pieces of Ling Cod
½   cup pine nuts
¼   cup white sesame seeds
¼   cup black sesame seeds
    (found in Asian markets or in
    Asian section of grocery stores)
1   cup unbleached white flour
2   large eggs, beaten
3   Tbs extra-virgin olive oil

Orange Ginger Sauce:
1   Tbs arrowroot or organic
    cornstarch
2   Tbs water
½   cup orange juice, preferably
    fresh squeezed
1   Tbs fresh grated ginger juice
1   Tbs organic cane sugar,
    agave, or honey
¼   tsp ground cinnamon
⅛   tsp sea salt

Optional: Use true cod, halibut, or other thick white fish or fish steak.

1. Preheat oven to 350°F. In a small blender, chop pine nuts coarsely and mix with sesame seeds. Set aside in a small shallow bowl.

2. Place flour in another shallow bowl. Beat eggs in separate shallow bowl and set aside.

3. Pat the fillets dry and dredge (quickly dip) in flour on one side. Then dip in beaten eggs and press into the seed mixture on the same side.

4. Preheat oil in medium frying pan on medium-high heat. Oil is hot enough to fry when a drop of flour begins to sizzle immediately. Place seeded side down and fry for 30 seconds or until seeds become light golden brown. You are not cooking the fish, just browning the seeds. Remove fish into a 9 x 13-inch baking dish with seed side up.

5. Bake for 6–8 minutes or until fish flakes easily when a fork is inserted into the thickest part of the fish.

6. While fish is baking, dissolve arrowroot in water and place in small saucepan with remaining ingredients. See below for "ginger juice." Simmer on low until it thickens and drizzle over fish.

Bites of Insight

To make ginger juice, grate fresh ginger against a small-holed handheld cheese grater until you get ginger pulp coming out of the other side of the grater. Take this pulp and squeeze it in the palm of your hand to release the ginger juice. Discard pulp. This is easier and quicker than mincing.

Jambalaya

(Serves 4–6)

Like so many dishes that become classic local fare, jambalaya was designed to use leftovers. Basically, anything goes. There are a wide variety of ways to make jambalaya: with chicken, sausage, shrimp, ham, even duck, or alligator. New Orleans Creole-style "red" jambalaya is made with tomatoes and chicken stock. Cajun-style "brown" jambalaya is made with chicken or beef gravy and often contains okra.

3   Tbs extra-virgin olive oil, divided
½   lb total of boneless chicken, cubed and/or shrimp, pork ribs, turkey, or ham
½   lb hot smoked sausage or smoked ham, diced
1   medium onion, chopped
3   cloves garlic, minced
¾   cup diced green bell pepper
4   stalks celery, chopped
5   oz can tomato paste
1   quart beef stock or chicken stock
3   cups crushed tomatoes or 28 oz can crushed tomatoes
3   bay leaves
1   tsp sea salt
¼   tsp ground black pepper
2   Tbs Creole seasoning blend or Cajun spice mix
½   cup chopped scallions

Optional: Sliced frozen or fresh okra

1. Preheat 2 Tbs oil in frying pan and brown the chicken on both sides. Remove and set aside. Brown the smoked sausage in the same pan and remove and set aside.

2. In a large pot, add 1 Tbs oil and sauté the onion, garlic, green pepper, and celery on medium heat until onions are transparent, about 2–3 minutes.

3. Add the tomato paste and stir until the paste browns. Browning the paste adds an additional depth of flavor to the sauce because the natural sugar in the tomato caramelizes, deepening the flavor and color. Continue stirring for 2 minutes.

4. Add beef or chicken stock, crushed tomatoes, bay leaves, salt, and pepper. Add Creole seasoning (and okra if you are using it). Cover and cook over medium heat for about 10 minutes.

5. Add precooked meat, chicken, or seafood and cook another 5 minutes. If you are using seafood, be careful not to overcook it. Check seasonings and adjust to your taste.

Wow! Turkey Burgers

(Serves 4)

I am told these are the best turkey burgers that people have tasted. See for yourself! Turn some of this mixture into turkey meatballs and turkey meatloaf to freeze for later dinners.

2	lbs ground free range turkey meat (1 lb breast and 1 lb dark meat)
1	Tb extra-virgin olive oil
1	small onion, minced
¼	cup minced fresh parsley
2	tsp dried tarragon
1	medium carrot
1	small zucchini
½	tsp garlic powder
1	tsp sea salt
¼	tsp ground black pepper
¼	cup natural vegetable oil for frying

1. Place ground turkey in a large bowl. Preheat oil in a medium frying pan and sauté onion for 2–3 minutes. Add parsley and tarragon and sauté 30 seconds longer. Add this to turkey meat.

2. Grate carrot and zucchini with vegetable (box) grater on the medium sized holes. Add to turkey mixture with remaining ingredients: garlic powder, salt, and pepper and mix well.

3. Form into burgers, 5–6 inches wide and 1 ½ inches thick. Place patties on cookie sheet or plate and continue forming burgers until all mixture is used. Make sure the burgers are evenly shaped all around and the sides are as thick as the center. Preheat oil in frying pan on medium-high heat. Test the oil by dropping a little bit of turkey mixture into the oil. If it begins to sizzle immediately, the oil is ready. Cook 3–4 burgers at one time. After about 4 minutes when burgers have browned, turn over and cook the other side. Cook another 4–5 minutes. Burgers will swell and puff up a little. Do not cover yet and do not pat them down. They should be firm to the touch when pressed in the middle. If not firm, cover, reduce heat to medium and cook another few minutes.

Serving Suggestion: To freeze for later use, form burgers but do not cook them. Unused mixture can also be made into small 2-inch turkey balls. Place turkey balls on an oiled cookie sheet. Bake in preheated 350°F oven for 5 minutes; shake sheet to roll balls; bake again for 5 minutes. Freeze to use in sauces, soups, and casseroles.

Bites of Insight

How can you tell when your steak or burger is cooked without cutting into it? Restaurant chefs will poke it and test for texture. If it is rare, it will feel soft like the skin between your thumb and index finger. If it is medium, it will feel as firm as the pad of your hand at the base of your thumb. Well done? It will be as firm as the center of the palm of your hand. Heat and time will vary depending on your cookware and whether you use a gas or electric stove. You will learn from experience how to get these just perfect without drying them out. There's no need for a meat thermometer....just poke it! I have used this technique without fail.

Spicy Orange Beef

(Serves 4)

The orange zest flavor with chili spices up this dish. The dark sauce is rich and satisfying.

¾ lb top round beef, fat trimmed (grass-fed is best!)
3 Tbs arrowroot or organic cornstarch, divided
1 tsp orange zest
2 Tbs extra-virgin olive oil
2 cloves garlic, minced
¼ lb string beans, halved (2 cups)
1 red bell pepper, seeded and cut into strips
2 carrots, cut into matchsticks
1 Tbs fresh ginger, peeled and cut into matchsticks

Sauce:
1 tsp grated orange zest
1 tsp low-sodium beef broth
¼ cup orange juice
2 Tbs soy sauce
1 Tbs organic cane sugar
1 tsp chili-garlic sauce or ¼ tsp crushed red pepper flakes

1. Slice beef into thin strips ¼-inch wide. Combine 2 Tbs of arrowroot or cornstarch and 1 tsp of the orange zest. Dredge (dip) beef slices into cornstarch mixture and place on a plate. Set aside for the moment.

2. Preheat oil in a large frying pan (or wok) over medium-high heat. Oil is hot enough when a bit of cornstarch mixture begins to immediately sizzle when placed in oil. Add beef and stir-fry quickly just to take the red color out. Overcooking the beef will toughen it. Remove beef and set aside. Cover to keep warm.

3. To the same pan, add additional oil if necessary, and garlic, string beans, red bell pepper, carrots, and ginger. Sauté for 2–3 minutes on medium heat. Remove and add to beef.

4. In a small bowl, combine 1 Tbs arrowroot or cornstarch, orange zest, broth, orange juice, soy sauce, cane sugar, and chili-garlic sauce. Stir sauce mixture thoroughly before adding it to frying pan. Stir constantly until mixture thickens and no lumps are present, about 2–3 minutes. Add beef and vegetables back into frying pan, heat to serve. Serve over brown rice.

Serving Suggestion: Add more vegetables such as snow peas or summer squash if you like. You can also substitute chicken or tofu for the beef.

Bites of Insight

Organic cornstarch is made from non-GMO corn (genetically modified) which I prefer. Arrowroot starch comes from the root of the arrowroot plant. It is invaluable in cooking when you wish to have a clear, thickened sauce, like a fruit sauce. Unlike cornstarch, arrowroot starch will stay clear during cooking.

Salmon Quinoa Cakes

(Serves 4–6)

A good way to use leftover salmon as this can stretch your food budget. Another sailing day picnic lunch for us!

½ cup quinoa
¾ tsp sea salt, divided
¼ cup green peas
1 Tbs extra-virgin olive oil
¼ cup minced onion
¼ lb precooked salmon, wild caught
2 Tbs finely chopped fresh dill
1 large egg, beaten
1 Tbs arrowroot or organic cornstarch
¼ tsp powdered ginger, or fresh minced ginger
⅛ tsp ground black pepper
natural vegetable oil for frying

Optional: Add 1 tsp capers for an added salty "punch."

1. In a medium sized pot, bring 1 cup water to boil. Rinse quinoa and drain. Add quinoa to boiling water with ¼ tsp salt, cover and reduce heat to medium-low. Simmer for 15 minutes. Add peas to the top of quinoa without stirring them and cover again. Let the peas steam for 5 minutes. Remove from heat and place quinoa and peas in a large mixing bowl to cool.

2. In a small frying pan, sauté onion for 2–3 minutes on medium heat. Add to the quinoa.

3. Using your fingers, crumble the cooked salmon into the quinoa. Add dill, ginger, ½ tsp salt, and pepper. Add egg and arrowroot or cornstarch. Begin to work this with your hands and start forming cakes about 3–4 inches wide and at least 1-inch thick. Set on a plate or cookie sheet and continue forming the remaining cakes.

4. Cool cakes in the refrigerator for an hour. This makes them easier to fry. Preheat oil ¼-inch deep in a large frying pan. Oil is ready when a little of the mixture begins to sizzle immediately. In order for the cakes to brown the oil must be kept hot. Keep the flame on medium-high and don't overcrowd the pan with too many cakes. Fry until the cakes are browned. Flip to the other side and brown again. Remove from pan and serve immediately with your favorite wasabi mayonnaise.

Spicy Salmon Rub

(Makes 4)

Wow flavor… both spicy and sweet. Serve with the mango salsa in my **Coconut Shrimp with Mango Salsa** *recipe in this chapter.*

2   salmon fillets, wild caught
3   Tbs extra-virgin olive oil

Dry Rub:
2   Tbs organic cane sugar
1   Tbs chili powder
1   tsp ground black pepper
2   tsp ground cumin
2   tsp ground paprika
2   tsp sea salt
½   tsp dry mustard
½   tsp ground cinnamon

1. Preheat oven to 350°F. Combine dry rub ingredients in a shallow bowl. Press each fillet firmly into rub, enough for spices to stick to fish on one side only.

2. Preheat oil in medium frying pan on medium-high heat. Place salmon top-side down in pan and fry for 1–2 minutes, long enough to "sear" on spices. Remove and place in baking pan, top side up and bake for 8 minutes. Alternately, after searing, finish cooking salmon in frying pan—flip salmon over, cover, reduce heat to medium-low and cook for 5–6 minutes or until salmon flakes easily. Or another option is to broil it in a toaster oven or conventional oven for 8 minutes on the medium rack after searing.

Serving Suggestion: Serve this with my *Herbed Couscous with Garbanzo Beans* from the *Salads that Satisfy* chapter, or *Hawaiian Cole Slaw* and *Crunchy Jicama Cabbage Salad* in the *Fresh Garden Salads* chapter.

Curried Coconut Tofu & Veggies

(Serves 4)

Although I'm a New Englander and was raised on meat and potatoes, I occasionally enjoy curry and this is one of my favorites.

2	Tbs light sesame oil
½	cup chopped onion
4	cloves garlic, minced
1	Tbs peeled and minced fresh ginger
1	cup chopped green cabbage
1	cup sliced carrots
1	cup cauliflower florets
1	lb firm tofu, cubed
½	cup vegetable stock or water
1	cup frozen peas
1	tsp sea salt
15	oz can light coconut milk
2	tsp curry powder
¼	cup chopped fresh cilantro (for garnish)

Optional: Small 15 oz can diced tomatoes

1. In a large frying pan, preheat sesame oil on medium heat. Sauté onion, garlic, and ginger for 2–3 minutes.

2. Add cabbage, carrots, cauliflower, tofu, and vegetable stock or water. Cover and simmer for 5–8 minutes. Stir in peas, salt, coconut milk, and curry. If using diced tomatoes, add them now. Cover again and simmer for 2–3 minutes.

3. Adjust flavors to your liking and garnish with fresh cilantro before serving.

Serving Suggestion: If you serve this with brown rice, couscous, quinoa, or any other whole grain, you are serving a dish high in protein and fiber. Skip the chicken or beef and serve with a green salad.

Mapo Doufu with Peppers

(Serves 4)

Asian flavor with lots of color! Serve over rice.

1   Tbs light sesame oil
1 ½ tsp toasted sesame oil
1   clove garlic, minced
½   cup minced leek bottoms
    (onions or scallions can be
    substituted)
½   cup chopped red bell pepper
8   mushrooms, sliced
    (shiitake or cremini can be
    substituted)
1   lb package firm tofu, cut into
    1-inch cubes
3   scallions, minced
    (for garnish)

Sauce:
½   cup vegetable stock or water
1 ½ tsp sake, white wine, or mirin*
2 ½ tsp soy sauce
½   tsp sea salt
1 ½ tsp ketchup
2   tsp arrowroot or organic
    cornstarch

1. Preheat both oils together in a large frying pan on medium heat. Add garlic, leek bottoms, and red pepper. Stir-fry for 2 minutes. Add mushrooms and sauté for 1 minute.

2. While mushrooms are cooking, combine water or stock, sake, soy sauce, salt, ketchup, and arrowroot in a separate bowl. Add to frying pan with veggies and simmer for 2 minutes while sauce thickens.

3. Add tofu cubes and reduce heat to medium for 3–4 minutes. Garnish with scallions.

Serving Suggestion: Tofu supplies the protein in this dish. Serve over brown rice or Udon noodles (Japanese pasta) for a delicious vegetarian meal.

Bites of Insight

Mapo doufu is a popular Chinese dish from the Szechuan province. It is often cooked with minced meat, usually pork or beef. Other variations of ingredients include water chestnuts, onions, other vegetables, or wood ear fungus, but it's always spicy.

* Mirin is a sweet wine vinegar that can be found in Asian markets.

Tofu Parmesan

(Serves 4)

This could be award-winning (at least among your family and friends). I was a private chef for a Hollywood actress (who shall remain nameless) and she requested this twice a week. I never let her know that it took only 20 minutes to prepare. I have fooled men who do not eat tofu and wowed children and adults alike with this simple and delicious dish!!!

1 lb extra firm tofu, drained
2 large eggs, beaten
1 ½ cups Italian bread crumbs
    natural vegetable oil
2–3 cups tomato sauce or
    prepared pasta sauce
8 oz mozzarella cheese, grated
    or rice mozzarella found in
    health food stores

1. Preheat oven to 375°F. In a shallow bowl, beat eggs with a fork. Fill another shallow bowl with bread crumbs.

2. Holding tofu horizontally, slice tofu into 8 even slices, each approximately ½-inch thick. Drain on paper towels. Blot with another paper towel on top to remove excess moisture.

3. Dip tofu first in egg mixture, then in bread crumbs, and lay on a plate. Continue until all the tofu is breaded.

4. The tofu does not need cooking so you are frying the tofu just to lightly brown the bread crumbs, not the tofu. Cover the bottom of a medium frying pan with ½-inch of oil. Preheat oil to high heat. To test oil for readiness, drop a small piece of tofu in the pan. If it begins to sizzle immediately it is ready. Place a few pieces of tofu in pan and fry until golden brown. Flip over and brown other side.

5. Spread tomato sauce on bottom of large baking pan. As tofu comes out of the frying pan, layer slices side by side on top of the sauce. Do not stack tofu or add sauce on top of tofu. Generously sprinkle with mozzarella cheese and bake for 15–20 minutes, uncovered, until cheese melts.

Serving Suggestion: Do not use a soft tofu as the water content is too high and it will stick to the pan or possibly crumble. Serve with a green salad.

Bites of Insight

Do not overcrowd pan or the oil will cool and the tofu will absorb too much oil. The trick to using very little oil in frying is that the temperature of the oil must remain consistent. This is achieved by not overcrowding the pan. Extra virgin olive oil should never be used for pan frying as it will foam at higher heats, causing the oil to cool, resulting in soggy tofu.

Sunrise Curried Tomato Stew

(Serves 6)

Bright and colorful. A deliciously warming stew...this is made from pre-frozen tofu that you should freeze several days ahead of time.

1 Tbs extra-virgin olive oil
½ cup diced onion
3 cloves garlic, minced
½ cup cubed red bell pepper
½ cup sliced carrots
4 small red potatoes, unpeeled, scrubbed, and quartered
28 oz can diced tomatoes
1 lb firm tofu, cubed, frozen and thawed
1 small Granny Smith apple, unpeeled and cored, cut into ½-inch pieces
1–2 Tbs curry powder
1 Tbs honey
1 tsp sea salt
¼ cup chopped fresh cilantro

1. Prepare tofu by draining and cutting into 2-inch cubes. Freeze at least three days ahead or longer. Freezing will make the tofu texture spongier and more absorbable, allowing more juices and flavors to infuse the tofu.

2. Defrost tofu completely and gently squeeze tofu in your hand over the sink to remove as much water as possible without crushing the cubes. Pieces will have a spongy texture. Set aside in bowl.

3. Preheat oil in a medium sized soup pot on medium heat. Sauté onion and garlic for 2–3 minutes. Add red pepper and sauté for another few minutes.

4. Add remaining ingredients: carrots, potatoes, tomatoes, tofu, apple, curry powder, honey, and salt. Cover and gently simmer for 20 minutes. Do not stir tofu; allow it to just simmer in the broth.

5. Add cilantro for garnish and serve immediately.

Serving Suggestion: Serve over brown rice, couscous, or quinoa to make a hearty protein dish full of vitamins and minerals. Serve with a green vegetable or salad.

Tempeh Reuben

(Serves 4)

If you like sauerkraut, you will love this sandwich!! A great vegetarian alternative to a classic East Coast favorite!!

8 oz tempeh
2 Tbs soy sauce
4 Tbs extra-virgin olive oil, divided
1 onion, sliced

Assemble:
8 slices rye or pumpernickel bread
4 slices Swiss or soy cheese (optional)
½ cup sauerkraut, drained and pressed dry
4–8 spinach leaves
3 medium tomatoes, sliced
½ cup Russian dressing

1. Standing tempeh on its narrow side, slice in half about the size of a slice of bread. Cut in half again. You'll end up with tempeh pieces big enough to cover a slice of bread but not too thick. Combine soy sauce and ¼ cup water in a shallow pan. Add tempeh pieces and marinate for 5 minutes on each side. Drain on paper towel.

2. Preheat 2 Tbs oil in medium sized frying pan on medium-high heat. Sauté sliced onions on medium heat until onions are wilted and brown, about 4–5 minutes. Remove and set aside.

3. Clean the pan and preheat additional 2 Tbs oil on high heat. Fry tempeh, browning on both sides. Place on paper towels and allow excess oil to drain off.

4. Lightly toast bread. If using cheese, place cheese on bread and toast in toaster oven or broiler until cheese melts. Assemble sandwiches with 1 slice of tempeh, sauerkraut, spinach leaves, sliced tomatoes, sautéed onions, and Russian dressing. Yum!

Serving Suggestion: Only buy tempeh that is organic. Organic standards do not allow for Genetically Modified seeds or GE seeds to be used. Approximately 90% of soy crops are from GMO or GE seeds. I prefer White Wave brand of tempeh as it has a firmer and milder texture than some others on the market.

Bites of Insight

Tempeh is a soybean cake that originated in Indonesia where the soybean was traditionally fermented in banana leaves. Tempeh might have small gray spots on it; this is a natural result of fermentation and does not mean the tempeh has spoiled. Tempeh is very high in protein and because it is fermented like soy sauce and miso, it is an easily digested protein.

Good for You Desserts

· · ·

Opposite: Silky Fruit Gelatin, see page 280

Good for You Desserts

"What? How can desserts be good for you?" Since desserts are an integral part of today's American diet, it is necessary that they be as wholesome and nutritious as possible. The guilt-meter goes way down when you make desserts with fresh organic fruits, whole grain organic flours, nuts, and natural sweeteners. These desserts can actually be nourishing, giving you added vitamins and minerals, as well as protein and unsaturated fats. However, they can be quite nourishing to your waistline as well. If you are one of the unfortunates who gain weight easily from carbohydrates, then view these desserts as occasional treats instead of daily fare.

When I was growing up, virtually every dinner was followed by a dessert. Although many of them were as simple as store-bought cookies, a dessert was always present. Some of my childhood desserts were from my mother's own wartime experiences in England. One dessert I fondly remember was white bread smothered in butter and sprinkled with brown sugar, then placed under a hot broiler until the sugar bubbled and hardened. The memory of that sweet, buttery crunch is still in my childhood taste buds. No, I haven't tried to make a healthier version; some desserts are just better left behind in childhood.

Another dessert was "snow candy," which was made from corn syrup (which I would not use today) and maple syrup cooked to a candy consistency and then drizzled over a pan of freshly fallen snow. I still remember my sister and I squealing with delight when we were sent outside to catch the fresh snow, knowing our favorite winter

treat would soon be melting in our mouths. As the sugar syrup hit the snow it would immediately harden and for days we would have ribbons of hard, maple-flavored candy.

Of course, there were always times when Mom was making chocolate cake or whipped cream and we would lick the bowl and beaters clean. Although none of these recipes are in this chapter (sorry), my version of my mom's apple pie is included. I have stepped it up a healthy notch or two from my mother's recipe. By the way, she was famous in our family for her pies—especially lemon meringue—and at 89 years old she was still making them!

When I became a mom, I too was in the habit of serving sweets on a daily basis. Although our diets changed and the quality of the ingredients improved, there were still far too many carbohydrates being consumed than we needed. Raising my children on a mostly vegetarian diet, they were already getting a fair amount of good quality carbohydrates from whole grains and beans dishes. Adding even a healthy dessert every day was just too much!

Sometimes a good hug can be better than a great cookie…
Are you eating sweets simply out of habit or an emotional need? When I asked myself that question, it was clear the sweet habit was stronger than the immediate food desire. Desserts soon took a backstage in my meal planning and became a treat that we would make once a week or so. Actually, this was a great way to get my boys into the

kitchen. I purchased a healthy cookie cookbook and let the kids pick out the recipe they wanted to make. When I made homemade bread, they were with me in the kitchen kneading their portion of the dough into cookies. They would decorate them with raisins and carob chips and shape them like clay. I do not remember them eating very many of these finished creations but they certainly had fun preparing them and "helping" mommy in the kitchen. We won't talk about the mess Mom had to clean up! I would have never imagined that one of my sons would also become a private chef to the stars!

Ingredients

Great flavor comes from the quality of ingredients you use, so chose carefully:

• **Oils** should be expeller pressed (this was formerly referred to as "cold pressed"). Although I use extra virgin organic olive oil for most of my cooking, I do not use it for baking. Spectrum Naturals (www. spectrumorganics.com) expeller pressed oils are found in health food stores and they are, in my opinion, some of the best vegetable oils available. For baking, I prefer using light organic sesame oil and sometimes sunflower oil as it leans more towards a "buttery" nature. Spectrum even produces a corn oil that is a rich golden yellow color and a great substitute for butter. Since the switch to ethanol fuels, however, quality corn oil is harder to find. Good expeller pressed oils smell like the seeds from which they were extracted: sesame, walnut, corn, almond, or sunflower seeds, etc. In some cases, butter is better, and when I do choose it, I always use organic butter. For more information about butter and oils refer to my chapter *Getting the Nutrition You Need*.

• **Flours** should be organic whole wheat flour and organic unbleached white flour. You can add nutrition boosters to many recipes to increase Omega-3, protein, fiber, and vitamins. Some of these boosters can be, but not limited to, wheat germ, wheat bran, ground seeds like flaxseed, hemp or chia seeds (for protein and Omega-3), fig butter, oat bran, and bean flour. Adding an additional tablespoon of any of these to a recipe will not change the texture of your dessert. If you use more than that, though, you will have to adjust the remaining ingredients.

• **Natural sweeteners** can include: pure maple syrup (my favorite), agave, honey, stevia, coconut sugar, evaporated organic cane sugar, molasses (which comes from the syrup of cane when boiled), barley malt, rice malt, or yucon syrup. Molasses is the highest in iron and trace minerals but is the most intensely flavored, so unless you do not mind everything tasting like gingersnap cookies, have another sweetener on hand. I never use artificial sweeteners, under any circumstance!

• **Stevia** is a great choice for those who need to watch their sugar intake. Stevia comes from a small fresh herb, and when it is in season, you may be able to purchase it at your local farmer's market. One tiny leaf is packed with intense sweetness. Stevia is a zero on the glycemic scale, so it will not increase blood sugar and is acceptable for diabetics. It is also available in stores in powder or liquid form. Follow the recommendations on the package for substitution.

• **Blue agave syrup** is a low glycemic sweetener from the agave cactus. This is the same cactus that is used to make tequila. It has a low glycemic index of approximately 27. Although good for calorie watchers, diabetics should use agave with caution. I always look for raw and organic agave syrup to be sure it's the real thing. There are highly processed versions of agave on the market. Avoid them! Coconut sugar is a great substitute and has a low glycemic index of 55. Look for it in your local health food store or online.

• **Dairy** ingredients can be substituted, if necessary, with unsweetened almond milk, rice milk, or light coconut milk found in health food stores and some supermarkets. Why do I not recommend soy milk? Please refer to my chapter *True Food* for more information about the cautions of soy milk. Try substituting almond milk, sesame oil, and honey for some of the ingredients in my *Cranberry Orange Nut Bread*!

• **Eggs** are a powerhouse of protein, vitamins, and essential fatty acids. The quality of the egg is determined by the environment and diet of the hen. It is natural for chickens to lay fewer eggs during their molting season. However, most commercially raised hens are kept in cages and stimulated to produce eggs year round. Additives in their meal can include antibiotics, phosphates, steroids, and food coloring to enhance the yellow yolk. Those eggs have a fragile shell and tasteless yolk.

Do you know what a healthy egg is? Cracking one should take some force; a healthy egg should not easily crack in your hand into several pieces. A strong shell means the hen received sufficient amounts of calcium in her diet. The truth is, most commercial eggs are too fragile and could never survive the hen sitting on them. Secondly, when the egg hits the pan, the albumen (clear part surrounding yolk) should hold together in a small circle not a watery pool that runs out to the edge of the pan. The yolk should be high, round, and deep yellow color. Most commercial eggs are a light color that is enhanced with food coloring additives. I encourage you to do a taste test, side by side, of a commercial egg typically purchased from a grocery store and an organic egg. See the difference and taste the difference. When I shop, I buy free-range, organic, hormone-free and antibiotic-free eggs found at my local farmer's market.

• **Baking powder** is my first choice over baking soda, and I always look for aluminum-free baking powder.

• **Spices or herbs** can enhance food flavors, but only if they are relatively fresh. Shelf life for freshness and flavor for dried herbs is six months and for dried spices is three years. Spices come from the bark, nuts, and seeds of plants and are more shelf-stable. Herbs are dried leaves and quickly lose their chlorophyll and flavorful oil. Most herbs are available organically grown whereas most spices are imported and many are not yet available organic.

• **Sea salt** has more minerals than the refined table salt we grew up with. Table salt contains additives to create its white color and to keep it from clumping. Sea salt is minimally processed and more minerally balanced. Please refer to my chapter *Getting the Nutrition You Need* for more information about salt quality.

Dessert Makeovers
You could make most dessert recipes in any cookbook

using healthier ingredients with great results. Virtually every item can be purchased organic these days, including chocolate. So my first step is replacing ingredients with an organic version. Secondly, I replace white sugar with organic evaporated cane sugar. Sometimes in a recipe, it is better to stick with the granulated version of sugar than to switch to a liquid version, like honey or agave. For instance, that famous chocolate chip cookie recipe right off the chip bag, the one everyone loves, does not come out the same when oil and honey are used instead of sugar and butter. The butter and sugar "cream" together to fluff the cookie and then melt into the chewy rich texture that we all know and love. So occasionally I will make these cookies, but I use organic butter, organic evaporated cane sugar, organic chocolate chips, and organic whole grain flour and get the same great results.

When you are substituting liquid fat (oil) for a solid fat (butter) in a recipe, remember to use a little less oil than butter. For example, if a recipe calls for ½ cup butter, I would use ⅓ cup oil. If you are using a liquid sweetener (agave, honey, maple syrup) instead of granulated (sugar or brown sugar) remember to back down on other liquid amounts found in the recipe. So, if it calls for ½ cup of milk or water, I would use ⅓ cup instead to rebalance the liquid-to-dry ingredient ratio. Since baking is a chemical reaction between the liquids, dry ingredients and leavening agents, upsetting the balance can result in a failure. Usually only a slight adjustment is necessary.

In addition to any added sweetener, natural as they may be, the whole grain flour in most of these recipes is fairly high on the glycemic scale. So if you have a health problem, limit and carefully select your desserts, no matter how healthy they may be.

Please experiment and enjoy the fun in creating new dishes with nourishing ingredients. Feeding my children nutritious foods gave them great health during their school years. That experience led me to write this book and pass this knowledge on to others. Enjoy good food, enjoy good health, and enjoy your life.

Best Ever Apple Pie

(Serves 6)

This apple pie has the perfect balance of sweet and tart. It will be the tallest apple pie you have ever made.

2   unbaked premade pie shells
6-8 apples (mixed varieties—
    Granny Smith, Braeburn, etc),
    peeled, cored, and sliced
¼   cup unbleached white flour
1   tsp vanilla extract
¼   tsp sea salt
1   tsp ground cinnamon
¼   cup brown sugar
¼   cup organic cane sugar

Topping:
1   large egg white
2   Tbs organic cane sugar

1. Preheat oven to 375°F. Position rack in the middle of the oven.

2. Peel and core apples. Slice into ½-inch pieces. In a medium sized bowl combine apples with flour, vanilla, salt, cinnamon, brown sugar, and sugar. Toss well.

3. Using a premade pie shell, fill your shell with the apples in a close circle. Layer the apples until all are used. The center will be raised and the pie will be tall.

4. Roll out your second pie shell topping and fit it over the pie. Crimp the edges and "flute" or use a fork to secure layers. In the center of the pie, cut a small cross slit hole to allow for steam to escape.

5. Whisk one egg white with ½ tsp water. Brush over pie and crust with a pastry brush, then sprinkle with organic cane sugar. This will give the pie a glistening, golden crust. Since the edges cook faster, either purchase a pie ring, or use aluminum foil to cover only the fluted edges.

6. Place pie in preheated oven for 20 minutes. Reduce heat to 350°F and remove the foil. Continue baking for 30 minutes. Test doneness with a knife in the center of the pie. The apples should still feel a little firm. Remove the pie and let it cool for at least 30 minutes before slicing.

Bites of Insight

When apples are just poured in a shell, there is too much space between the apples and results in a fallen crust after baking. Layering the apples in a tight circle on the bottom of the pastry shell helps to avoid this. This makes a great high and dense pie that won't collapse after baking.

Blueberry Cobbler

(Serves 8)

Cobblers were named after the old stone cobble streets because of the cobbling effect of the fruit and cake batter.

Dry Ingredients:
½ cup whole wheat pastry flour
1 cup unbleached white flour
¼ cup organic cane sugar
2 tsp baking powder
¼ tsp sea salt

Wet Ingredients:
2 large eggs, beaten
1 tsp vanilla extract
¼ cup natural vegetable oil
½ cup almond milk

Fruit Filling:
4 cups fresh blueberries, about 1 ½ lbs (or other berries in season)
1 Tbs unbleached white flour
¼ cup organic cane sugar
¼ tsp sea salt

1. Preheat oven to 350°F. In a large bowl combine all dry ingredients: both flours, sugar, baking powder, and sea salt.

2. In a separate bowl combine wet ingredients: eggs, vanilla, oil, and almond milk. Then combine both dry and wet ingredients together, making sure to mix thoroughly.

3. Wash and drain blueberries and place in an oblong 9 x 13-inch baking dish. Sprinkle with 1 Tbs flour, ¼ cup sugar, and ¼ tsp sea salt.

4. Pour batter slowly over the blueberries, making sure to cover them all. Place immediately in a preheated oven for 25 minutes, or until the batter turns a golden brown and a knife inserted in the center of the cobbler comes out clean.

Serving Suggestion: If you are using frozen blueberries, thaw and drain thoroughly before placing them in the baking pan, and add 2 Tbs flour to the fruit instead of one. When in season, add peaches to the blueberries for a terrific combination. Serve with *Cashew Cream*, whipped cream, or ice cream.

Chocolate Dipped Strawberries

(Serves 4)

Everyone's favorite, and much easier than you would think. Don't be intimidated—even kids can dip berries!

1 pint large, fresh strawberries
12 oz package semi-sweet
    chocolate chips

Variation: For Tuxedo Strawberries, it is a two step process. Follow directions provided but use white chocolate. Let berries cool completely. Repeat process with dark chocolate dipping only on two sides just enough to create the "lapel" effect of the tuxedo. A "V" shape of white chocolate should be exposed. Using a pastry bag with a fine point, dot chocolate buttons on the white "shirt." You can purchase tubes of icing in black or brown colors for this step. Let them dry thoroughly and enjoy this elite dessert.

1. Rinse strawberries in a colander and place in a single layer on paper towels to thoroughly air dry. Chocolate will not stick to wet strawberries. Choose premium strawberries that are large, free of bruises, firm, and have leaves still intact. Line a cookie sheet with aluminum foil, waxed paper, or parchment paper.

2. Using ½ cup of chocolate chips at a time, place them in a glass bowl and microwave for 30 seconds. Remove and quickly stir the chips. Replace in microwave and repeat. On the second try, the chips will melt as you stir vigorously. This process has to be done quickly. You may also use a double boiler—see instructions below.

3. Gather melted chocolate in a deep tablespoon or soup ladle. Grab one strawberry by its stem or leaves and lay it down on its side into the chocolate. Moving quickly, swirl the strawberry onto the other side completely coating with chocolate. Work fast as the chocolate will begin to cool quickly and thicken, making it harder to dip the berries.

4. Lay coated strawberries on the cookie sheet, leaving plenty of room between them. Cool at room temperature until the chocolate hardens, about 15 minutes.

5. Refrigerate loosely wrapped strawberries when the chocolate has completely cooled. Too soon will turn the chocolate a smoky, dull color. Consume within two days as they will deteriorate quickly.

Bites of Insight

Instead of a microwave, use a small pot placed in a larger pot that has 2 inches of water in the bottom. Bring the water to a boil and place chips in smaller pot. Begin to stir as soon as you see the chips melting. The chocolate stays soft for a longer period of time giving you more time to dip the strawberries.

Chocolate Coconut Bars

(Makes 9 large bars)

Can you say decadent? Rich with chocolate, nuts, and coconut....a wow combination.

Crust:
1   cup quick-cooking rolled oats, toasted
½   cup oat flour
½   cup unbleached wheat flour or sorghum flour
4   Tbs organic butter (or light oil)
⅓   cup maple syrup, honey, or a combination of both
1   tsp vanilla extract

Topping:
1   cup semi-sweet chocolate chips
½   cup chopped walnuts
¾   cup shredded unsweetened coconut
¼   cup maple syrup
1   tsp vanilla extract
1   large egg plus 2 egg whites
2   Tbs unbleached wheat flour

Optional: You can add ¼ cup of dried cranberries or dried goji berries to increase antioxidants in these fabulous bars.

1. Preheat oven to 350°F. Grease an 8 x 8-inch square baking pan with oil or butter.

2. Mix rolled oats, oat flour, and wheat flour together. Add butter, breaking it up with a fork so mixture resembles coarse meal. Pour in maple syrup and vanilla and mix thoroughly. Press mixture evenly over bottom of prepared baking pan. Bake for 10-12 minutes. Remove and let cool for 10 minutes.

3. Meanwhile, mix topping ingredients together. Spread topping evenly over oatmeal crust once it has cooled. Bake for 20 minutes or until some of the coconut is golden. Remove from oven and let stand for 10 minutes or until cooled before cutting into bars.

Note: To make these gluten-free, replace wheat flour with sorghum flour, found in most health food stores.

Cranberry Orange Nut Bread

(Makes 1 loaf or 9 slices)

The cranberry and orange juice combination gives this bread just the right amount of tartness. Buy extra bags of fresh cranberries to freeze and enjoy this colorful holiday bread year round.

Dry Ingredients:
2 cups organic unbleached flour
1 ½ tsp baking powder
½ tsp baking soda
½ tsp sea salt
1 cup organic cane sugar (or
   ¾ cup honey; mix with wet
   ingredients)

Wet Ingredients:
1 large egg, beaten well
¾ cup orange juice
2 Tbs natural vegetable oil
1 Tbs grated orange zest
1 tsp vanilla extract

1 cup fresh cranberries
½ cup chopped walnuts or
   pecans

1. Preheat oven to 350°F. Generously grease and lightly flour a rectangular loaf pan.

2. In a medium sized bowl, mix all dry ingredients together: flour, baking powder, baking soda, salt, and sugar. In separate bowl mix together egg, orange juice, oil, orange zest, and vanilla.

3. Fold wet mixture into dry mixture until thoroughly mixed. There should be no lumps left.

4. In a food processor, pulse the cranberries until they are roughly chopped in half. This will allow the loaf to rise more easily and slice better. Gently fold in cranberries and chopped nuts into your mixture.

5. Pour into loaf pan and bake on the middle rack of the oven for 60 minutes or until knife comes out clean. Cool 10 minutes and turn pan over to dislodge loaf onto board.

Bites of Insight

I make a few loaves of this bread several weeks in advance of the holidays and freeze them. Tightly wrap the cooled loaf in plastic wrap and then wrap again with aluminum foil. This will prevent loaves from getting freezer burn. The bread will thaw in an hour. I suggest slicing your bread for the basket when it is still a little frozen. It will make it easier to slice and the pieces will continue to thaw in the basket. These make great gifts too.

Date and Walnut Bread

(Serves 9)

Another great bread that I just love. Can you tell I love walnuts? They contain Omega-3 too!

Dry Ingredients:
2 cups whole wheat pastry flour
2 tsp baking powder
1 tsp ground cinnamon
½ tsp sea salt

Wet Ingredients:
⅓ cup natural vegetable oil
⅓ cup maple syrup
1 tsp vanilla extract
2 large eggs, beaten
¾ cup milk (cow's, almond,
    or rice)
2 tsp grated orange zest

¾ cup chopped dates (date
    pieces are best and available
    around the holidays)
½ cup chopped walnuts

1. Preheat oven to 350°F. Generously grease and lightly flour a rectangular loaf pan.

2. In a medium sized bowl mix together all dry ingredients: flour, baking powder, cinnamon, and salt.

3. In a separate bowl combine all wet ingredients: oil, maple syrup, vanilla, eggs, milk, and orange zest.

4. Combine wet with dry ingredients and mix until all lumps disappear. Fold in dates and walnuts.

5. Pour into prepared loaf pan and bake for 50 minutes. Check with a cake tester or knife. If it comes out wet, bake for another 5 to 10 minutes, or until cake tester comes out clean. Cool on rack for at least 10 minutes before removing from pan. Turn loaf pan over to dislodge loaf and cool another 10 minutes before slicing.

Note: Also a great recipe for making ahead and freezing for the holidays. Instead of ordinary dinner rolls with holiday dinners, I offer a basket with sliced cranberry bread, date and walnut bread, and corn bread, all of which I made weeks before to save time.

Bites of Insight

For orange zest, using a handheld small holed grater, grate just the rind from the orange. Make sure not to get any of the white pithy part. Move quickly around the orange to get just the outermost peel.

Fresh Fruit Crisp

(Yields 4–6 servings)

One of my favorite ways to serve fruit—no matter what fruit is in season!

Crisp Topping
Dry Ingredients:
2   cups quick-cooking rolled oats
⅓   cup whole wheat flour or unbleached flour
¼   cup brown sugar (or more to taste)
½   cup chopped walnuts
½   tsp ground cinnamon
½   tsp sea salt

Wet Ingredients:
4   Tbs organic butter
¼   cup natural vegetable oil
⅓   cup maple syrup

Fruit Filling:
3   cups of blueberries (or any berry), apples, or peaches
2   Tbs arrowroot or unbleached white flour
¼   cup organic cane sugar

1. Preheat oven to 350°F. Grease an 8 x 8-inch baking pan.

2. Wash and drain fruit. If using fruit with a peel, remove and slice into ½-inch slices. Place fruit at the bottom of square baking pan, sprinkle with sugar and arrowroot. If you are using very ripe fruit, it will have more juice, so use a little more arrowroot or flour to bind the fruit together.

3. Toss dry ingredients together for crisp topping. Next, work in butter and oil with your hands, just until mixture resembles coarse bread crumbs. Add maple syrup and stir gently to combine. Layer this over fruit and place in oven; bake uncovered for 30 minutes or until crisp, golden brown and fruit is tender but not mushy.

Variation: Instead of your own crisp topping, purchase your favorite granola from the health food store (I love the vanilla almond and the ginger granolas) and sprinkle that on your prepared fruit. Cover with aluminum foil and bake for 25 minutes or until fruit is tender but still holding together. If it is not covered, granola can dry out too much and burn.

Bites of Insight

Arrowroot is found in the spice section in grocery stores and can be used as a substitute for cornstarch. Since 90% of corn is genetically modified, I only use organic cornstarch found in health food stores. I find arrowroot works well when my recipe calls for starch to thicken.

My Favorite Carrot Cake

(Serves 8–10)

I love carrot cake. If you are trying to avoid dairy serve this with **Cashew Cream** *(found in this chapter) instead of* **Cream Cheese Icing**. *Either one is fine…it's your choice.*

Dry Ingredients:
1   cup whole wheat pastry flour
1   cup unbleached white flour
2   tsp baking powder
2   tsp baking soda
½   tsp sea salt
2   tsp ground cinnamon
1   cup raisins
½   cup chopped walnuts (optional)

Wet Ingredients:
1 ¼ cups honey
½   cup natural vegetable oil
    (sesame, corn, canola,
    safflower)
4   large eggs, beaten well
2   tsp vanilla extract
3   cups grated carrots
    (approx. 1 lb carrots)

1. Preheat oven to 350°F. Oil a 10-inch springform pan or an oblong 9 x 14-inch glass baking dish, or two 8 x 8-inch cake pans. Dust bottom of pan with flour and shake off excess. You can also use parchment paper cut to the size of the bottom of the pan for very easy cake removal.

2. In a bowl, combine all the dry ingredients together and mix well.

3. Combine honey and oil together in a medium sized bowl. Add beaten eggs and vanilla and stir again. Combine wet and dry ingredients together, stirring until all lumps are gone. Fold in carrots, raisins, and walnuts if you are using them.

4. Evenly distribute batter in baking pan(s) and bake for 45–50 minutes or until a cake tester or knife inserted in the center of the pan comes out clean. If you are using one pan, it will take longer to cook than if you divide the batter into two pans. Completely cool before removing cake from pan. Ice cake with *Cream Cheese Icing*.

CREAM CHEESE ICING

1 ½ cups cream cheese,
     softened (not whipped)
½   tsp vanilla extract
6   Tbs maple syrup (or honey or
     agave syrup)

Combine all ingredients in a blender or use an electric mixer and blend until smooth. Ice cake and enjoy!

Peanut Butter Snow Balls

(Makes 2 dozen 2–inch balls)

A great after-school snack! I kept these in the freezer for my kids and their friends. They liked them ice cold too!

2   cups natural peanut butter
    (must be freshly ground)
⅓   cup raisins or currants
⅓   cup raw sunflower seeds
¼   cup sesame seeds (optional)
⅓   cup shredded coconut
½   cup barley malt

Optional: Add ¼ cup carob chips or chocolate chips

1. Thoroughly mix together all ingredients except barley malt.

2. Add barley malt and mix until everything holds together. If mixture is dry and crumbly, add more barley malt.

3. Form mixture into balls by placing a small amount about the diameter of a quarter into the palm of your hands and roll until a ball is formed. Roll balls in shredded coconut and sesame seeds, if using, and serve. Store excess in an airtight container or freeze them. This helps cut back on impulse snacking…mostly from mommy.

Serving Suggestion: These "protein balls" are high in protein, calcium, iron, and other minerals and are a good pick me up for the kids. If you are signed up for snack day at your child's school this is a great recipe. As an in-between-meals snack, these are good for anyone who needs to put weight back on. You can easily substitute freshly ground almond butter for the peanut butter with great results.

Bites of Insight

Barley malt is a thick, sweet syrup found in health food stores. It is made from malting barley grain. It is similar to molasses, but is lighter in flavor. You can also use honey or rice syrup instead of barley malt, however only use ⅓ cup of honey as it is not as thick as barley malt.

Roasted Fresh Figs with Goat Cheese

(Serves 4)

Serve three figs per person if offered as a dessert. As an appetizer, serve one or two. These are even yummy as a part of a healthy and delicious breakfast!

12 figs (Brown Turkey or Mission)
¼ lb goat cheese, softened
1 tsp minced fresh rosemary or
   ¼ tsp dried rosemary
¼ lb prosciutto, sliced lengthwise
12 toothpicks

1. Preheat oven to 400°F.

2. Score each fig by slicing it half way down the middle and then across. Place on cookie sheet.

3. In a bowl, combine rosemary and softened goat cheese. Stir until blended.

4. Slice prosciutto into long pieces (long enough to wrap around fig with some overlap).

5. Place half a spoonful of cheese mixture inside each fig and wrap prosciutto around it. Secure with toothpick.

6. Place back on the baking sheet and bake on middle rack of oven. Roast until prosciutto begins to "sweat" and figs are shiny, approximately 10–12 minutes. Transfer figs to platter and garnish with rosemary sprigs if you used fresh rosemary. Serve immediately.

Bites of Insight

In temperate climates, figs come into season twice a year, once in early summer and again in autumn. Black Mission figs are among the most readily available and are often sweeter. However, Brown Turkey figs are larger and easier to handle while stuffing, although not as sweet. Their sweetness combined with the tartness of the cheese and the saltiness of the prosciutto delivers a complexity of intense and satisfying flavors. Choose figs that are a little soft because they will be the sweetest. If you are buying figs a few days ahead pick ones that are still a little firm and without blemishes.

Real Pumpkin Pie

(Serves 6)

I don't know why we wait for the holidays for this creamy and satisfying pie. It is best, though, when winter squash are freshly harvested. Almost any winter squash variety, except for acorn, will work.

2 cups pumpkin puree
  (see *How to Cook Pumpkin* on
  following page)
1 unbaked premade pie shell
2 large eggs
$^2/_3$ cup milk (or half and half or
  light coconut milk)
1 cup organic cane sugar
1 tsp ground cinnamon
½ tsp ground ginger
½ tsp ground nutmeg
¼ tsp ground cloves
1 tsp vanilla extract
½ tsp sea salt

1. Preheat oven to 425°F.

2. In a large bowl, whip eggs with milk and add sugar. Add remaining spices, vanilla, and salt. Mix again and fold in pumpkin puree until completely blended.

3. Roll out your pastry and place in an 8-inch pie dish and flute the edges. Cover the edges with a pie edge protector or with aluminum foil. See instructions in my *Best Ever Apple Pie* recipe in this chapter. Pour pumpkin mixture in shell and bake for 15 minutes on center rack of oven.

4. Remove foil or edge protector, reduce oven temperature to 350°F and bake an additional 45 minutes or until the pumpkin is set. It should not jiggle in the center when you gently shake the pie. Pie is done when knife placed in center comes out clean and pie does not look loose in the center. It usually has a crack in the center when set. If it is still too soft in the middle, bake for another 10 minutes. Let pie cool at least 30 minutes before cutting. Real pumpkin pie deserves real *Whipped Cream* or my *Cashew Cream* in this chapter.

WHIPPED CREAM

½ pint heavy whipping cream
½ tsp vanilla extract
2 Tbs organic cane sugar or
  maple syrup

Whip with electric mixer on medium until cream creates peaks.

HOW TO COOK PUMPKIN

The surprising truth is pumpkins (Jack O' Lanterns) are not the best choice for pumpkin pies. They are watery, stringy, and usually not very sweet. My suggestion is to use a dense, sweet variety of winter squash such as Hubbard, Banana, Butternut, Buttercup, Hakaido, Kobocha, or Fairytale pumpkin. A popular canned pumpkin pie that is widely used is made with Hubbard squash. Hubbard grows large, dense, and sweet with little water. Baby food companies use this squash for their pureed "pumpkin" baby food.

To make puree:
Slice the squash in half and scoop out the seeds. Put a little water in the bottom of a baking dish, and put squash flesh side down. Bake at 350°F for 30–60 minutes depending on the size of the squash pieces. When squash is tender remove, cool, and scoop out the flesh. It may be necessary to process this in a food processor to make a smooth, thick puree. If the puree is watery put it back in the baking dish and return to oven to bake covered for another 20–30 minutes, so that it dries out more.

If the squash is too large to cut, poke knife holes in several places around the top of the squash and bake whole for 1½ hours. After baking, cut, remove seeds and string, and scoop out pulp. Refrigerated, squash can be stored for up to five days. You can also freeze this pulp for up to six months for later use.

Yield:
7 lbs pumpkin will yield 3 ½ lbs of puree
1 lb pumpkin equals 4 cups when diced, sliced, or grated, or 2 cups pureed

Silky Fruit Gelatin

(Serves 6–8)

This is a healthier version than the commercial gelatins available which contain food coloring, artificial colors, and too much refined sugar! This is a guilt-free desert so make plenty for your family!

1   quart natural apple-strawberry juice, or any variation (preferably organic)
4   Tbs agar agar
1   pint strawberries or other fresh fruit

Optional: You can use any natural juice as a base: apple-strawberry, peach, blueberry, apple, or coconut. Use any fresh fruit combination you wish.
I have combined peaches and blueberries with wonderful results.

1. Pour fruit juice in a 2 quart pot, add agar agar flakes, and cover. Bring to a boil, reduce heat immediately. Simmer on low for 5 minutes until flakes have melted.

2. Clean and slice strawberries. When the agar flakes have melted, turn off heat and add sliced strawberries. You don't want strawberries to cook as they will turn gray and mushy.

3. Pour into a mold or dish. Allow to set at room temperature for a couple of hours, or an hour in the refrigerator.

Note: Agar agar is a natural, tasteless and odorless sea vegetable that will gel just about any liquid. See *Bites of Insight* chapter for more information.

Cashew Cream

(Yields 1 ½ cups)

This is a very rich and delicious dairy alternative to whipped cream or ice cream. Still high in calories but a great source of fiber and good healthy fat.

1   cup presoaked raw cashews
1   cup unsweetened almond milk
½   tsp vanilla extract
1   Tbs agave or honey

1. Place all ingredients in blender. Blend on high until creamy, approximately 3-4 minutes. This takes some time to make sure all pieces are blended smoothly. It should be smooth and creamy like real cream. Add a little more milk if necessary. This will keep in the refrigerator for up to 5 days. It will get stiffer in the refrigerator after a few hours. If it is too stiff, add a little more almond milk and stir.

Sunflower Crunch

(Makes 2 cups)

We sometimes make batches of this crunch, put it in decorative jars and give them as gifts during the holidays.

2   cups raw sunflower seeds
⅓   cup barley malt
⅛   tsp sea salt

1. Preheat a large frying pan on medium heat. Add sunflower seeds and a pinch of sea salt. Do not use oil. Continue stirring to prevent seeds from burning. When a few seeds turn a very light brown, usually around 8–10 minutes, they are ready for the barley malt. Do not let seeds turn a dark brown or they become bitter.

2. Add barley malt, stirring as you pour. Add just enough malt so the seeds start to stick together, adding more if necessary. Stir for about a minute until barley malt begins to "string." You are cooking the water away from the barley malt and "sugaring" the syrup. When that happens, the barley malt starts to show "strings" as you stir it.

3. Lightly wet a cookie sheet to prevent mixture from sticking. Quickly spread mixture flat, forming an even layer. You can use the back of a large wet spoon to help you spread seeds in a single layer.

4. Allow to harden for 10–15 minutes. If seeds are sticky, too much malt was used. If seeds didn't stick together, not enough was used or you didn't let the barley malt "string" enough. It is too late to fix anything now, so make a note for next time.

Bites of Insight

Seeds can also be toasted in the oven on a cookie sheet, but they tend to burn easily, so watch them very carefully. I find using my toaster oven is the best way to watch the seeds and prevent burning. Other seeds can be used in place of sunflower seeds such as roasted chopped almonds or cashews. You can also use honey, rice syrup, or agave syrup instead of barley malt. Experiment with the quantity as you may have to use less because some of these sweeteners have more liquid than others.

Streusel Apple Coffee Cake

(Serves 9)

This cake supplies us with protein, high fiber carbohydrates, vitamins, and minerals. So eat it, it's good for you and is a great afternoon pick-me-up.

Dry Ingredients:
1 ¼ cups whole wheat flour
¼ tsp sea salt
2 tsp baking powder

Wet Ingredients:
½ cup milk (cow's, almond, or rice)
⅓ cup maple syrup
2 large eggs, beaten
2 Tbs natural vegetable oil
⅓ cup natural applesauce
½ tsp vanilla extract

Streusel Filling:
½ cup coarsely chopped walnuts
⅓ cup coarsely chopped raisins
2 Tbs wheat germ
2 tsp ground cinnamon
⅓ cup maple syrup
1 Tbs organic butter
1 apple (Rome or Granny Smith), peeled, cored, and thinly sliced

1. Preheat oven to 375°F. Oil a 9-inch round glass pie pan or an 8 x 8-inch square baking pan.

2. In a medium sized bowl, combine dry ingredients: flour, salt, and baking powder. Mix thoroughly.

3. In a separate bowl, combine milk, syrup, eggs, oil, apple sauce, and vanilla. Mix thoroughly. Combine dry and wet ingredients together and mix until all lumps are gone and blended smooth. Pour half of the batter into the oiled pan. Set aside the remainder.

4. Layer slices of apple on top of batter, allowing them to overlap. Sprinkle half of the streusel filling over apples, and pour remaining batter over that. Sprinkle remaining streusel filling on top. Bake for 30–45 minutes or until cake tester or knife inserted in center of cake comes out clean.

Serving Suggestion: This cake freezes well when wrapped with plastic wrap and then placed in a plastic bag. Great for a quick snack with tea or on-the-run breakfast. The whole wheat flour, wheat germ, and nuts all contain protein.

Walnut Date Bars

(Serves 9–12)

Bet you can't eat just one! There's something very satisfying about these bars that makes it hard not to eat more than one.

Crust:
1   cup quick-cooking rolled oats
2/3 cup whole wheat flour
1/3 cup maple syrup
4   Tbs butter or natural
    vegetable oil

Filling:
1   large egg
1/2 tsp vanilla extract
1/4 cup maple syrup
1/4 tsp sea salt
1/2 tsp baking powder
1/3 cup shredded coconut
2/3 cup chopped dates
2/3 cup chopped walnuts
    whole walnuts (for garnish)

Optional: Add 2 Tbs wheat germ to boost the nutrition.

1. Preheat oven to 350°F. Combine oats, flour, maple syrup, and butter or oil together and mix well. Oil an 8 x 8-inch square baking pan and press mixture evenly into the bottom. Put on the middle rack in the oven and bake for 15 minutes. Remove and set aside to cool.

2. Combine the filling ingredients listed. Mix thoroughly. Spread this filling evenly over the crust in the pan. If using whole walnuts, place 9 walnuts evenly on top where you will cut into bars.

3. Return to oven and bake for an additional 20 minutes. Cut into bars as soon as you remove it from the oven but wait until it cools before removing bars.

Bites of Insight

The best dates for baking are the date pieces that are coated with oat flour. They are available in most stores around the holidays. Bars will store very well for up to two weeks in a covered container. You can vary the recipe by using raisins, figs, or dried apricots instead of dates. Try almonds or pecans instead of walnuts.

Bites of Insight

Tips Cooks Love!
Over 145 tips, techniques, and shortcuts that will make you a better cook!

Save Time Shopping

↝ Plan weekly menu and grocery lists. Sunday is the best time to shop with shorter waiting times in checkout lines.

↝ Organize grocery list by area or section of your favorite store to avoid back-tracking to departments.

↝ If you need smaller portions of an item, ask the produce manager to cut produce sold by the pound in a quarter or a half, such as cabbage. Separate bananas, clusters of grapes, or broccoli, or anything else sold by the pound. You don't have to buy the whole bunch but stores are hoping you don't know that. For instance, ask the butcher to separate a package of chicken into smaller packages.

↝ Call ahead and place orders with the butcher, seafood, or deli counters so it will be ready for you to pick up.

Save Time Cooking

↝ Organize and prep by having all the ingredients and equipment ready and available. Chefs call it *mise en place.*

↝ Keep a bowl for vegetable scraps on the counter or tie a plastic bag to one of the drawer handles for quicker and easier cleanup.

↝ Cook simultaneously on as many burners as you can. Think ahead to tomorrow's meals and prep some of the ingredients ahead.

Save Cleanup Time

↝ Pour water into dirty pots and pans while they're still hot to prevent food from sticking. This results in a lot less scrubbing later.

↝ Line your baking pans with parchment paper or foil for less cleanup.

↝ Clean as you go, wiping counters and washing dishes. I do this to allow my mind to reorganize the next few steps I have to do in cooking. It's a mental break that clears my mind.

Agar Agar

Agar Agar is a natural seaweed that will cause any liquid to gel. Agar Agar is made from several varieties of seaweed that are tasteless and odorless. Compare this to commercial gelatin, which is made from the collagen in cow and pig bones, hooves, noses, ears, and tissues. These slaughterhouse remains are first pre-treated with a strong acid to loosen the collagen protein. Boiling then releases the remaining collagen which is then dried into what we know as gelatin, the main component of many popular fruit flavored desserts. Did I mention the added artificial colors, flavors, and sugar? Makes it an easy choice to avoid gelatin, doesn't it?

Agave

Agave is the syrup from the Blue Agave (Agave Tequilana), the same cactus used to make tequila. Agave is composed mostly of fructose and glucose and has a lower glycemic index than sugar and is one and half times less sweet.

Almonds

Almonds are more alkalizing and higher in calcium than other nuts. One ounce of almonds contains as much calcium as ¼ cup of milk. You'll also get 35% of your daily allowance of vitamin E. The fat in almonds is monounsaturated (the good fat) and contains no cholesterol. Almonds contain many healthful nutrients: magnesium, phosphorus, zinc, folic acid, phytochemicals, and are high in healthy fiber.

Apples

Try to use organic apples when possible. Commercially grown apples are sprayed more than fourteen times during their growing process! They will retain some of these pesticides and herbicides. Peeling does not remove all these chemicals.

Arrowroot

Arrowroot comes from the tuber root of an arrowroot plant. It can be substituted for cornstarch in most dishes. Arrowroot powder also makes a great thickening agent when you want to prepare a clear sauce. In comparison, cornstarch tends to make the sauce appear cloudy. Arrowroot tolerates acidic ingredients better than cornstarch so it is perfect for a sweet and sour dish. As a cornstarch substitute use:
• 2 teaspoons arrowroot flour = 1 tablespoon cornstarch. Use 2 tsp to 1 cup of liquid for sauce.

Asparagus

Asparagus has no fat or cholesterol and is low in sodium with less than 4 calories per spear! Asparagus is a nutrient-dense food high in folic acid and is a good source of potassium, fiber, vitamin A, B6, and C, and thiamin. A 5 oz serving provides 60% of the recommended daily allowance for folacin which is necessary for blood cell formation, growth, and prevention of liver disease. Asparagus is a member of the lily family. Under ideal conditions, an asparagus spear can grow 10 inches in a 24-hour period—now that's fast!

Baking Soda and Aluminum-Free Baking Powder

Baking powder a leavening agent, and it's usually called for in recipes where there are alkaline (as opposed to acidic) ingredients. Baking soda (sodium bicarbonate) is one of the ingredients in baking powder, which, when moistened, releases carbon dioxide, which causes baked goods to rise. The tinny flavor that you might detect in baked goods could be because of the baking powder used. Use aluminum-free baking powder for a better taste.

Barley as a Soup Base

If you like a creamy, thick soup, don't rinse the barley. Just add cooked barley directly to the soup. However, if you like a clear broth soup, place cooked barley in a colander and rinse under running water for a few minutes while turning the barley with a spoon to remove the starch.

Barley Malt

Barley malt is sweet syrup produced from sprouted whole grain barley. Similar to honey in texture but closer to molasses in flavor, it is about half as sweet as white sugar and has a lower glycemic index than either of these. It can be found in health food stores. Malted barley is used to make beer, whiskey, malted shakes, malt vinegar, candy, and some baked goods.

Bell Peppers

Red peppers are the ripe version of green peppers. They are on the "dirty dozen" list of foods most heavily sprayed with pesticides and herbicides. I always buy organic bell peppers to avoid these sprays. Visit www.ewg.org for their "dirty dozen" list of foods to avoid and foods that are safe.

Blanching

Blanching vegetables results in firm, brightly colored vegetables. Bring a small pot of water to boil, add vegetables (one type at a time) and boil on high for

30 seconds to 2 minutes depending on the vegetable. Remove with slotted spoon and place in a bowl of iced water to stop the cooking. Drain and add to your recipe.

Blueberries

When using blueberries in a recipe, always mix with the dry ingredients first. This coats the berries and prevents the leeching of the purple juice into the batter. Quickly mix the wet and dry together right before cooking your griddle cakes or muffins. If using frozen blueberries, just add them directly to the dry ingredients. The berries will defrost while cooking.

Bok Choy

Bok choy adds a light, sweet flavor, and crisp texture. Bok choy is high in vitamin A, vitamin C, and calcium, but low in calories. The Chinese commonly refer to bok choy as pak choi or "white vegetable." Baby bok choy, also called Shanghai bok choy, is a smaller, younger version of the same vegetable.

Bonito Flakes

Bonito flakes are very thin freeze-dried fish flakes, and can be purchased in any Asian market. Bonito is used widely in Japanese cooking to enhance flavor in soups, stews, stocks, and sauces. You may also garnish soups with bonito flakes.

Broccoli

Ounce for ounce, cooked broccoli has almost twice as much vitamin C as orange juice. Broccoli is one of the most nutrient-dense foods and contains generous amounts of folic acid which may prevent some birth defects. Broccoli is beneficial in warding off heart disease, strokes, and some cancers.

Broccoli Raab

Broccoli raab is not related to broccoli but to the turnip family. Originating in the Mediterranean and China, it is actually a descendant of a wild herb. This vegetable is a source of vitamins A, C, and K, as well as potassium.

Broccoli Stems

Broccoli stems have a wonderful flavor and remain crunchy when cooked in stir-frys. They are great in salads such as broccoli slaw or in vegetable dips, or can be used as a base for broccoli soup. To prepare, remove outer peel carefully with a knife. Then slice or chop into smaller pieces.

Bulgur Wheat

Bulgur wheat is parboiled, dried, and partially debranned whole wheat. It is sometimes confused with cracked wheat, which is crushed whole wheat grain that has not been parboiled.

Buttermilk

Commercial buttermilk is made by adding a lactic acid bacteria culture to pasteurized whole, skim, or nonfat milk. After the addition of the culture, the milk is left to ferment for 12 to 14 hours at a low temperature (optimum 69°F). It is usually labeled cultured buttermilk and may be salted or unsalted. Yogurt can sometimes be substituted for buttermilk.

Capers

Capers are actually the bud and fruit from the flower of the caper bush. Capers are pickled and add a zippy and briny flavor to a dish. Add to sauces, gravies, and poultry or seafood dishes.

Carrots—Baby

Carrots have 10 times more vitamin A than a peach, and 30 times more than an egg! Carrots provide calcium, potassium, and fiber. But the popular "baby" carrots are one-tenth the nutritional value of a regular carrot. They are made from the broken carrots that are shaved and shaped into a "baby" carrot. True baby carrots taper into a sharp point at the end and still have part of the stem visible.

Carrots—Heirloom

Celtic literature refers to carrots as "honey underground." Carrots became popular in England only during the reign of Elizabeth I. Carrots were eaten daily in Ireland, Scotland, and Wales and were originally red or yellow, until a hybrid orange variety was developed. The Queen of Holland liked it and as it matched the color of her Coat of Arms, she declared that the orange variety would henceforth be referred to as the carrot. Leave it to a woman! Red and yellow carrots are now called heirloom carrots.

Celery

Celery is on the "dirty dozen" list of foods most heavily sprayed with pesticides and herbicides. I always buy celery organically grown to avoid these sprays. You can go to www.ewg.org for their "dirty dozen" and "safe" list of foods.

Cheese Alternatives

For those who need to avoid dairy, there are a few good cheese alternatives at health food stores. Rice cheddar and mozzarella cheese come in a block or shredded, which melts faster. Almond cheese comes in several flavor varieties and is a tasty alternative. Or a vegan variety of cheese, Daiya, is quite good.

Chicken—Cleaning and Prep

Rinse chicken breasts and pat dry. Place breast skin-side down on a cutting board with the fattest side away from you. With a sharp knife held horizontally, slice off the top of the thickest part of the chicken to make the breast an even thickness. Your chicken will cook evenly if the breast is cut in this way.

Chicken—Cooking

Cooking chicken with the bone-in may impart more flavors to the meat and keep it moister, but it takes longer to cook. Boneless chicken can be cooked in half the time.

Chicken Stock for Soup

When making soup, always use a fresh, bone-in, skin-on chicken. A skinless chicken breast will not be as tasty. You need the fat from the skin and bones for flavor. After the chicken is cooked you can remove most of the fat by removing the skin.

Chioggia Beets

This Italian beet variety has a distinct candy stripe pattern of white and red rings once it is sliced. However, once cooked, the stripes disappear and the beet becomes pink. They are delicous sliced raw into salads or cooked for soups, pickles, and side dishes.

Chocolate—Melting

Instead of a microwave, use a double broiler. If you don't have one, place a small pot in a larger pot that has 2 inches of water in the bottom pot. Bring the water to a boil and use the smaller pot to indirectly melt the chocolate.

Coconut Milk

Coconut milk is a great substitute for heavy cream in many soups and stews or in dishes when you want that strong Asian flavor. If you want a creamy texture without the strong coconut flavor use "light" coconut milk instead, which has a mild flavor and can replace heavy cream or half and half in many recipes.

Corn

Ninety percent of corn and corn products are genetically modified. As of this writing, all corn used for feed is grown from genetically modified seeds. Additionally, Monsanto has released their BT sweet corn seed which is also GMO. Read more about GMO in Chapter 1.

Corn Flour
This comes from a corn kernel called dent or flint corn, not the corn on the cob we are accustomed to eating as a vegetable. This is the final milling of this grain and it is the base for cornflake cereals, corn chips, corn tortillas, and other corn snacks.

Corn Grits
Yellow corn grits are used to make polenta. See *Good Ole' Polenta* recipe in my *Vegetables—Nature's Bounty* chapter. Corn grits are simply coarse ground whole grain corn called dent or flint corn. One more step of milling would result in corn flour. I prefer the yellow variety, found only in health food stores, because it has more flavor than the white grits most commonly available.

Cornstarch
Unless it is organic, all cornstarch comes from genetically modified corn. More than 90% of our corn crops are now genetically modified. Read more in Chapter 3, *Adapting Your Favorite Recipe*. You can find organic cornstarch (GMO-free) at your local health food store.

Couscous
Couscous is made from processed and refined wheat flour. It is not a whole grain but more similar to pasta. If you need to avoid wheat for any reason you'll have to avoid couscous. However, the couscous recipes in this book can all be substituted with quinoa, which is a delicious wheat and gluten-free, high-protein whole grain.

Cracked Wheat
Cracked wheat is made from spring wheat (soft wheat) as opposed to winter wheat (hard wheat), a darker wheat that is higher in gluten or protein. Cracked wheat is simply cracked and it cooks quicker than whole wheat.

Creamy Soup Base
Almost any soup can be made creamier by adding blended beans. Other than canned refried beans, bean paste is not something you can buy. However, if you want to have a thick white cream base for a soup, for instance, blend a cup of cooked white kidney beans (cannellini beans) and add to the soup during the last few minutes of cooking. Coconut milk is also a good cream substitute.

Cremini Mushrooms
Cremini mushrooms, also called baby bella mushrooms, are juvenile versions of the portabello mushroom. The cremini mushroom is a close relative of the white button mushroom. The French name for portabello is *Champignon de Paris* (Paris mushroom). Phytonutrients found in shiitake, maitake, and reishi mushrooms have been the subject of anti-cancer research. More recently, however, common button and cremini mushrooms have been shown to have anti-cancer properties as well.

Currants
Dried Zante raisins are called currants. They are very small and intensely sweet. They are not the same as the red or black currants used in cuisines throughout Western Europe. Currants are high in antioxidants, potassium, and vitamin C. One cup of currants gives you as much vitamin C as three large oranges. Dried currants are very similar to raisins, and are a great substitute in many recipes calling for raisins.

Curry
Curry is not a singular spice but a spice blend of up to

a dozen herbs and spices. Curry is available in a wide range of heat and intensities depending on the blend. Be careful if you are sensitive to hot or spicy flavors. I find that curries sold at Asian and Indian markets range from very hot to "OMG hot!" Some very hot curries will usually state the BTU on the label. BTU stands for British Thermal Units and it measures the heat output, so you know it's super spicy. It is safe, however, to purchase curry in most health food and grocery stores as they tend to be milder. You can increase the heat in a mild curry by adding some cayenne pepper, chili powder, or fresh ginger to your taste.

Cutting Vegetables
Cut vegetables in such a way that they will cook evenly. If you are making a stir-fry, cut thinly to facilitate quick cooking. Harder root vegetables such as carrots can be cut larger for soups or stews. And faster cooking veggies, like snow or snap peas, can be cut into bite-size pieces or not at all.

Cranberries
Dried cranberries are high in antioxidants. See Chapter 2 *Antioxidants Protect Your Health*. Fresh cranberries will contain more vitamins and less sugar than dried. One third of a cup of dried unsweetened cranberries contains 26 grams sugar and 2 grams fiber. Additionally, the drying process substantially reduces the amount of vitamin A and vitamin C.

Dates
The easiest dates for baking are date pieces that are coated with oat flour. They are available in most stores around the holidays.

Dried Fruit
Dried fruit is high in vitamins and minerals, but also high in concentrated sugar calories as well. If you are on a low glycemic diet or are trying to lose weight, this should be an occasional treat.

Eggs
It's easy to tell if an egg is fresh or weeks old. A fresh egg shell might take a few hard cracks on the side of a bowl to break. The albumen will surround the yoke with little water runoff. Albumen, the clear jelly-like substance that turns white when cooked, has more protein than the yolk. A fresh egg yolk will have a deep yellow color and it will sit high and round. A fresh egg that has been hard-boiled is difficult to peel because the moisture in the egg doesn't allow for an air pocket between the albumen and the shell. An older egg will dehydrate, creating a larger air pocket between the albumen and the shell. Once boiled, these eggs are easier to peel. An older egg will have a thinner shell that breaks easily, a more watery albumen, and a pale yolk that is flat with a lighter color. A fresh egg will sink in a glass of water, a stale egg will float—toss it.

Evaporated Cane Sugar
Evaporated cane sugar undergoes less processing than refined sugar does. Therefore, it retains more of the nutrients found in sugar cane. It has a fair amount of calcium, potassium, riboflavin, and niacin. If you are watching your calories, be cautious as this is still a high-calorie sweetener.

Expeller Pressed Oils
Expeller pressed refers to oils that have been extracted from the seed by simply soaking and pressing. These oils are superior in flavor and nutrition. They are referred to as natural vegetable oils in my recipes. For more information, read *Clarifying the Fat* in Chapter 1. They are found mostly in health food stores.

Figs
In temperate climates, figs come into season twice a year, once in early summer and again in autumn. Black Mission figs are among the most readily available and are often sweeter and are the variety used for drying. Brown Turkey figs are larger and easier to handle while stuffing, although not as sweet.

Green Kadota figs are larger yet. Choose figs that are a little soft because those are sweetest. If you are buying figs a few days ahead, pick ones that are still a little firm and without blemishes.

Flaxseeds
Flaxseeds and flaxseed oil are an excellent source of Omega-3. They can be added to cookies, breads, hot cereals, or morning protein shakes. Use oil in salad dressings, but never cook with flaxseed oil.

Fried Foods
In Chinese medicine, fresh ginger and fresh radishes are considered helpful in digesting oils and fats.

Grating Fresh Ginger
For grated ginger, there is no need to peel! The easiest way to get ginger juice from fresh ginger is to simply grate the ginger directly on a small handheld cheese grater. Make sure it has small holes in it so that the ginger comes out as a soft juicy pulp. Take a small ball of this pulp in the palm of your hand and simply squeeze the ginger juice directly into your dish. This is much easier and quicker than peeling, slicing, and dicing the ginger.

Gravy
To make a roux or gravy, start by melting 2 Tbs of butter in a small frying pan. Add 1 Tbs of flour and stir for 2–3 minutes. Slowly pour in broth as you use a fork or wire whisk to break up the flour lumps. Add broth a little at a time so that lumps will not form. To make white gravy, use milk, milk substitutes, or cream instead of broth.

Herbs—Dried
Dried herbs can be exchanged for fresh herbs in most recipes, but dried herbs do not have the same intensity and freshness. When a recipe calls for fresh herbs and you want to substitute dried, decrease quantity by one third. When the recipe calls for dried and you want to substitute with fresh herbs, increase quantity by three to account for water.

Herbs—Fresh
Wash the entire bunch in a large bowl of water, shake off excess water. Hold a bunch of herbs on a chopping block and mince the amount you need. No need to tediously remove individual herbs. This works best with fresh herbs such as curly parsley, Italian parsley, dill, and cilantro.

Fresh Herbs—Storing
Put your bunch of fresh herbs in a shallow but wide-mouthed jar. Fill with water, cover with a plastic bag, and refrigerate. This will keep the herbs fresh for more than a week.

Hulled Barley
Hulled barley is the natural unpolished whole grain. It's a little chewier and more flavorful and preferred over pearled barley. It contains protein, vitamins, and minerals. Pearled barley is polished which means the bran/fiber and the germ have been removed. This results in an 80% nutrition loss! Pearled barley is like white rice and hulled barley is like brown rice...big difference! Choose hulled!

Hydrogenated Fats
These fats are usually chemically extracted from seeds and then boiled at high temperatures. Hydrogenation stabilizes the oil so it is "shelf stable" for up to one and a half years. The oil is pushed through hydrogen gas, then deodorized, bleached, and degummed. For more information, read *Clarifying the Fat* in Chapter 1.

Jicama

Jicama (pronounced hick-a-ma) is a round root vegetable from Mexico that has a fresh, juicy, crunchy texture. It tastes like a cross between an apple and a potato. Use jicama in salads or stir-fry dishes.

Juicing a Lemon

To juice a lemon without a juicer, roll lemon on a cutting board by pressing down with the palm of your hand to soften. Slice in half and hold one half in one hand and with the other hand, push a fork into the center of the lemon. Have a strainer placed over a small bowl ready to catch the juice. Twist your hands in opposite directions, while squeezing the lemon at the same time. The juice will come pouring out.

Kale

When purchasing kale, look for dark, even green color with firm, fresh leaves. Wilted kale is a sign of water loss. Varieties of kale include curly leaf, red leaf, and a flat leaf variety commonly referred to as Tuscan kale or dinosaur kale. Kale is available year-round but for the best flavor, buy it in the fall and winter. Like the rest of the cabbage family, kale gets sweeter with cold nights.

Kombu

Kombu (kelp) is a sea vegetable rich in nutrients and one of the most alkalizing vegetables you can eat. It is mildly flavored and can be added to soups, beans, and stews. It is a rich source of protein, minerals, and vitamins. Recommended amount is a 2–3 inch piece per pot of beans or soup. Kombu is available in health food stores or Asian markets.

Leafy Greens

Kale, collard greens, mustard greens, turnip greens (tops), watercress, Swiss chard, and parsley are just a few leafy greens that are high in calcium, beta-carotene, vitamin E, and iron. For best results, either cook in boiling water without a lid or sauté in olive oil.

Leeks

To clean leeks, cut across the leek where the white and green parts meet. Keep top and bottoms separate. Cut down the long white part and rinse thoroughly, making sure to separate the leaves. Cut down again lengthwise and then chop crosswise into ½-inch pieces. For the green upper part, discard old, tough outer leaves until you get to the tender green leaves. Chop as you did the white part and keep separate. Soak in water to help remove dirt.

Mapo Doufu

Mapo doufu is a popular Chinese dish from the Szechuan province. It is often cooked with minced meat, usually pork or beef. Other variations of ingredients include water chestnuts, onions, wood ear fungus (a type of mushroom), or other vegetables, but it's always spicy.

Marinades

To avoid contamination, don't use a marinade for a dressing if it had raw meat marinating in it. The exception would be if you cook the marinade and then turn it into a finished sauce.

Mirin

Mirin is a sweet rice wine with a low alcohol content that is used in Japanese cooking, especially for glazing and sauces. You can substitute mirin with dry sherry or sweet marsala, or you can dissolve ¼ tsp sugar in ¼ cup white wine or sherry.

Miso

Miso is a paste made from fermented soybeans and is the base for miso soups. Miso comes in a variety of flavors, from a salty "beefy" flavor to a light and sweet flavor. Traditional miso soup starts with kombu dashi (kombu or kelp stock). The kombu can be minced and added back to the soup or saved and cooked with other dishes such as beans. Miso can be found in health food stores or Asian markets.

Mustard

The first appearance of mustard-makers dates back to 1292. Dijon, France, became a recognized center for mustard-making by the 13th-century. One of the most famous Dijon mustard makers was Grey-Poupon, hence the name of one of the most delicious prepared mustards.

Mustard Greens

Mustard greens are also known as Chinese mustard. They have a distinct horseradish/mustard flavor and are used widely in Asian and Indian cooking. Soul food dishes include ham hocks with mustard greens. Mustard greens are high in vitamins A and K. Steaming any bitter greens will bring out their bitterness. That's why I like to boil or sauté bitter greens with extra virgin olive oil.

Nori

Nori is the seaweed used to wrap Japanese sushi rolls. It is a good source of protein, containing 4.65 grams of protein in 1 cup. Nori is also high in iron, calcium, vitamins B and C, and many minerals. My family snacks on nori sheets and loves them.

Nuts

Soaking nuts and seeds in water for several hours makes them easier to digest and process into a creamy product. If possible, always use raw organic nuts for your milks and creams.

Oil Spray

Cooking oil spray can be used to coat measuring spoons or cups so that syrupy food like honey, agave syrup, etc. will slip off easily. Use it to spray your hands when forming the *Wow! Turkey Burgers* in *To Meat or Not to Meat* chapter. Or lightly coat your knife blade to keep dried fruit and garlic from sticking.

Omega-3 Essential Fatty Acids (EFA)

Omega-3 essential fatty acids help to reduce inflammation. Cold water fish, fish oils, and flaxseed oil are some sources of this anti-inflammatory oil. Most Americans get fifteen times more Omega-6 (pro-inflammatory) than Omega-3. Many diseases result from inflammation so consuming more Omega-3 rich foods can protect us from disease and premature aging.

Orzo

Orzo is simply rice-shaped pasta. Orzo is the Italian word for barley. It describes the shape and size of the pasta. Orzo is popular in the Mediterranean nations and the Middle East. The best orzo comes from durum semolina wheat, a hard wheat variety that retains its shape during cooking.

Pan Frying

To test oil for readiness, drop a few bread crumbs or a little of the food you will be frying into the pan. If it begins to sizzle immediately, the oil is ready. The trick to frying lightly is to keep the oil temperature consistent, which is achieved by not overcrowding the pan. Overcrowding the pan will cool the oil and result in a soggy, oily dish. Extra-virgin olive oil should never be used for pan frying as it will foam at high heat. The trapped air bubbles cool the oil, also resulting in a soggy dish. Crispy, lightly fried food is only achieved when the oil remains hot throughout the process. Sesame, sunflower, or canola oil are best for pan frying.

Pasta vs. Noodles

Pasta and noodles are interchangeable in my recipes. According to the National Pasta Association, in order for noodles to be classified as noodles, they should contain 5.5% egg solids by weight. Noodles are usually rolled and cut to form long bands or thin rods. They can be made from rice flour, mung bean starch, buckwheat flour, or durum wheat. Pasta is much lighter and under Italian law should be made with only durum wheat. Pasta can be made into many shapes and the dough is often extruded as macaroni, fusilli, and spatzle.

Peanuts

Peanuts are in the legume family and, unlike tree nuts, grow under the ground. Aflatoxin mold often grows on peanuts stored in warm, humid silos. Aflatoxins have been found in pecans, pistachios, and walnuts, as well as milk, grains, soybeans, and spices. However, aflatoxin levels are checked and regulated in the U.S. My whole family and I prefer almond butter.

Peeling Garlic

The easiest way to peel garlic is to place a clove on your cutting board and hold your knife blade flat side down on top of the clove. With your other hand, make a fist and hit the blade with a hard smack. It will crack the clove and split the skin, making it easier to peel.

Peeling Onions

If you presoak an onion for 10 minutes you will avoid irritated eyes, and the onion will peel much easier. To cut onions into wedges, leave root end on when removing the skin. Stand the onion up with root end on top and slice through this root end in half. Take each half onion and repeat this step. You will have 6 wedges of onions held together by a piece of the root end still intact.

Peeling Tomatoes

To peel tomatoes, drop in boiling water for one minute, remove, and cool. Peel should slip off easily.

Unsoaked onion is harder to peel   *Soaked onions are easier to peel without tears*

Remove stem end   *Cut in half*

Thin slices down onion   *Sliced but in one piece*

Slice across

Perfect Apple Pie

When apples are just poured in a shell, there is too much space between the apples and this results in a fallen pie crust once baked. Layering the apples in a tight circle on the bottom of the pastry shell helps to avoid this. This makes a great high, dense pie that won't collapse after baking.

Polenta

Polenta is coarse-ground cornmeal used in traditional Italian dishes. Polenta was commonly eaten as porridge or gruel in the early 1900s. Polenta is still considered a peasant food in some parts of the world. Polenta was also eaten with buckwheat, farro, and chestnut flours. Cooked polenta can be shaped into balls, patties, or sticks. Fried polenta is popular in Southern Brazil.

Pomegranate Seeds

Pomegranate seeds are high in vitamins C and K, potassium, iron, and fiber, and are low in calories (80 per serving). Pomegranates are especially high in polyphenols, a form of antioxidant purported to help reduce the risk of cancer and heart disease. In fact, pomegranate juice, which contains health-boosting tannins, anthocyanins, and ellagic acid, has higher antioxidant activity than either green tea or red wine.

Protein Powder

For a vitamin/protein boost you can add a scoop of protein powder to your drink. Be careful in your selection as many of them are designed for weight gain and contain considerable amounts of sugar. To replace a meal, one serving can have 300 calories but should also have a good amount of vitamins and minerals. Egg-based, whey, or rice-based protein powders are more digestible than soy protein powders. Read the labels.

Quinoa

Quinoa (pronounced keen-wah) is native to South America and was once considered the "mother seed" of the Incas. Quinoa is a nutritional powerhouse that supplies all nine essential amino acids, including lysine, making it a complete protein. Quinoa is an excellent option for vegans, and for anyone wanting to add non-meat proteins to their diet. Quinoa also contains one of the highest plant-based iron levels. It's an excellent source of manganese, magnesium, copper, phosphorus, and fiber. Quinoa is also naturally gluten-free, making it a great choice for those following a gluten-free diet.

Radish Tops

Another amazingly nutritious, misunderstood vegetable is radish tops. Radish tops have a mild taste, are tender, and can be added to raw salads, soups, or a stir-fry. They are as nutritious as other leafy greens.

Rice

Short grain brown rice will make sweet, sticky rice. Long grain rice is better for pilafs as the grains will remain separate. Most whole grains double in volume when they are cooked. If you want two cups of cooked rice, start with 1 cup rice and 2 cups water. For rice recipes and for more information on cooking whole grains, see *Amber Waves of Grain* chapter.

Rice Syrup

Rice syrup is made from malted brown rice and is similar to barley malt. Rice syrup is mildly sweet and a good choice when you need ingredients to hold together. It can be found in health food stores.

Rice Vinegar

Organic rice vinegar is found in most stores and is less acidic than white vinegar. Distilled white vinegar is very acidic. Distilling and pasteurization kills the beneficial bacteria that unpasteurized vinegar contains.

Roasting Bell Peppers

To roast peppers, place pepper directly on the grill and char the skin on all sides. Or lightly oil skin and place in a pan directly under broiler. Continue turning until the entire pepper is blackened. Remove and place in a covered bowl for five minutes. This allows steam to separate and loosen the skin from the meat of the pepper. To remove skin, rub off with your fingers. Using running water to remove the skin will remove the roasted flavor.

Roasting Corn on the Cob

To roast corn on the cob, boil or steam shucked corn for 5 minutes. Remove from heat and drain. Have grill on high heat. Brush corn with butter or oil and a little salt. Place on grill and turn every minute for even browning. To grill corn with husks, first remove outer tough green husk. Pull back but do not remove inner husk. Remove silk and brush corn with butter. Pull husks back up and tie with kitchen twine to secure. Place on grill for 20–30 minutes while turning frequently.

Salad Dressing

When mixed with vinegar or lemon juice, broccoli, string beans, snow and sugar peas, and green peas will lose their bright green color after a while. To avoid discoloring, keep the dressing on the side or toss with dressing a half hour or so before serving.

Sesame Seeds

Sesame seeds that are found in grocery stores are usually hulled. They will be bright white in color, usually expensive, and can go rancid quickly. Natural sesame seeds are unhulled and have varying degrees of light brown coloring. These will last longer, are less expensive, and are found in most grocery stores that have an Asian food aisle, health food stores, or Asian markets.

Shallots

Shallots are a small root vegetable with a copper papery skin that looks similar to a large garlic clove. It is a variety of onion but has a sweeter, milder, yet richer, and pungent flavor. They can be stored for at least 6 months. Use in soups, stews, roasted vegetable dishes, and just about anywhere you would use onion or garlic.

Shocking Method

The shocking method is a sure-proof method to cook a noodle or pasta *al dente*—still firm and slightly chewy. In a large pot, bring 2 quarts of water to boil, add noodles and stir. After several minutes, when water reaches a full rolling boil again, add ¼ cup of cold water. This shock will reduce the water boil. Wait until water is at a full boil again and repeat. This method allows the heat to penetrate to the inside of the noodle at the same time it cooks the outside. This results in an evenly cooked noodle. Most pastas and noodles will need three shocks before they are cooked. Angel hair takes only one shock, but always taste-test noodles before taking them off the stove.

Soba Noodles

Soba noodles are made from buckwheat flour and wheat flour and have a unique flavor. Some varieties are 100% buckwheat for those who want gluten-free options. Soba noodles are found in most grocery stores that have an Asian food aisle, health food stores, or Asian markets.

Soup Making

The key to good soup making is not to use too much water. Water should cover the vegetables by two inches. Simmer only until vegetables are tender. Periodically check to see if water is reducing too much. Add remaining water near the end of cooking when you will be seasoning. Most vegetable soups can be cooked in less than 15 minutes. Chop the vegetables that need the longest cooking and add them in first. While they are simmering, chop the next vegetable and so on. Layering your vegetables according to cooking time requires no need for stirring.

Soy Products
Ninety percent of soybeans are genetically modified! So please look for organic soy products. I recommend only fermented organic soy products.

Soy Sauce
Soy sauce and shoyu are the same sauce, just a different name. Tamari traditionally meant wheat-free. Produced for thousands of years, soy sauce is made from fermented soy beans mixed with some type of roasted grain (wheat, barley, or rice), injected with a special yeast mold, and liberally flavored with salt. After being left to age for several months, the mixture is strained and bottled. Use it to flavor soups, whole grain dishes or stir-frys.

Spaghetti Squash
Spaghetti squash is a wonderful low-carb alternative to pasta. If the squash is cooked just right, you will be able to pull strings out of the squash with a fork. Overcooking will result in a soft but tasty vegetable.

Spice Rub
Make a spice rub in advance by combining 2 Tbs brown sugar, 2 Tbs ground paprika, 4 tsp ground cumin, 2 tsp sea salt, and 1 tsp ground black pepper. This is great for chicken thighs, fish filets, and sweet potato fries.

Sprouting Grains and Beans
Grains, beans, nuts, or seeds triple their nutritional value when sprouted. To soak beans, for example, place in water overnight. Drain and rinse the next morning. Place a mesh netting over top (you can purchase sprouting jars from a health food store).

Keep the jar upside down leaning on a tilt against something so that air can circulate while excess water drains. This prevents grain and beans from fermenting in too much water. Rinse once or twice a day for 3 days when a root will begin to form. It is then ready to add to recipes and salads.

Summer Squash
Yellow summer squash, also called crookneck squash, is a member of the gourd family. It is in the same class as zucchini, patty pan, and other hybrid varieties with an edible thin skin. They are mildly sweet and best when eaten in season, early to late summer. Choose squash that are small, shiny, and firm-skinned, free of blemishes or bruising.

Sunflower Seeds
Sunflower seeds are best purchased raw. Toast them yourself in a dry frying pan or in a toaster oven at 325°F for 8 minutes. Store-bought roasted sunflower seeds can quickly go rancid.

Sweet Potatoes
Sweet potatoes are relatively low in calories and have no fat. They are rich in vitamin A and potassium, having five times the RDA of vitamin A. The yam, a tuber, is a member of the lily family, and the sweet potato is a member of the morning glory family.

Tahini
Tahini is a paste of ground sesame seeds and is similar to soft nut butter. It has a nutty sweet flavor and is great for creamy salad dressings. Tahini contains a good amount of calcium and B vitamins. Use it in dressings, gravies, and sauces. Look for tahini in grocery or health food stores.

Tangerine Oranges
Tangerine oranges are a broad class of oranges that include mandarin and clementine, among others. They have a distinct thin, loose peel and have been dubbed "kid-glove" oranges.

Tempeh

Tempeh is a fermented soybean cake with a meaty texture. It originated in Indonesia where soybeans were traditionally fermented in banana leaves. Tempeh is high in protein and is easily digested because it is fermented like soy sauce and miso. It has a higher content of protein, dietary fiber, and vitamins than tofu. Tempeh has a firm texture and strong flavor. Because of its nutritional value, it is used worldwide in vegetarian cuisine and many consider it a meat substitute. Tempeh might have small gray spots on it; this is a natural result of fermentation and does not mean the tempeh has spoiled.

Testing Meat for Doneness

How can you tell when your steak or burger is cooked without cutting into it? Restaurant chefs will poke it and test for texture. If meat is rare, it will feel soft, like the skin between your thumb and index finger. If meat is medium, it will feel as firm as the pad of your hand at the base of your thumb. Well done? It will be as firm as the center of the palm of your hand. There's no need for a meat thermometer…just poke it! I have used this technique without fail.

Toasted Sesame Oil

Toasted sesame oil has a delicious unique flavor and is best in Asian dishes. It has a shorter shelf life because it is toasted, so keep it refrigerated and it will last three to six months.

Toasting Seeds

The best way to prevent burning is to toast seeds for 5 minutes in a preheated toaster oven at 325°. Seeds can also be toasted in the oven on a cookie sheet, but they tend to burn easily, so watch them very carefully.

Tofu

Tofu is very high in protein. Tofu is made from cooking cracked dried soybeans. This results in a milky liquid, which then sets into a cheese-like consistency. An 8 oz serving has the same amount of protein as a 5 oz hamburger. The fat in tofu is unsaturated and contains about 85% water. If calcium sulfate is added (not all tofu contains this), the tofu is a good source of calcium. It also contains a fair amount of iron, phosphorus and B-complex vitamins. Soft or silken tofu varieties are a good choice in dressing or sauce recipes. Firm and extra firm tofu varieties contain less water and are best used in entrée recipes.

Tomatoes

Tomatoes are a fruit and refrigeration will spoil their delicate texture and sweetness. Always store tomatoes at room temperature. Leave them in a basket on the counter out of direct sunlight and they can last up to a week or more. Tomatoes are high in lycopene, which has many health benefits. Tomatoes originated in South America and were introduced into Italian cuisine only a few hundred years ago.

Turmeric

Turmeric is a spice that gives an intense yellow color to a dish and is the main ingredient in curry powder. Its active ingredient is curcumin and it has a distinctly earthy, slightly bitter, slightly hot, peppery flavor. Long known for its anti-inflammatory properties, recent research has revealed that turmeric is proving beneficial in the treatment of many different health conditions from cancer to Alzheimer's disease. Add it to soups, stews, sauces, dressings, even cookies!

Vinegars

Vinegars are made when the fruit sugar of apples (or grapes) is converted into alcohol by a process called yeast fermentation. Next, the alcohol is converted into acetic acid by a process called acetic acid fermentation. Vinegars should be unpasteurized (unheated) so as to maintain this active culture. Spectrum Naturals and Braggs are the only brands I know of that do not pasteurize their vinegars. These unpasteurized vinegars help restore your intestinal flora, similar to what yogurt does. These vinegars will continue to ferment so keep them refrigerated.

Wakame

Wakame is used traditionally in Japanese cuisines in salads and miso soup. For a 50 gram serving, wakame contains 22 calories, 1.5 g of protein, 4.5 g of carbohydrates, less than .5 g of fat, and a little fiber. Wakame provides a variety of minerals including calcium, iron, magnesium, phosphorus, potassium, and trace amounts of zinc, copper, manganese, and selenium. In addition, wakame contains beta carotene and folate, along with low levels of vitamin K, vitamin C, niacin, choline, and vitamin E. It can be purchased in most health food stores or Asian markets. I use it in most of my soups, including my *Marvelous Minestrone* in *For the Love of Soups* chapter.

Walnuts

Walnuts are a source of Omega-3, an essential fatty acid that has an anti-inflammatory effect in our bodies. Most Americans do not get enough of this EFA. Walnut oil can be used for salad dressings and cooking.

Whole Oats

Whole oats (also called oat groats) are the natural form of oatmeal before it is "rolled" as in rolled oats, or "cut" as in steel-cut oats. They contain more vitamins and minerals than the processed variety and haven't oxidized because they are still whole. Of all the varieties of oatmeal available, this is the king of nutrition.

Wild Rice

To shorten cooking time, cook wild rice for 30 minutes covered and then let it rest for about a half hour or more. It will continue to absorb water. The grain is cooked properly when it splits open. Otherwise it will be chewy, starchy and will not absorb any dressing. All rice dishes can become dry and hard in the refrigerator so start with rice that is cooked on the softer side.

Yams

What we call garnet yams are actually just a different variety of sweet potatoes. True yams are native to Africa and vary in size from a few ounces to over 100 lbs with over 600 varieties. Compared to sweet potatoes, yams are starchier and drier with flesh colored in white, pink, or brown, with a rough and scaly texture. Yams can be found in international markets sold in precut pieces.

Zest

Zest is the minced or grated thin outer layer of citrus fruits. There are several ways to remove the zest. (1) Using a vegetable peeler, gently peel off a thin layer of a lemon or orange. Be careful not to get the white pithy part as it is very bitter. Mince with a knife. (2) Use a zester, specifically designed for this purpose. (3) Use a handheld small holed grater and grate just the rind. Grate lightly around the fruit to get just the outermost peel.

Acknowledgments

This cookbook would never have been written if it weren't for all the wonderful people who came through the many kitchen doors where I have taught. Over the years, thousands of students have acknowledged my skills and requested my recipes time and time again. Their desire to learn inspired me to create new flavors, textures, teaching techniques and eventually to write this book. Many of you have become friends who continue to encourage and support me.

The conception, gestation and birth of any book is a miraculous process, and the word "acknowledgment" doesn't even begin to do justice to the creative and supporting roles that so many people played in this adventure. I had an amazing team of kitchen testers, designers, editors, and others who helped shape this book.

To those who walked this creative road with me and kept me focused on the goal, my sincere appreciation:

My dedicated recipe testing team in Santa Barbara, and San Luis Obispo, CA. Your interest, positive feedback, and encouragement spurred me on.

Janet Valentine, whose artwork brought character to these pages, you shared additional design ideas that added so much to the book.

My copyeditor and word guru, Maryjean Ballner, who scrutinized the manuscript at every stage (and sometimes twice). Your patience and humorous suggestions kept me on track and helped make this book into something I am very proud of.

Josh Shaub at www.VeryNaturalPhoto.com, whose passion for food, photography talents, and amazing creativity brought life to my recipes.

Laura Patrizi, who pulled everything together to assemble what now you hold in your hands—I can't thank you enough for your skills in editing and talent in formatting and design, as it was a tremendous part of this project.

Celia Fuller, thank you for your hard work and for skillfully managing this complicated process. Your professionalism was much appreciated.

Mary Ann Kohrs, my chef assistant extraordinaire who has worked with me tirelessly for the past few years and is my right hand in the kitchen always anticipating what I need before I do. My gratitude for your loving commitment is great.

To more friends, unnamed and unnumbered but not unremembered, who read the manuscript at different stages and offered their insights, wisdom, enthusiasm and suggestions.

In addition to those who worked directly on the book, I appreciate the loving support and encouragement from my friends and family. To some of my closest friends, Kiki Corbin, Marilyn Grosboll, Susan McIntire, Marilyn Miller, Margaret Carmen and to my lifelong best friend and sister, Parris, thank you all.

And most important, I want to thank my readers. May you find good health through the knowledge and recipes I've shared in this cookbook.

To your health!
Suzanne Landry, 2013

Index

Note: Page references in *italics* refer to photographs.